JUKEBOX SATURDAY NIGHT

More Memories of the Big Band Era and Beyond

by
RICHARD GRUDENS

Author of
The Best Damn Trumpet Player,
The Song Stars,
The Music Men,
and *Snootie Little Cutie*

CELEBRITY PROFILES PUBLISHING
Box 344 Main Street
Stony Brook, New York 11790-0344
(516) 862-8555

CANDID PHOTOS BY
C. CAMILLE SMITH, GUS YOUNG, ROBERT DE BETTA

Library of Congress
Catalog Card Number 99-74213

ISBN 1-57579-042-1

Published by:
Celebrity Profiles Publishing Inc.
Div. Edison & Kellogg
Box 344 Main Street
Stony Brook, New York 11790-0344
(516) 862-8555
Fax (516) 862-0139
E-Mail Ricwrite4 @ aol.com

Cover photo 1948 Wurlitzer by Stony Brook Camera
Paul Basirico / James Presant

Edited by Mary Lou Facciola

Printed in the United States of America

 PINE HILL PRESS, INC.
Freeman, S. Dak. 57029

Artie Shaw and his band, 1953. *(Richard Grudens Collection)*

TABLE OF CONTENTS
JUKEBOX SATURDAY NIGHT
More Memories of the Big Band Era and Beyond

PART ONE

PART TWO

PART THREE

PART FOUR

PART FIVE

FOREWORD

by Ann Jillian

(Courtesy of Camille Smith)

In 1984 Richard Grudens first interviewed me while I was performing with Bob Hope at Westbury Music Fair on Long Island. Richard's been a friend and supporter ever since, always fair, always reporting an honest account of my career activities to his readers throughout the years.

This new chronicle Richard has written about some of our musical heroes is the fourth in a series and profiles bandleaders, musicians, arrangers, singers and other participants of what's been identified as *America's Golden Age of Music*, the period beginning with the roaring 1920's, right though the war years and beyond, an unbroken line through the frenetic rock and roll period, with enough of it's greatness continuing today. Performers like me have benefited greatly from these early innovators of music.

In *Jukebox* you will read about the musically productive life and career of the great bandleaders Artie Shaw, Les Brown, and Red Norvo, through personal interviews which are totally readable with interviewing techniques that allow his subjects to be extremely forthcoming.

Remembrances of the early dance bands of Paul Whiteman, Casa Loma, Leo Reisman, Jean Goldkette, Vincent Lopez, Ted Lewis, and Coon-Sanders are featured, as well as stories of the celebrated ballrooms where people like you, and perhaps your parents, danced happily to the music they loved.

The Meadowbrook, the Glen Island Casino, the Graystone, the Sunnybrook, the Cocoanut Grove, the Palomar, and Tune Town, among others, are profiled here for your fond recollection or first introduction.

Richard talks with some of the surviving, unsung songwriters of the age: Ervin Drake, who wrote "It Was A Very Good Year" and "I Believe;" Jack Lawrence, who wrote "Linda" and "Tenderly;" George David Weiss who wrote "Mr. Wonderful" and "What A Wonderful World;" all great songs that made the bands and their vocalists so popular during that august melodic period.

Last, but not least, he also presents to you the renowned broadcasters, the radio disc jockeys who brought the music into your home or car, and yesterday's and today's European bandleading counterparts of yesterday's and today's American Big Bands.

You can always be certain that the facts as presented in this book are completely accurate, for Richard Grudens specializes in what Big Band vocalist Connie Haines calls "the truth as we all lived it" accuracy, always checking with his subjects or their associates or survivors before placing their life's work into public print.

As a veteran actor, singer and entertainer who has been there, working Broadway, Las Vegas, Tahoe, Atlantic City, many places on Bob Hope's USO tours, singing the songs that were popular in this era, and on lots and lots of television, I recommend this chronicle to you as an enjoyable flashback into a time considered by so many as musically unique.

Jukebox Saturday Night is a pleasing trip down memory lane. Sit back, enjoy an hour or two, and re-live those wonderful, musical days of our lives.

Ann Jillian,
Sherman Oaks, California
March 1999

BAND LEADERS IN THE 1950's

Top Row L-R: Stan Kenton, Lawrence Welk, Les Brown, Harry James, Ray Anthony, Freddy Martin, Orrin Tucker.
Bottom Row L-R: Sam Donahue, Woody Herman, LeRoy Anthony, Jerry Gray.
(Photo files of Audree Kenton)

INTRODUCTION AND ACKNOWLEDGMENTS

by Richard Grudens

It's been over thirty years since George T. Simon's original, definitive book *The Big Bands* with a foreword by Frank Sinatra was first published, and fifteen years since Leo Walker's fifth printing of the original *Big Band* Almanac was first compiled in 1978.

After publication of my first book , *The Best Damn Trumpet Player*, featuring interview pieces with Lionel Hampton, Harry James, Benny Goodman, Count Basie, Ray Anthony, Woody Herman, and Buddy Rich sprinkled among some singers and personalities of the Big Band Era, I authored two additional books on the singers, *The Song Stars*, about the lady singers, and *The Music Men*, about the men singers, along with myriad other material to complete, I thought, a trilogy.

Upon reviewing the three books, Dr. Stanley Cohen, President of Five Towns Music College in Dix Hills, New York suggested an additional volume be added to the trilogy that would focus on the remaining Big Bands not portrayed in the first three to complete what he felt was begun — a complete, cohesive presentation of data told through surviving participants of music's Golden Age while these icons are still with us.

"We have added all three of your books to our library and to our bibliography of Graduate Course offerings. The additional book will round out the texts,"he said. His concept is to utilize the four books as texts which would be the basis of a graduate course covering exponents of swing music of the Big Band Era for future students to consider and comprehend.

With the new book in mind, I telephoned George T. Simon at his New York City home and talked with him about compiling information for a new Big Band book. "Of course! It's a great idea. A refresher and updating is needed, and, if you need any help, call me, " he said.

All four books acknowledge the bands, large and small, famous and obscure, old and new. In compiling interviews, information, and quotations, I have long ago decided that all the facts must be accurate. No fudging. No poetic license. No guessing. Acting as the old radio news writer I once was, I realized that truth and accuracy were paramount. As Connie Haines said, responding to my *comments* request on *The Music Men*, "You always tell the truth about the Big Band Era, *as I lived it.*" Maria Ellington Cole and Kathryn Crosby expressed similar comments.

The title *Jukebox Saturday Night* suggests the age of the Big Band Era and earlier, when roadside houses, which featured playing recordings on commercial machines, were known as *Juke joints*, or *Jook joints*, suggesting a synonym for sex, dance, and music. The word *juke* is much like its sister phrases *rock 'n roll* or *funk*, a combination of words that black society of the time spawned in shanty bars and café's located in poor, agricultural areas of Southern America.

According to J. Krivine's 1977 book about the jukebox, also entitled *Jukebox Saturday Night:* "Saturday night was for good times. Juke bands or gin mill piano players would perform. When electrically amplified recording machines were introduced, they became known as *juke boxes*. Rather than hiring a band, these places utilized first the phonograph, then the *juke box* arrived."

Jukebox Saturday Night will profile some great bands and some not so great. Among them Artie Shaw's and Les Brown's bands, two of the best. Red Norvo's story is less known but as valid as any. We lost Red Norvo in early April, just before the book's first printing.

As with each book, I received lots of assistance. First, my special thanks goes to my friend and mentor Frankie Laine. Frank is eighty-six and still recording. We have been friends for almost twenty years. Frank and his exemplary management of life and career has always been an inspiration to me. Secondly, I thank Connie Haines, whose biography we are authoring together, for her immeasurable help and infectious enthusiasm.

I sincerely thank Ruth Ellington and her sons Stephen and Michael for insight about the great Duke Ellington; Joe Pardee and lovely Lynn Roberts for their assistance with Harry James; Big Band writer Bob Melvin for his comments on the Dorseys; my friend, bandleader Larry O'Brien and his amazing group of youngsters who keep Glenn Miller's precious music active worldwide; the spirited and gracious Audree

Kenton for help with her Stanley, whose legacy she protects and promotes; Doris Day and Stumpy Brown for help with Les Brown; and Portia Norvo, for help with her dad, Red Norvo.

Thanks, too, to Anthony DiFlorio III for all-around encouragement and direction; Anthony Agostinelli of "The Network," vocalist Anita O'Day and Milt Bernhart for help with Stan Kenton; Andy Murcia for help with his wife, Ann Jillian; Don Kennedy of "Big Band Jump," who keeps our kind of music going strong; my dedicated editor, Mary Lou Facciola; Tess, *marvelous* Tess Russell, who finds those unfindable subjects with charm and grace, even when she is lying in her sickbed from where she frequently telephoned me; author George T. Simon, who started it all with his prolific contributions in *Metronome* Magazine; Frank Esposito of *Remember When* magazine for his ideas and research; the champion of the Big Bands, Roy Belcher of Big Bands International in England; Frank Touhey of Montpellier in Cheltenham, England, and bandleader Ray Anthony of Los Angeles, who distribute all those wonderful Big Band recordings. And a special remembrance of William B. Williams, along with thanks to Jack Ellsworth, whom I consider to be the two best broadcasters of *our kind of music* ever.

I thank my immediate family, my wife, Jean, and son Bob, for their patience because I wind up ignoring their need for my presence. They have grown used to me sitting in front of my Mac Classic with the little black and white screen and serving me tea and apple pie at an appointed hour. They know where my heart lies while each book is composed. Writers somehow have to find a way to make it up to their families.

So, turn and absorb the pages written about the dance bands, ballrooms, Big Bands, songwriters, vocalists, arrangers, broadcasters, and European counterparts, all contributing to the legacy of the Big Bands.

Doris Day once told me that she plays music when she reads, trying to capture the mood of the book. Good idea! Play Glenn Miller recordings as you absorb each word of the Glenn Miller chapter. Perhaps play "Begin the Beguine" with Artie Shaw or "Artistry in Rhythm" when reading about Stan Kenton. It sets the mood and colors each chapter melodically. That's exactly what I do while I write about each of them.

Richard Grudens — Stony Brook, New York
April 25, 1999

A note from
MILT BERNHART

PRESIDENT of the
BIG BAND ACADEMY OF AMERICA

Milt Bernhart, Redondo Beach, CA, 1999 *(Courtesy of Milt Bernhart)*

I've felt for as long as I can remember that records have an important role to play in the scheme of things — pleasure, education, promotion...all of that and more.

But they can't come close to the real live thing. If you are too young to have heard Duke Ellington and His Famous Orchestra then...you never will. But you say you've heard recent re-releases, and what do I mean, it's not the same?

That's just what I mean...**it's not the same!** The playing on the record may be fabulous, but the player was playing to a microphone, not an audience in most cases. And that makes a big difference (in my humble opinion). The microphone hears all, but couldn't care less. It's more than a rumor that the best music ever — was not recorded. Is that bad? No! It's wonderful. You had to be there. Am I reaching you?

And if you were there, you may have even tried to describe what you heard to someone who wasn't there. Didn't work, did it?

You just had to be there!

Like life itself, you go with the bumps. It's worth it.

And besides...for all of us, both performers and listeners, there's more good music just up ahead. Don't you hear the orchestra warming up, and the excited buzz of the audience as they find their seats? Anticipation is in the air. Music is about to claim us.

Thank you, God.

Hollywood Palladium premiere opening. Halloween Eve, 1940. "You had to be there!" *(Richard Grudens Collection)*

Quite A Party!

(L-R) Buddy Rich, Woody Herman, Willard Alexander, Benny Goodman, Count Basie, Stan Kenton, and Mel Tormé at a party for Willard Alexander, 1955. *(Courtesy Audree Kenton)*

The Song
JUKEBOX SATURDAY NIGHT

by Stillman & McGrane

Moppin' Up Soda Pop Rickeys
To Our Heart's Delight,
Dancing to Swing a Real Quickie
Jukebox Saturday Night

Goodman and Kyser and Miller
Help to make things right,
Make a Hot Lick with Vanilla
Jukebox Saturday Night

They Put Nuthin' Past Us
Me and Honeylamb,
Making one Coke Last Us
'Til It's Time To Scram
Money, We Really Don't Need That,
We'll Make Out All Right,
Letting The Other Guy Feed That,
Jukebox Saturday Night

After sippin' a soda
We Got a Scheme
Somebody Else Plays the Record Machine
It's So Easy to Use Pet Names
When You Listen to the Trumpet of Harry James
(trumpet solo)
We Love to Hear the Tenor Croon
Whenever the Inkspots Sing a Tune
(vocal group sings)
Money! We Really Don't Need That
We'll Make Out Alright,
Lettin' That Other Guy Feed That

JUKEBOX SATURDAY NIGHT

Band Leader, Paul Whiteman, 1929 *(Richard Grudens Collection)*

PART ONE

THE EARLY DANCE BANDS

GET READY, GET SET, LET'S DANCE!

Proliferating throughout the Big Band Era, the musical organizations of Benny Goodman, Artie Shaw, Duke Ellington, Glenn Miller, and Tommy and Jimmy Dorsey attracted colossal crowds at America's dance pavilions, theaters and hotels. Earlier, those very same venues hosted dozens of pioneer dance bands. The unique musical congregations of Paul Whiteman, Fred Waring, Vincent Lopez, Wayne King, Casa Loma, Fletcher Henderson, Coon-Sanders, Ted Lewis, Jean Goldkette, Leo Reisman, Gus Arnheim, and Isham Jones set the stage for the dynamics that was to come.

In the grand ballrooms of New York's Waldorf-Astoria, Biltmore, Savoy, and Roosevelt hotels and at rural small-town locations like the Sunnybrook Ballroom in Pottstown, Pennsylvania, enthusiastic dancing partners could swing to all the great dance bands in the early decades of this century.

Paul Whiteman's King of Jazz Orchestra

Paul Whiteman's 1920 landmark recordings of "Whispering" and "The Japanese Sandman" spurred national interest in jazz dance music in the days when radio was still a novelty, television far off into the future, and sound films still ten years away. Showcased at San Francisco's Fairmont Hotel (long before Tony Bennett left his heart there) and Los Angeles' Alexandria Hotel, both songs enjoyed unexpected, spectacular success. With their catchy, infectious phrasing, you'll find yourself whistling and humming those tunes over and over all day long.

A recording contract followed as well as a long run at the Palais Royale in New York City. Paul Whiteman and his mis-named King of Jazz Orchestra was on top of the beat that people were dancing to in what is considered the beginning of the Jazz Age, even though Whiteman was hardly considered a jazzman. His world-famous orchestra employed some of the later greats of pop and jazz music including Tommy and Jimmy Dorsey; arranger and composer Ferde' Grofe; arranger Bill Challis; vocalist Bing Crosby; legendary cornetists Bix Beiderbecke and Henry Busse; guitarist Eddie Lang; vocalist Mildred Bailey; violinist Joe Venuti ; cornetist Loring "Red "Nichols; saxist Frankie Trumbauer; composer, pianist Hoagy Carmichael; pianist, leader and arranger Lennie Hayton; saxist, bandleader Roy Bargy; trumpeter, bandleader Bunny Berigan; trombonist and leader Jack Teagarden; trumpeter Charlie Teagarden, trumpeter Billy Butterfield, and many others, a virtual *who's who* of American popular music. Even the great entertainer Al Jolson was once backed by Whiteman on the original "Kraft Music Hall" radio show.

I personally enjoyed the almost daily acquaintance of Paul Whiteman at his NBC studio office in the early fifties. An NBC studio page, I observed him frequently while directing visitors to his office, always receiving a personal thank-you and sometimes a fatherly arm about the shoulder. At the time I did not fully realize his significant contribution to the music of the Jazz Age. Remember, it was Paul Whiteman who premiered George Gershwin's classic composition "Rhapsody in Blue" to the world at an Aeolian Hall concert, New York City's then sanctuary of classical music, on February 12, 1924, with the composer himself at the piano. Paul Whiteman's King of Jazz Orchestra with thirty-four all-stars was the biggest name and the most creative force in the music business during that period.

The Casa Loma Orchestra

The Casa-Loma Orchestra, originally named The Orange Blossom Band, began playing dance music at the Glen Island Casino in New Rochelle, New York, and the Colonnades in Manhattan's Essex House. The Casa Loma name originated when the Casa Loma Hotel in Toronto, Canada, went bankrupt and the band's manager, Jean Goldkette, sent the now-unemployed Orange Blossom Band on tour, re-naming it the Casa Loma Orchestra. Orchestra members, always outfitted in bow ties and tails, were also its board of directors, each man receiving an equal share in the profits, making it a cooperative band. It became the nation's favorite dance orchestra - not a hot band - but sweet and popular. On one 1939 Decca album alone, the group recorded composer Hoagy Carmichael's "Rockin'Chair," "Georgia On My Mind," "Riverboat Shuffle," "Little Old Lady," "Lazy River, "and, of course, the ultimate standard "Stardust."

With a playing style that was considered new and different, alto-sax player Glen Gray, who eventually became the band's leader, led the Casa Loma Orchestra to great commercial success. My longtime friend Bill Challis arranged some of the organization's lasting charts, as he did earlier for the Goldkette band and later for the Whiteman band. "Smoke Rings," written by H.Eugene Gifford and Ned Washington, was the Casa Loma theme. This now very classy orchestra continued running strong, especially when they succeeded Ray Noble's Orchestra at the celebrated Rainbow Room up on Radio City's 65th floor, lasting until the Second World War began, when it disbanded. Some say Casa Loma initiated the swing craze by the prolific use of *riffs* (repeated phrases by

Casa Loma Orchestra at NBC Studios, 1937 *(Richard Grudens Collection)*

alternate sections of the band) and an energetic approach to the unmistakable intonation of their brass and reed sections.

I recall Buddy Rich telling me that he enjoyed listening to the recordings of Casa Loma when he was at home between engagements and in the mood for "some very good music." The photo here of Casa Loma is the front -face of a promotional postcard I found recently in an outdoor memorabilia show at Cold Spring Harbor Park on Long Island.

Jean Goldkette's Prolific Orchestra

Jean Goldkette, a former French concert pianist, led a star-filled concert-style musical group rather than a dance band, and he also managed other bands. Jimmy and Tommy Dorsey, Joe Venuti, and Bing Crosby's favorite guitarist Eddie Lang, Bix Beiderbecke and arranger Bill Challis were all Goldkette employees. When Goldkette, who also owned the Graystone Ballroom in Detroit, discontinued his short-lived band, after a stunning farewell engagement in New York's Roseland, a number of his players migrated to Paul Whiteman's King of Jazz Orchestra.

Leo Reisman's Society Orchestra

In the early twenties Leo Reisman's Orchestra played strictly sweet dance music. A true society dance band, its muted brass, silky saxes, and singing violins achieved notable success. At the age of ten Reisman was handed a violin by his dad and a year later he became the leader of his grammar school band. At twelve, young Leo began plugging songs in W.T. Grant Department Stores for Houghton & Dutton Music Publishers.

After studying at the New England Conservatory of Music in Boston, he led a big band in the Egyptian Room of the Brunswick Hotel. Reisman, a busy entrepreneur, maintained and managed over 20 bands at one time, all by different names, thereby becoming a music impresario, being hailed by many as a genius of the music world.

Leo Reisman, about 1929 *(Richard Grudens Collection)*

Reisman tried to bring to Boston all he had heard in New York, especially the success of Whiteman with Gershwin's music. Leo Reisman's bright group of musicians performed for thirteen straight years in the Waldorf's prestigious Wedgewood Room (later re-named the Empire Room), employing the first female big band singers Mildred Bailey and Lee Wiley. Reisman's long list of vocalists on recordings included: a young Bing Crosby crooning "Brother Can You Spare a Dime;" Fred and Adele Astaire vocalizing Broadway's The Band Wagon on RCA's first long-playing recording score in 1931—just before Astaire's Hollywood career began; Astaire's definitive recording of Cole Porter's "Night and Day" from the movie *The Gay Divorcee* in 1932, and Harold Arlen's - yes, Harold Arlen's vocal on a 1933 recording of his own composition "Stormy Weather," which he composed with lyricist Ted Koehler.

Reisman's career spanned 44 years, over twenty in the recording studio alone. He was directly responsible for the careers of both Benny Goodman and Dinah Shore, among others, and was the very first to feature a black artist in his orchestra. At first resisting jazz, for him an unacceptable innovation of music, he later accepted the idea, adapting it to his personal style.

Fred Waring's Pennsylvanians

Charming and handsome Fred Waring, whom most know as a leader of Fred Waring's Pennsylvanians singing group, started his first band in 1916 with his brother Tom as vocalist. After first trying to make it as a dance band at the Colonial Theater in Richmond, Virginia in the early twenties, he later developed his singing musical-show organization instead. First, he developed a quartet of banjo players; then, further developing in radio on Detroit's WWJ, he moved his group to Philadelphia, calling them Waring's Pennsylvanians. Tom and Fred Waring would perform their own

Fred Waring, 1938, while at NBC radio *(Richard Grudens Collection)*

vocals on recordings like "Collegiana," becoming one of the best-known orchestras on radio from 1933 onward. He started at CBS where

5

he adopted his signature tune, "Breezin' Along with the Breeze," but wound up at NBC in the late Thirties, appearing on "Chesterfield Time" and later "The Fred Waring Show," where I first knew him. His office secretary, Cora, once told me that it was Fred who invented the famous Waring Blender while working at the Shawnee Inn he owned on 600 acres in Pennsylvania.

Fred Waring's Pennsylvanians triumphantly performed in Paris at Des Ambassadeurs during a European tour in 1928. *Variety* described Waring's players as "one of the most imitated groups on radio, especially those great choral arrangements for the rocking chair crowd."

Coon-Sanders Nighthawks

Radio's Aces was the Coon-Sanders Nighthawks sobriquet, as if they needed one. Carlton Coon, drummer and vocalist, and pianist-arranger Joe Sanders led this collegian-type, partner-led dance band from Kansas City on WDAF, with rollicking rhythms and cheery greetings. True radio dance band pioneers, Coon-Sanders Nighthawks performed requests sent to the studios via a Western Union ticker installed in the studio. It was probably the first request (radio) show. Arranger Joe Sanders was the first to spread saxophone section voicing, inserting a vocal into almost every selection. Coon-Sanders played jazz, calling it *concert jazz.* Two good-looking, personable guys, their music was peppy, original and unique for the times, which accounted for their success. Mel Torme' first sang with Coon-Sanders Nighthawks.

Coon-Sanders Nighthawks record album cover of 1962. (Richard Grudens Collection)

The ten piece group first arrived in Chicago in 1924 and scored so well at the Lincoln Tavern and Congress Hotel that, when MCA booking agency promised the popular Blackhawk Restaurant a top-flight band in 1926, Coon-Sanders got the job, broadcasting nightly over WGN, sometimes sharing the mike with Wayne King's and Ted Weems' orchestra.

Coon-Sanders Nighthawks took to the road and when they played at Angell Park Pavilion in Sun Prairie, Wisconsin in 1931, they earned thousands of new fans playing often requested songs "Ball and Chain," "What a Girl," "Georgia on My Mind," and "St.Louis Blues. "With a lengthy stay at New York's Hotel New Yorker and a recording session for RCA Victor, they returned to Chicago and played in the famed College Inn at the Hotel Sherman. That "once in a lifetime band" Coon-Sanders disbanded with the early death of young Carleton Coon in 1932. Joe Sanders tried vainly to lead his own band, mostly in the midwest, but it simply didn't live up to the former days of Coon-Sanders.

"Vincent Lopez Speaking"

Vincent Lopez brought his piano and his well-trained musicians into focus playing his signature tune "Nola," thus becoming one of the most prolific dance bands in America during the 1920s. His famous deep-baritone introductory opening words on his WJZ radio program, "Hello, everybody. Lopez speaking," became household words and made him a national figure on radio. In 1925 his band also performed in London at the Hippodrome and the Kit-Kat Club.

Vincent Lopez, 1924. "Lopez Speaking," he'd say. *(Richard Grudens Collection)*

Ted Lewis: "Is Everybody Happy?"

The great Ted Lewis thought himself a jazz musician, but he really wasn't. He certainly was a show business phenomenon showcasing an impressive list of sidemen: Benny Goodman, Jack Teagarden, Mugsy Spanier, Jimmy Dorsey, and Fats Waller, to mention a few. Ted's famous catchphrase "Is everybody happy?" and his theme "Me and My

Ted Lewis and his band, 1929. *(Richard Grudens Collection)*

Shadow," as well as his enduring performance of his own composition "When My Baby Smiles at Me" while sporting an old battered top hat, were all household words during the 1920s, as he and his almost-corny show band devoted enough time to the dance field to be considered an important part of it.

Ted Lewis started at Coney Island in Brooklyn, New York, in 1916 with intentions of becoming a vaudeville act. The band went on to play in top vaudeville houses here and in Europe, especially London's Hippodrome and the famous Kit Kat Club, and for many years up into the '60s and '70s at New York's Roseland and Latin Quarter and at Las Vegas' Desert Inn, where he had his final appearance in the Inn's famous lounge where he always drew great nostalgic crowds.

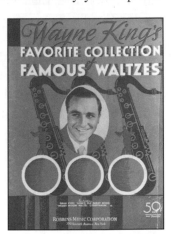

The Waltz King-Wayne King

Wayne King's Orchestra was a true dance band. His theme, "The Waltz You Saved for Me," identified this incomparable group of musicians who were featured at the Trianon Ballroom in Chicago in 1927 and later at Atlantic City's Steel Pier. His eight year tenure at the famous Aragon,

Wayne King sheet music, 1929. *(Robbins Music Corp.)*

8

where he was crowned "The Waltz King", popularized him nationally over network radio, featuring the vocals (and whistling skills) of Elmo Tanner, Charles Farrell, Buddy Clark and The Barry Sisters.

The Great Fletcher Henderson

Another landmark group of fine musicians was Fletcher Henderson's orchestra who started up in New York City at the Club Alabam in 1923, followed by a tenure beginning in 1925 at the Roseland Ballroom for the ensuing five years. Fletcher Henderson and his devoted following of happy dancers were the talk of New York. His orchestra featured an absolute all-star group of players that included Edgar Sampson, Don Redman, Walter Johnson, Benny Carter, Rex Stewart, Sid Catlett, Louis Armstrong, Roy Eldridge, Coleman Hawkins, and other later greats to be. A virtual showcase of some of the best black jazz musicians of all time.

Some say that Henderson's style, compositions and arrangements may have been the catalyst for the formation of the Big Band Era popularized by Benny Goodman employing his charts back in 1935. (It was Henderson who wrote and arranged "King Porter Stomp.") In 1982 Benny Goodman told me that the time spent recording with Henderson's arrangements were his happiest years in music.

Fletcher Henderson and his jazz-flavored pioneer band, who concentrated mostly on smooth dance tempos, toured the forty-eight states playing a variety of ballrooms, hotels, and theaters, then toured Europe twice, the first time in 1929. He disbanded shortly after World War II, when he semi-retired, concentrating on arranging for other orchestras and the Hollywood movie studios.

Gus Arnheim's Cocoanut Grove Orchestra

Gus Arnheim's Cocoanut Grove Orchestra performed regularly for dancers at both the Cocoanut Grove and the Ambassador Hotel in Los Angeles. Here, bandleader Stan Kenton got his start, as did Bing Crosby and the Rhythm Boys (later featured with Paul Whiteman),vocalists Russ Columbo and Andy Russell, and sideman musician Fred Mac Murray (Yes, Fred MacMurray before those movie glory days). Arnheim's 1930s radio show from the Cocoanut Grove was two hours long and heard from "coast-to-coast," as they said in those days, describing network radio programs. Arnheim and his Orchestra appeared in the 1929 movie *The Street Girl*.

Isham Jones Dance Band

The Isham Jones Brass, 1934. George Thow, Clarence Willard, Johnny Carlson, Sonny Lee and Red Ballard. *(Richard Grudens Collection)*

Another one of the early dance bands was Isham Jones, who began it all in 1919 when he formed a small ensemble in his hometown of Coaltown, Ohio. Jones played both piano and saxophone equally, and even learned to play the string bass. Jones was a prolific songwriter as well. He found a home for his musical group at the College Inn, where the band remained for five years. His songs are evergreen dancing songs: "I'll See You in My Dreams," "You've Got Me Crying Again," "When My Dream Boat Comes Home," "Swinging Down the Lane," "It Had to Be You," great tunes all. Bandleader Woody Herman was both a sideman and vocalist with Isham Jones before forming his first Herd. Jones' band was very popular in Atlantic City at the famous Steel Pier,

10

where so many bands played for the dancers of the thirties, as well as in performances at New York's Lincoln Hotel and Denver's Elitch's Gardens.

After retiring because of bad health, Isham Jones returned to New York in 1936 and was featured for a while back at the Lincoln Hotel. His was a sweet ensemble of great music.

Ben Pollack, Bandleader Maker

Ben Pollack, 1936. *(Richard Grudens Collection)*

Ben Pollack's band spawned an impressive number of important musicians who later went on to great fame as bandleaders in the Big Band Era. Try Glenn Miller, Benny Goodman, Jack and Charlie Teagarden, Charlie Spivak, Jimmy McPartland, and in a later band, an unknown named Harry James. Some list! Pollack was originally a drummer, and, like his playing, a very dynamic, hard-driving man. He was a rather unhappy kind of musician, but musically excellent. His never-ending quest to form new bands, winding up as leader of a small dixieland group of players, never worked out, mostly due to his on-again, off-again interest in bandleading.

Epilogue

The reign of the early dance bands punctuated the beginning of a time that musically dominated the lives of both its participants and audiences identified as both dancers and listeners. The formation of these pioneer groups of musicians spawned new and even greater organizations that grew into a phenomenon we recognize as the dawn of the Big Band Era, that is, the birth of America's Golden Age of Music that mesmerized the next several generations of its fans. The dance bands had a great impact on America's popular culture and came to a climax beginning in the late Thirties when the Big Band explosion began to make its mark on the musical landscape.

11

THE GREAT BALLROOMS

One of the first hotels to host a dance band was the St. Francis Hotel in the heart of San Francisco way back in 1913 when it hired Art Hickman's small band to play its prestigious Rose Room. In 1915, a visitor, famed theatrical producer Florenz Ziegfeld, heard them play and brought the eight-piece band, which consisted of piano, trumpet, drums, violin, trombone, two banjos, and bass, to New York to play in the Ziegfeld Follies revues and other nearby venues, perhaps initiating the dance band craze at the dawn of the Big Band Era. The Hickman band

Frank Dailey's Meadowbrook of Cedar Grove, New Jersey. In two versions — before and after addition of the porch. *(Big Band Jump)*

later showcased a string and sax section and is believed to be the first dance band to employ the use of saxophones.

THE MEADOWBROOK

On Pompton (Turnpike) Avenue in Cedar Grove, New Jersey lies an important artifact of the Big Band Era, Frank Dailey's Meadowbrook, where just about all the bands played. Unlike most ballrooms of those times The Meadowbrook is still intact, although it is a shadow of its former self. The Meadowbrook was like a large motel with second story porches, with awnings over the large windows on the first floor, and shutters flanking the side windows. It was painted white with a grassy knoll rising in front with center steps that led to the entrance.

Tommy Dorsey's Orchestra played "I'm Getting Sentimental Over You" there, and Glenn Miller's masterpiece "Moonlight Serenade" was frequently heard in this popular showcase. Frank Dailey, who lived nearby, opened the Meadowbrook in 1930, hoping to showcase his own band, The Meadowbrook Syncopators.

"In the late evening of Tuesday, March 12, 1940, if you were listening to NBC radio, you would have heard Glen Gray's orchestra playing its theme song, 'Smoke Rings'," according to Bill Buchanan, who recently wrote an article about the Meadowbrook for the Montclair, New Jersey, *Times*. "During that period, the major networks featured late night Big Band broadcasts from many nightclubs, hotels, and ballrooms throughout the country. Billy May's arrangement of 'Pompton Turnpike' played at the Meadowbrook put the hoofers in the fast lane with its tempo, and the growling trumpet was that of Billy himself.

"Across the radio dial you could also tune in to the Big Bands from the Raymore Ballroom in Boston, the Mayfair Restaurant at the Van Cleve Hotel in Dayton, Ohio, and the Rustic Cabin in Englewood, New Jersey, where Frank Sinatra was discovered by Harry James, who was listening to these very broadcasts when he discovered Sinatra.

"These late night radio programs were passports to fame for the bands, because young people would hear the broadcasts from distant places, and when the band arrived in their own city, fans lined up to greet them."

"The Meadowbrook complex on Route 23 in Cedar Grove has long been shuttered, and surrounding shrubbery has reclaimed the once sparkling landscape. But if you meander up the steps and listen carefully at the entrance door, you may still be able hear the music from another time played by the Big Bands you love."

THE SUNNYBROOK BALLROOM

"In those days there were no tables or chairs in the entire ballroom," according to Jim Wardrop, author of *Let's Head for the Brook!* - The Story of the Sunnybrook Ballroom, "No liquor was served - just soft drinks and soda fountain treats. The dress code required a jacket and tie for guys, and nice dresses for the girls. Zoot suits (overexaggerated clothes) were often seen on the jitterbugs and gators around the bandstand. The age of admission was eighteen. A ticket cost seventy-five cents for the big-fee name bands. Dances were held from 8:30 PM to 2:30 a.m. with forty-five minute sets of music."

As with most ballrooms, especially during the Depression years, groups of teens filled a car and headed for a place like the Brook.

"The Brook has been a 67 year fixture, consisting of a large swimming pool, picnic area, ballroom and restaurant," according to Big Band music aficionado Carl Harner, a long time resident of nearby Boyertown, Pa., who remembers the Brook. "Over the years I have been surprised at the number of people I meet all over the Philadelphia area who used to go there. It was an amazing place in its heyday."

"In cold weather everyone's hat, coat, and boots were thrown on huge piles in the corners of the ballroom," Wardrop writes, "Crowds jammed the Brook eager to strut their stuff on the large Norwegian maple floor."

All the name bands played the Brook at one time or another. Hal Kemp was a frequent visitor. Charlie Spivak played more New Year's gigs than anyone. Frank Sinatra, Connie Haines, and the Pied Pipers first introduced "Sunny Side of the Street" with Tommy Dorsey right there on the Sunnybrook stage. When Connie Haines and I worked on revising her biography in late 1998, a glance at an entry in her private diary of 1940 read, "Saturday, April 20 - We played Pottstown's

Sunnybrook tonight. I went over really well. The kids liked me. But, the bus ride back made me sort of sick, though."

On his last civilian tour in 1942, before he formed the Army Air Force Band, Glenn Miller played the Brook on February 28th and drew 7,200 fans. "The room was so crowded most of the kids stood in place all evening as there was no room to dance."

THE TUNE TOWN BALLROOM

"I remember back in 1937 very well," says Vince Rowe, a former big city music writer. "The scene was a small mid-western community completely devoid of live entertainment. My thirst for this new music came from radio broadcasts and records. Then I traveled to St. Louis where the real thing existed: The Tune Town Ballroom."

Vince had made plans to see the great Chick Webb at Tune Town. He knew his style and all the personnel of the band. "That wondrous dance emporium that I'd heard so much about (you may remember the Count Basie recording "Tune Town Shuffle" in honor of this popular danceland location) was filled with dancers-jivers and jitterbugs elbowing and jostling for a few feet of swing space. I went right to the bandstand, and there in full flower with instruments blaring was the great thirteen piece Webb orchestra."

Chick Webb was there, a man of the hour: "Chick, the littlest big man there ever was — the leader and number-one drummer, was leading his beautiful band. It was exciting and thrilling to stand there and watch these great musicians play 'Stompin' At the Savoy,' 'Don't Be That Way,' 'If Dreams Come True,' and 'Organ Grinder's Swing.'"

Almost unnoticed was a young girl sitting shyly on a straight-backed chair to the right of her leader: "She didn't attract much attention until she got up to sing. When that happened, all dancing stopped and everybody crowded around to hear this young talent perform. And was she so good singing her own wonderful song, that nutty novelty nursery rhyme 'A-Tisket, A-Tasket' (written with my old friend, band-leader Van Alexander) that she had lost her yellow basket," Vince recalled, "It was none other than our later 'First Lady of Song,' Ella Fitzgerald, when she was just nineteen."

15

On that big band summer night in 1937, Vince Rowe and hundreds of others got a thrill and a memory at the Tune Town Ballroom in St. Louis, Missouri, that has lasted a lifetime.

THE STARLITE BALLROOM

The Starlite Ballroom, 1940. *(Courtesy of Big Band Jump)*

In Hershey, Pennsylvania, the Starlite Ballroom was a legendary venue, catering to dancers who came by trolley from Harrisburg and Lebanon beginning way back in 1917.

In the early days and into the '40s, men who wanted to gain entrance to the Starlite had to wear neckties and coats and the women, dresses only. If you forgot your tie it would cost you a quarter for a house tie rental. Top bands played the Starlite, but it is said that Lawrence Welk failed to draw enough patrons to make a profit.

The Starlite was centered in an area among trees and parklike settings alongside a lake. Cool breezes kept the dancers from being steeped in sweat while dancing. With a whopping 23,000 sq. ft. dance floor and thousands of yards of fabric draped from the ceiling to help create a luxurious atmosphere, the Starlite Ballroom enjoyed success right up to the 1970's. That stately old pavilion closed it doors in 1977

16

and was demolished, leaving, as Carl Sandburg once said, "only the grass which covers all."

THE VALENCIA BALLROOM

The Valencia in 1934. *(Courtesy of Big Band Jump)*

In 1939 the Valencia Ballroom of York, Pennsylvania, celebrated its tenth year of presenting some of the greatest attractions of the Big Band Era like Kay Kyser, Tommy Dorsey, Casa Loma, Horace Heidt, Sammy Kaye and most of the other prevalent bands of the time. Although York was rural, people would travel as much as two hundred miles to attend dances there. By 1959, the Valencia's rule was over, a church taking its place through the '80s. The building is still there perhaps echoing the beautiful sounds of the Big Bands it hosted over more than twenty years.

THE GRAYSTONE

When ballroom dancing swept America, the Graystone Ballroom in Detroit. once owned by bandleader Jean Goldkette, with its great central chandelier with mirrors that reflected sparkling light and its domed ceiling that was covered with colored fabrics, became the place to be seen during the 1920s until the end of the war.

"The mezzanine around the entire ballroom is canopied and replete with inviting chairs and divans where guests may rest or lounge while enjoying the music and a full view of the dancers below," boasted the management in ads. Many of the Big Bands played engagements in this fine ballroom. Eight thousand people a week patronized the Graystone Ballroom in its heyday. "In 1930 we opened at the Graystone Ballroom. Charley Horvath and Charley Stanton were in charge and they said there were only two great dance bands in the country, Jean Goldkette's Victor band and us-the Fletcher Henderson band," according to cornetist Rex Stewart, whose greatest glory was his eleven years with Duke Ellington, "We had men like Buster Bailey, Don Redman, and Russell Smith working with us then."

THE GLEN ISLAND CASINO

Just the other day, Graham Pass of BBC radio inquired about the existance of the famed Glen Island Casino, which he wanted to visit in April, 1999, while on a Big Band visit to New York. A simple inquiry revealed that this great romantic spot that showcased the Big Bands of the 1930's and '40s was gone, replaced by the Glen Island Country Club, its original building totally re-designed, not a trace of the old look left.

The Glen Island Casino was located on Long Island Sound in New Rochelle, New York. The softly lit main ballroom, graced with very high French - styled windows that overlooked the water, was on the second floor. The natural wood walls enhanced its beauty.

Glenn Miller opened there in May of 1939, followed by Glen Gray's Casa Loma Orchestra. Glenn Miller's shows were produced as live radio shows. The Glen Island Casino represented glamour and prestige, where only the best and most popular bands were featured.

More Dance Band Ballrooms

The Savoy and Grand Terrace Cafe' in Chicago, the Palomar in Hollywood (where Benny Goodman single-handedly unleashed The

Swing Era one night in 1934), the Benjamin Franklin Hotel in Philadelphia, and in New York the Arcadia, Roseland (both Manhattan and Brooklyn versions),the Cafe Rougé in the Pennsylvania Hotel, all very popular in the '20s,'30s and '40s, especially with Glenn Miller's Orchestra.

The Biltmore Hotel and Cocoanut Grove in Los Angeles, the Mark Hopkins and Palace Hotels in San Francisco, the Taft, Lincoln, Commodore, and New Yorker Hotels in New York, also booked notable dance bands as did the Marine Ballroom of Atlantic City's Steel Pier in New Jersey and The Rainbow Room, high up on Rockefeller Center's 65th floor, where Ray Noble's Orchestra with vocalist Al Bowlly prevailed for so many years, and where Glenn Miller discovered his special "sound."

When the Trianon and Aragon Ballrooms first opened in Chicago, many other towns and cities tagged their newly-opened ballrooms by the same names. Most bands played popular dance music, although jazz-oriented groups began executing a new style they called *swing*. The prestigious Ritz Carlton Roof in Boston was a favorite gig for Duke Ellington, as the Hippodrome in Baltimore was for Glenn Miller in his early days.

During the 1920s, Roseland, a very popular ballroom located at 51st Street and Broadway in New York City, employed two rotating bands as a standard policy. Sam Lanin, a former member of John Philip Sousa's world-famous military band, directed the first Roseland band. Alumni of Lanin's various bands went on to become leaders of a number of groups formed during the Big Band Era. Jean Goldkette's Orchestra played Roseland, too, and in the off-season toured New England ballrooms.

A dashing Artie Shaw at Paramount Studios. *(Richard Grudens Collection)*

PART TWO

ARTIE SHAW

The "Begin The Beguine" Band Begins

What an exhilarating experience conversing with renowned band-leader Artie Shaw. Artie's depth as a thinker and reputation as a constantly analyzing musician follow him from his restless days as an outspoken bandleader right up to today. Artie Shaw is 89 years old but talks and acts like 50.

For the past two weeks I spent much time preparing for our forthcoming telephone date from his home in Newbury Park, California, listening to his recordings from the early days and reading available material about his musical life, past and present. But no form of preparation was enough.

We faced off phone to phone, and, suspicions confirmed, it was not an easy interview, although it was at times dramatic, funny, and, for certain, stimulating. By contrast, Les Brown's interview for this book was warm, soft and cuddly. Red Norvo's was somewhat stressful only because of his chronic hearing problem. but the Artie Shaw interview session was like navigating through white water — very difficult at best, but strangely gratifying.

But, hold on, I think we are getting ahead of ourselves. Let's back up to the year 1910 where he was born Arthur Jacob Arshawsky in New York City. He was raised in New Haven, Connecticut from the age of eight; he played saxophone there in the high school band. After some effort as a player with the school's Peter Pan Novelty Orchestra, he joined Johnny Cavallaro's local band, where, at fifteen, he was the youngest member, and where he learned the many harsh lessons of a musician's life, Artie Shaw then headed to Cleveland and finally Chicago for a while, carefully honing his playing and arranging skills with Joe Cantor's Far East Orchestra, Austin Wylie's band, and Irving Aaronson's Commanders, "...working every night until 3 A.M., then

21

heading for the 'Negro district' to sit in with Earl Hines and go till day-light. One had to get away from the respectable band to play some jazz," Artie noted. Playing with and watching musicians like trumpeter Mugsy Spanier and clarinetist Frank Teschemacher influenced the young clarinetist.

"I was the kind of guy who listened to everybody, that's how I learned," he said. "Sure, it's easier when someone can show you how to do what you want to do. But the big thing is to learn - some way - just so you do learn. My home grown method of learning may be tougher - but once you do learn it my way, you don't easily forget what you've learned. But, I didn't know I wanted to be a bandleader. It never entered my mind. It just happened as anything happens," Art went on. Although he swears he patterned his music after no one in particular, he swears he remembers it all as "…nothing but work, work, work, until from time to time I got tired and quit for awhile —which, as you know, I did a number of times when I felt I had to."

Artie Shaw returned to New York as a freelance player for CBS, appearing in concert in a clarinet-and-strings quartet that didn't really work out. He was nineteen and had to remain in New York because of an accident where a man stepped in front of his car and, as a result, died. He was forced to stay on for legal reasons. At the time Artie Shaw knew no one at all in New York.

Trecking uptown to listen to jazz players, he met and was befriend-ed by Willie "The Lion" Smith in Harlem. "I had never heard piano playing like that in my life." Artie joined in with Smith and went on to meet bandleader Chick Webb and a young and then-healthy kid vocal-ist, Billie Holiday. "There was the great Jack Teagarden and his younger brother Charlie, Eddie Condon, Gene Krupa, Benny Goodman, Wingy Manone and the whole Chicago crowd who also had come to New York about the same time as I did to try their luck in the Big Apple."

Artie encountered the now legendary jazz cornetist Bix Beiderbecke, who was on the downgrade after leaving Paul Whiteman's King of Jazz Orchestra, now a pitiful wreck of a man, unable to control his drinking that was interfering with his cornet playing. He also met Jimmy Dorsey, who had already established himself and would come around now and then and play in their jam sessions. And, Artie encountered a successful Tommy Dorsey; a flat-broke, struggling Bunny Berigan, who was trying to earn a living as a trumpet player, and a young piano player named Joe Bushkin, who later played with Tommy Dorsey. "We hung out at Plunkett's, a hole-in-the-wall joint under the Sixth Avenue El at 53rd Street and Ninth Avenue, where I met a music conductor from CBS who got me an audition and a part-time job with Red Nichols' band. As a result, I got to play first saxophone in the CBS staff orchestra. I was only 20 years old." Artie began focusing on becoming "somebody," driving himself through hard work and a "feverish need to know about things."

PLUNKETT'S

There was a number of passwords used at Plunkett's in those days, according to Esquire's 1947 Jazzbook. In those free and easy days tabs represented more of the business than cash. There were two booths in the small back room, but they were seldom used except for a siesta or the occasional visit of an angry wife. Every day the barreled beer arrived at Plunkett's in a different truck: a florist's delivery car, a milk wagon, or even a hearse. Eddie Condon's dressing room, the icebox Tommy Dorsey talks about, was loaded to the ceiling with thousands of dollars' worth of instruments — everybody's — from Jimmy Dorsey's famous collection of gold saxophones to Peewee Russell's crud- caked clarinet, or Bix Beiderbecke's cornet in a corduroy sack, and even Joe Venuti's fiddle and Jack Teagarden's and Glenn Miller's trombones. The camaraderie at Plunkett's was something special. Why, when the Dorsey Brothers started their orchestra, Jimmy Plunkett was their manager. The bar was about ten feet long and on the shelves above it were a half-dozen nondescript beer steins. In the telephone book Plunkett's was listed as The Trombone Club.

Between gigs, Artie applied his earnings as a radio studio musician, one of that elite group of excellent instrumentalists, to finance a general education in the hope of becoming a writer. He purchased a small farm in rural Bucks County, Pennsylvania, where, for about a year, he wrote a book about legendary cornetist Bix Beiderbecke, but scrapped it because he wasn't satisfied with the results. He returned to New York. I began working my head off in the radio and recording studios, making several hundred dollars a week playing on soap and cereal programs. Now and then there would be a recording session, a distinct improvement on the sickening advertising music I was forced to do. I also tried to go back to arranging. I dreamed up a little piece of music, a composition I entitled 'Interlude in B Flat,' drawn from ideas supplied by Mozart and Brahms - people and stuff like that.

"I played it at a swing concert with the help of two violin-playing friends, a violist, a cellist, and added guitar, string bass, and drums for the sake of rhythm, It was such a huge success that agents kept calling me." Art refers to Joe Helbeck, a night-club owner who had invited him to participate with his then small group to perform for the benefit of Local 802 of the musician's union at the Imperial Theater. Artie called his group Arthur Shaw's Swing String Ensemble, fusing strings with brass, an unheard of effect at the time. The excellent results prompted Tommy Rockwell, who headed the Rockwell-O'Keefe Booking Agency, to ask Artie to form a permanent band. Some have called that concert a milestone in jazz history, as being the first real jazz concert.

During the summer of 1935, Artie put together a regular band just after some valid efforts with Bunny Berigan's band. Artie performed on that original famous recording "I Can't Get Started" that remains a hit even today.

"The first gig with my new band —I called it Art Shaw and his Orchestra — was at the Lexington (Hotel) in New York," Art continued, "playing what we did best. I had two fellow musicians from Aaronson's days, tenor saxist Tony Pastor and Lee Castle playing trumpet. I also added a string quartet that was a different approach. Jerry Gray set this up. He was a jazz fiddle player and a very good arranger."

I reminded Art that his first band sounded much like Dixieland: "Well, everybody sounded like everybody in those days. What's Dixieland, anyway? Maybe shades of that sound entered our brain, I don't know."

If you listen to those early 1936-37 Brunswick recordings "It Ain't Right," with Peg La Centra on vocal, "Thou Swell," "Sugarfoot

Stomp," and a swinging version of "Goodnight Angel," you'll see what I mean. They were the pre-"Begin the Beguine" stardom days. The band had four strings, three brass, and only two reeds. Artie and Jerry Gray did all the arrangements. Then the "Begin the Beguine" band arrived :

"When we recorded Cole Porter's 'Begin the Beguine' in 1938, we soared, even though it was the 'B' side. That tune was nowhere, and suddenly a guy named Artie Shaw comes along and makes a record of it with a totally different arrangement, and it becomes a hit. How do you figure it?" Artie said, "You seek perfection and settle for what you get."

The arrangement developed for Artie Shaw's "Begin the Beguine" transpired in Boston where they had a long engagement at the Roseland-State Ballroom. "I asked Jerry to re-arrange 'Begin the Beguine,' a tune that the band liked to fool around with. I wanted to get the attention of the (ballroom) dancers, and it did. Jerry wrote a strong introduction for that reason. He substituted a modified 4/4 beat for the original beguine rhythm."

I told Artie that New York's WQEW radio had just conducted an annual listener's poll of the 156 best recordings of all time, and that his original version of "Begin the Beguine" came in number one.

"It was a good recording, I'm not surprised that it has stood up this long."

"And your 'Stardust' was number eight."

"Yeah, I heard that. That's fine."

"And 'Frenesi' was forty-one."

"Well, that proves my point. It's all relative, isn't it. It's like art - very subjective. I really don't follow polls - never have. I only care whether I achieved close to what I wanted to do. Everytime you go into a studio, you have an idea of what you want to do. Somebody has to come out on top no matter what you do. But, what does it really mean? How do you measure that?

"You have no idea what's going to happen when you make a record. All you can do is make the best record you can. I didn't follow the idea of make success - make things what people wanted. I tried to do what I wanted and to do it as well as I could do it. Some of it worked. I call myself an eighty-percent loser."

"Your fans and I think you are a ninety -percent winner."

"No - no, no! If I was a ninety-percent winner, I'd be a zillionaire. A ten-percent winner is very big."

After the "Begin the Beguine" (with "Indian Love Call" on the "A" side) success, the Shaw band began recording for Bluebird and included the bouncy, jazzy "Back Bay Shuffle" (which Artie still enjoys; the "ghost" band playing it quite differently today, he says) and "Nightmare," that Artie composed in his hotel room during that Boston stay, which became his eerie-like band theme.

Artie Shaw and Helen Forrest, 1938. *(Richard Grudens Collection)*

Another kind of musician, jazz singer Billie Holiday, sang with Artie Shaw's band for the Boston engagement in Roseland-State, until she decided to quit. She was tired of the racism dished out to her mostly on Southern tours, being replaced by co-band singer Helen Forrest. Artie composed and arranged a tune especially for Billie entitled "Any Old Time" which eventually became a hit - now a standard - a tune loved by the musicians themselves. It is magnificent, to say the least. Find the original version and listen carefully. It's pure Shaw and Holiday excellence. You will come to love the work of Artie Shaw and Billie Holiday for this recording alone. As a footnote: After recording the song with Billie, the record company (RCA) would not release it, citing Billie as not being commercial. "So I told Billie about that and that I had to record it with somebody else," Artie explained, "So I used

Helen Forrest, and they released the record. Stupid, but true! Billie was a remarkable singer. I chose her because she was a singer I could afford at the time and the only singer that could keep up with the band. Helen Forrest was also very good. She learned a lot from Billie; she sat next to her for a while. They split up the work. I always thought that later, Helen sounded a lot like Billie…same kind of feeling."

Just before Christmas 1998, when I asked Helen Forrest about her association with Artie Shaw, she complimented Billie Holiday's singing, saying, "I loved Billie's singing and listened to her phrasing quite a bit." And, she went on, "My favorite recording with Artie was 'All The Things You Are.' Artie always made sure that I was comfortable doing my songs in my own style. After all, Artie was my first Big Band leader."

In choosing which musicians would play in his band, Artie described it to me this way: "I hired the guys who I thought could play what I wanted to hear and what we needed from them as musicians. If they couldn't make it after they played with us for a while, you learned pretty soon who could and who couldn't handle themselves. I kept guys who I thought had potential, and weeded out the guy who couldn't blow. Les (sax player) Robinson said, 'What do you see in me?' and I said, 'I heard what you are trying to do.'"

Of all his sidemen Artie respected drummer Buddy Rich and tenor sax player Georgie Auld. "Buddy was a difficult musician, hard to harness, but he had something to say with his percussion, and he said it well and it helped my band at the time. Georgie Auld was also a hard headed musician who sometimes went against my musical grain. But, like Buddy, he kept the band going with his energy and skills and became, like Buddy, a major asset."

Then the inevitable November 1939 Artie Shaw question: "Why did you give up leading and playing so suddenly by walking out on your band at the Café Rouge in New York and taking off for Mexico on an unscheduled vacation, vowing never to return to bandleading? —I know you have been asked this question a million times, but there's nothing like getting the answer directly from Artie Shaw," I inquired carefully.

"It wasn't sudden. It was a build-up of disillusionment with what I was doing. I wanted to play music, and an audience wanted me to play

'Begin the Beguine.' It gets a little old after a while. We needed a little chance to play 'something' once in a while. I wanted to play real music, not music just for dancers, or treat it all as a business like the bands of Guy Lombardo or Sammy Kaye were doing."

Artie had left the band in the hands of Georgie Auld, who fronted what he called Georgie Auld and His Artie Shaw Orchestra, but it only lasted three months or so without Artie, who was south of the border in Acapulco resting up, playing in local jam sessions, always thinking and planning new and exciting new ways to play and present music, and collecting Mexican-Latin style music to bring up North.

When Artie returned from this unscheduled "vacation," he brought along a tune which, when recorded, became a major hit. The title was "Frenesi." "No one expected that great success. I didn't think - my God—'Frenesi' - the last thing on Earth we expected was for that to take off. It seemed about as far removed as possible from what they would call 'mainstream' hit music in those days. But it did. It went crazy," Artie told my colleague Fred Hall for his 1989 book *Dialogues in Swing*.

I love that tune. I don't know why, but when the recording begins with those lilting string phrases and percussion, then breaks into Artie's clarinet solo, I become instantly emotional. At the same time I try to recall why it affects me so, but to no avail, however deep I reach into my nostalgic brain.   By this time, it seemed Artie Shaw could not escape from success. His new orchestra was one of his finest. It had a string section and stars like Billy Butterfield on trumpet and Johnny Guarnieri on guitar and harpsichord (a new instrument for jazz-playing), Ray Coniff on trombone, Lennie Hayton on piano, and later Hot Lips Page on trumpet, Lee Castle and Max Kaminsky on trumpet, and Georgie Auld on tenor sax. Artie's memorable "Concerto for Clarinet" was recorded during the "Frenesi" period. "It came out of a film I was working on for Warner Brothers with Fred Astaire. I wrote the piece for Fred, who was gonna do a dance around it. So I wrote a thing called 'Concerto for Clarinet.' It was a framework kind of piece, part blues and part jazz. It was a lot like a thing I once did at a Paul Whiteman concert earlier, only less extensive."

When America entered the war in 1941, Artie Shaw joined the Navy and, as a Chief Petty Officer, led a Navy band on downright dangerous tours in the South Pacific entertaining the troops: "We arrived at Pearl Harbor on Christmas Day, 1942. Our band was called Navy Band Number 501, with players like trumpeter Max Kaminsky and drummer Davy Tough. Our base was New Caledonia. We set out on a 'tour' of the New Hebrides, the Solomons, spots like that. We played on ships, in jungles, on airfields, and anywhere they booked us. We hopped from place to place to place - jungles mostly. Not that we had any choice. On flight decks we were lowered into the ship, just like when we played the Strand or the Paramount in New York, only the stages there were raised like a giant elevator. On battleships we played under the big guns. We had a number of close calls when the Japs decided to bomb the ships we played on. We stayed on in Australia, however, and traveled up and down that whole continent before we began to come apart. Our instruments were in bad shape, as were our bodies. It was combat fatigue, and it was impossible to go on, so we shipped back to the U.S. I was in the Oak Knoll Naval Hospital for a few months, pretty much washed up, to say the least."

For a while Artie organized another band and recorded for Musicraft Records. Mel Torme's Meltones, a young and new group hailing from Chicago, recorded some very nice sides including "Get Out of Town" and "What Is This Thing Called Love," and songbird Kitty Kallen recorded a splendid version of "My Heart Belongs To Daddy," which she still talks about today. Artie still wasn't happy, just always unsettled and wanting.

Artie Shaw went East and settled down for a while in Norwalk, Connecticut, after trying Hollywood and being involved making movies. "I was at last able to write. For me, it was more important than playing a clarinet or leading a band."

Some consider Artie Shaw's small groups - his band -within - a - band groups like the pre-war Gramercy Five (named after a New York telephone exchange), who played lightweight, jazz-oriented material, as an excellent approach to creative music. Some choices were "Summit Ridge Drive" (which became a million seller, named after a street on which Shaw lived at the time of the recording), "Special Delivery

Stomp," "My Blue Heaven," and the breezy "The Grabtown Grapple," featuring, at different times, trumpeter Roy Eldridge, guitarist Barney Kessel, drummer Nick Fatool, trumpeter Billy Butterfield, guitarist Johnny Guarnieri, bassist Jud DeNaut, drummer Lou Fromm, bassist Morris Rayman, and pianist Dodo "The Moose" Marmarosa.

As a last musical stand, Artie Shaw resumed recording with an extension of the Gramercy Five group featuring guitarists Tal Farlow or Joe Puma and pianist Hank Jones. There were memorable sessions with this group including terrific versions of "S' Wonderful," "Little Jazz" (also a sobriquet for Roy Eldridge), "Love Walked In," "Summertime," "Lady Day" (as a tribute to Billie Holiday, known as "Lady Day"), and "Dancing On the Ceiling."

"Didn't you get some satisfaction doing that body of work with the small groups like The Gramercy Five? You had people like trumpeter Billy Butterfield and guitarist Johnny Guarnieri —"

"And I had guys like (pianist) Dodo Marmarosa and (trumpeter) Roy Eldridge. And I had guys like (pianist) Hank Jones and (guitarist) Tal Farlow."

"You have to be satisfied with some of those things."

"True. Satisfaction is doing it. The misery is having to keep doing the same thing year in and year out. I can't stand it. Nobody could stand it. Why should we play the same thing over and over just because it was successful? Some people put up with it; I didn't. A guy like Glenn Miller was a businessman. To me his was boring music. Very boring charts done over and over and over."

"Well, a lot of Goodman and Miller has stood up over all these years with the public and their ghost bands enjoy immense success even today with the reissuance of CDs and appearances on cruise ships and in Vegas and Atlantic City," I argued.

"Maybe some people like that. I don't. You see, as far as I was concerned the only good white bands in those days were me and Dorsey …and Goodman. Nobody played better than Goodman, but he had no musicality. I mean within his scope he was excellent. You see - it's not a foot race. I don't know how you can gauge who's better. It has nothing to do with better because there's no criteria. Just because you run a mile and say this guy got there quicker, so he is *better*. How do you say who's better, Rembrandt or Picasso? Completely, there is no such thing as a criteria by which you can say 'this is the best,' unless you define your terms. But I had to go on to make a living, pay my bills, and help my mother at the time. But you need an audience and you have to be playing for somebody. You attract an audience and they give you money and you pay your men. The audience doesn't come —you can't pay your men. That means you're out of business. See what I'm getting at."

Artie Shaw gave it all up in 1955, setting down his clarinet on the shelf forever.

We talked about his "ghost band" still operating today under the baton and clarinet of the capable Dick Johnson. "I remembered talking to band booker Willard Alexander in the mid-eighties when he was bugging you to get a ghost band going."

"Well, Dick has been doing it for some years. He's as good

Current leader Dick Johnson. *(Richard Grudens Collection)*

as good can be. But, I wouldn't like it. And, that term 'ghost band' - I hate it - I'm not a ghost. It's just a *band*."

"Woody Herman coined the phrase 'ghost band,' I reminded him.

"How did you find Dick Johnson?"

"Someone sent me a record of his small group. The guy said Dick had grown up on me, and I could tell it was true from listening to the record. He's a remarkable musician. So, a few years later when Willard (Alexander) pushed me for a new band, I thought of this guy Dick Johnson."

"Have you traveled much with the new 'ghost band'?"

"I traveled with the (ghost) band to get it established when we first put it together. I wanted to make sure it was working right — it takes a few weeks to shake a band down. So I went out on the road with it for a few weeks. It was with a Tony Bennett and Rosey Clooney show. That was it! I'm actually doing a concert out here at the end of the month (October 1998) at the Wilshire Theater in LA for KLON radio, although

I don't really like playing for the public anymore. I'm going to put the band together, rehearse the band—stand in front of it... and give the downbeats...that's it."

"What else are you doing? I know you have written three books besides your *Trouble With Cinderella* bio."

"That's what I do now. I have been working on a very long (book)—one, but I can't find any way to edit it down. I've had a broken leg for two years which is driving me *crazy*. That doesn't help. Editing is very difficult...writing is re-writing. Constantly. Someone once said, 'A work of art is never finished — it's abandoned.' A pretty good line...(we laugh)."

"What would you have done differently if you had to do it all over again?" I inquired suddenly and carefully.

"Well, knowing what I know now? Well...I certainly would not have done what I did. I would have kept going another year or so and I'd have been a multi-zillionaire. I would have gone with it long enough so I wouldn't have to think about money for the rest of my life."

Artie was recently invited to participate with Les Brown and Ray Anthony in England for the BBC back last August. But he declined for obvious reasons.

"I told them no. I simply do not do those kinds of things anymore."

"So what do you do every day of your life?"

"First, I get up and breathe...devoutly! After that I do what I want to do...that's mostly writing — it's an addiction, and ...I read a lot...tremendous amount of reading. But, I am not a fan...I'm not interested in reading about Peggy Lee or Helen O'Connell. I read completely different material. Anyway, most of those musicians and bandleaders were not exactly brain surgeons...I ran into that problem with Ken Burns who's doing that (television documentary) show on jazz - and his executive producer...Lynn Novack...who did most of the baseball show, says it's very difficult to get them to say anything...trouble with them...they don't know much...that's also the trouble with most writers...anyone can put sentences together...but what do they have to say? That's what's important. Tolstoy, who was a pretty good writer, and Dostoyevsky, they had something very important to say. That's what I read."

"You converse during interviews more than most subjects, Artie,"

"I'm sure that's true. Another thing about the band business is that all musicians know is how to blow a horn. They're all Johnny one-note people. So what are you going to talk about. I mean…which way do you play a middle B? Which finger do you use?"

I explained that writers like me may approach things from a different perspective.

"Well, you're trying to identify with the public and what they like. I know what I like, and I tried to do it. *Who's Who*…after fifty years they ask you for an epitaph. So, I give them the first one which is 'He did the best he could with the material at hand. But, the material in my hand was not very good. But, I did the best I could.' A lot of the music that was being played was not very good. Although, some of it was very good. I never will be satisfied. You know what my new epitaph is…simplified…the new one is 'Go Away.' (We laugh loudly together.)That's how much I feel about that. I mean, what's an epitaph? You're gone…who gives a damn? Some say, 'I want to be buried at so and so, or in so and so…' who cares where you are buried. Such a stupid thing to be occupied with. I guess people have this damn awful ego problem. Me! Me! Me! The center of the Universe…in other words…people are narcissistic. Everybody is at the center of the Universe…new gods for old…in America we have 260 million Universes. No wonder we get into trouble. Pretty sad."

Artie Shaw, despite his irreverence towards others in his field and personal negative feelings of disillusionment in the way music is controlled by people other than musicians, remains an important figure in the history of the Big Band Era. When he worked, and how he worked, he was the best. I have the feeling that from the very beginning Artie Shaw wanted to be a writer, finally causing him to place his instrument aside forever in favor of his pen, his true first love. But, in retrospect, it was his talent with the music that punctuated his life's work, not his pen. Millions have thrilled to his impeccable renditions of some of the best music of the Age.

Artie Shaw retired in his prime, a major loss to music. To Artie Shaw the best was rare, and the biggest wasn't necessarily Big.

Artie Shaw was Big and Artie Shaw's work is Rare, and he has survived on his own terms.

Les Brown, Doris Day's favorite band leader. *(Richard Grudens Collection)*

LES BROWN AND THE BAND OF RENOWN

In 1940, at the age of eight, I distinctly recall my first encounter with a Big Band. The scene was the New York World's Fair; the band was Les Brown's Band of Renown. The vocalist, a Cincinnati-born seventeen year old attractive blond youngster with freckles on her face, Doris Kappelhoff, had recently acquired a permanent sobriquet: Doris Day. I remember the thrilling, full band sound at the Dancing Campus Pavilion. It forged a considerable impression. But, my Aunt Irene urged me on to the other sights and, glancing back over my shoulder as the rich sounds diminished, I was drawn further and further away from the music I would come to love for a lifetime.

Today, some 58 years later, world-famous bandleader Les Brown and I shared a priceless conversation from his comfortable California home. We talked about Les' early experiences in music, including those World's Fair days, and about our mutually favorite group of musicians — Bob Hope's long-time (over fifty years) employees — Les Brown and The Band of Renown.

Les Brown had always wanted to lead a band. Even at 87 years old, Les is still an active bandleader working four or five "gigs" a month. His band is listed in the *Guinness Book of Records* as the longest running Big Band in history. He had just returned from London, England, where he, bandleader Ray Anthony, and bandleader, arranger Billy May were honored as special guests of the BBC Big Band Legends in Concert held at famous Ronnie Scott's in Birmingham, England.

Les' early life in Reinerton, Pennsylvania, was a happy one living with a baker-father who always led a local brass band, playing mostly John Philip Sousa marches, who fiercely encouraged and fostered his talented son's aspirations in music.

"Encourage me! Are you kidding? He forced me stay in the bake shop and practice. He did not encourage me; he was my boss and practically forced me to play, which probably explains why I have always been too easy with my own band members over the years."

Les' dad lived to the age of ninety-two, fortunately able to enjoy his three sons' successes in music, including, of course, Warren and Stumpy.

Before college, Les attended the Ithaca Conservatory of Music where he learned demanding arranging skills. He wound up at Duke University in North Carolina in 1936, initiating his career as the bandleader of a twelve-man group of undergraduates (his scholarship obligation) called the Duke Blue Devils Band. The band lasted for a year, after some limited traveling, performing at both Playland Casino in Rye, New York, and Budd Lake, New Jersey.

"We weren't bad for a college band, but we didn't make much money in those days, so we broke up. Anyway, the parents wanted their sons back in school."

For a short period Les arranged for the Isham Jones, Larry Clinton, and Red Nichols bands. "It was sort of a year-off thing. I worked freelance before I reorganized a new band of my own again."

In 1938, Les returned to Budd Lake to lead a local band. "I met my wife Clare at Budd Lake that year. We got married, and we stayed married, and that was that."

Searching for future recording artists, Ely Oberstein, the head of RCA Victor, realizing Les' talent, lured him into forming a Big Band, then promptly booked him into the Edison Hotel in New York for three months: "I received a hundred dollars a week, which was quite a bit of money. Joe Glaser, who was also Louis Armstrong's manager, took us on. He got us booked into the Arcadia in New York and into the 1939-1940 World's Fair in Flushing Meadow (New York)."

"Those were our developing years with the band, Richard," Les continued, "It was where we started it all. Doris Day had just joined us. The audiences really loved her. She not only sang well, but had a good voice on recordings, which made her an additional asset."

DORIS DAY

"Richard, people ask me why I left the Bob Crosby band to go with Les Brown. It's an old, old story. Bob actually told Les

Doris Day today. Check out the message. *(Richard Grudens Collection)*

about me. I was very young then and my work with the band had to do with a commercial they had on a radio show, but they became agency contract-bound to feature a girl called Bonnie King on the commercial. They were stuck with this girl even though they didn't like it. So they tried to locate other work for me. I didn't know Les Brown or even much about his band either. They spoke to him and asked him to come to the Strand Theater in New York where I was appearing with Bob Crosby.

"Well, he did just that. He came right backstage and said, 'I want you to sing with my band, I loved what you did in there.' My mother and I were invited to hear his band, and we loved it. I met all the guys and they were great. Bob Crosby told me that Les was going to be a big success and that it would be a wonderful thing for me to do. So that's how I did it, and was I happy that I did. I adored every minute of it and I love him and all the guys. They're all still my buddies, and one of them, Ted Nash (sax player), moved here with his wife because they were coming up to visit me all the time and fell in love with Carmel (California).

"Enough of that! See," she added, "I told you it was a long dull story, right?"

"Not really, Doris. Readers will want to know it right from your heart - directly from you to them," I explained.

"I also have to say — Les was, and still is, a marvelous man, and, despite his youth at the time, was a strong father figure for me. He was also a first-class musician. He played the clarinet and did his own arrangements. Unlike Glenn Miller, Benny Goodman and Tommy Dorsey, Les' band sound was staccato, amplified by his theme, 'Leap Frog,' and he had wonderful arrangements full of twists and surprises."

"Our first engagement with Doris," continued Les, "was at Mike Todd's Theater Café in Chicago in 1940. Gypsy Rose Lee was the headliner and we did two twenty-minute dance sets with Doris singing four or five songs. Her pay was seventy-five dollars a week. By the time she left me in 1946, it had risen to five hundred. I'd say that, next to Frank Sinatra, Doris was the best in the business on selling a lyric."

DORIS DAY

"We had great bus trips. Sometimes they were a little bit long. We also were able to get jobs at a hotel or a theater. That kept us in one place at least a week, mostly two, sometimes three. The bus trips were the most fun. I adored them because of the guys; they were the greatest and all we did was laugh as we traveled from place to place."

I asked Doris about some of the locations she appeared at with the band:

"The Glen Island Casino in New Rochelle (New York) was a wonderful place to work and we adored it. We really loved the classy Hotel Pennsylvania in New York, and the College Inn at the (Hotel) Sherman in Chicago was another favorite place along with the (Hollywood) Palladium in Los Angeles. Les loved working the Palladium, and he still does."

"Why did we call Doris *Do-Do.*? ...I guess that was because it was *D* for *Doris* and *D* for *Day*...and just for affectionate fun," said Les, "I don't know, we just did. She was the band's kid sister. She made a big hit with a song called 'Sentimental Journey.' One of my arrangers, Ben Homer, and I wrote the melody. I got lyricist Bud

Les Brown and Do-Do Day, 1944. *(Courtesy George Simon's Big Band Book)*

Green of "Once in a While" fame to put it into words. Once I heard Do-Do sing it, I knew for sure we had a hit on our hands."

Doris Day had first performed "Sentimental Journey" in the Cafe Rougé at the Hotel Pennsylvania in New York, where the band was appearing. The song became a symbol for homesick servicemen. The recording still rates high on recent polls of the most popular recordings of all time.

DORIS DAY

"'Sentimental Journey' was a World War II song and the first time I sang it at rehearsal I knew it was going to be a smash hit. And, of course it was! The guys that were in the service, especially overseas, went ape over it, and it became a huge hit for us. When we first played in New York, Les wouldn't play it over the air because he didn't want another band to get a hold of it and record it before he could."

"And right about then, after Do-Do left us the first time, we did an entire summer at Log Cabin Farms in Armonk,New York, from July 4th until Labor Day, and we had a radio wire every night…and every afternoon, too. The band was just building and the radio exposure did it for us and we went big from there. The boys really enjoyed that summer, living in local houses and having a chance to play baseball, tennis, and lots of swimming."

The band's first real hit, "Joltin' Joe DiMaggio," with a vocal by Betty Bonney, who succeeded Doris for a while, occurred in 1941. Fifty years later, the recording enjoyed a revival during the anniversary of the unbroken, record-setting 56 game hitting streak that DiMaggio established with the New York Yankees baseball team.

Les claims that Doris was inadvertently responsible for his long-time association with show business legend Bob Hope:

"Someone took Doris' 'Sentimental Journey' recording to Bob Hope, when Bob was sort of looking for a new singer for his radio show. When he heard the recording, he decided to hire the band, but that did not include Doris. He had Frances Langford singing and was reluctant to let her go because of their long association. It's ironic, though, because he hired Doris a year later, but had to pay her more because in the meantime 'Sentimental Journey' made a star out of her."

"After Doris left the band, how did you manage to get her to come back?"

"Well, I'll let Doris tell you that story."

DORIS DAY

"After I had my baby (Terry), I was singing again at WLW in Cincinnati, doing the late show - called 'Moon River.' It was

just me and a fabulous organist. I sang three beautiful ballads every night and we were on at midnight, of all hours. WLW was a 50,000 watt station so it went everywhere. Les was traveling in automobiles with the band and they had the radio on and heard me -'That's Do-Do!,' he said, screaming aloud in the car, and he now realized that I had started to sing again after having (her son) Terry. That's how he tracked me down and convinced me to return and it was the best thing I ever did in my life. I loved the band. It was a great, swinging band and I loved the musicians. We just had a great time and Les was a dreamboat."

My favorite Doris Day/Les Brown recording is "My Dreams Are Getting Better All the Time." "Well, that was my arrangement," Les said, "I doubled up the tempo on that recording because the song was kinda dull sounding. Doris is so sweet on that tune." The recording of "You Won't Be Satisfied" is another Doris Day unforgettable:

> *Oh, you won't be satisfied until you break my heart,*
> *You're never satisfied until the teardrops start,*
> *I tried to shower you with love and kisses,*
> *But all I ever get from you is naggin' n' braggin'*
> *My poor heart is saggin'.*
> *The way you toss my heart around's a cryin' shame,*
> *I bet you wouldn't like it if I did the same,*
> *You're only happy tearin' all my dreams apart,*
> *Oh, you won't be satisfied until you break my heart.*

Les Brown has had subsequent lady singers in the band over the years:"Lucy Ann Polk was different than Doris. Eileen Wilson and Jo Ann Greer also did very well with us. They each had their own style, I would say."

The recordings of "Bizet Has His Day" and "Mexican Hat Dance" have also been early Les Brown successes. In 1958 the band won the *Downbeat Magazine* "Best Dance Band" poll for the fifth consecutive year and was voted "The Favorite Band of 1958" in *Billboard's* poll of the nation's disc jockeys. The Les Brown Band always had the best reputation of any band around:

"I ran a tight ship," Les declared, "The band was clean with no drinking, no drugs, or hard language while working. I didn't discipline the fellows too much, you know, I was opposite to what Glenn Miller was- he was too tough and I was too easy. Maybe that's why all the musicians stayed on so long. (He chuckles). Life in my band was a little too easy, now that I think about it. The truth was that over time all the guys began thinking alike and phrasing alike, so we had a smooth, steady sound."

Another reason for Les Brown's great success was the presence of former Paul Whiteman and Kay Kyser arranger Van Alexander. Earlier, in 1938 (until 1943), Van had organized and conducted his own band shortly after arranging for Chick Webb. The band toured the East coast at places like the Paramount, Loew's State, and Capital Theaters in New York, as well as a very long engagement at Roseland. A who's who of great musicians got their start with Van: drummer Shelly Manne, bassist Slam Stewart, trumpeter Charlie Shavers, drummer Don Lamond, trombonist Si Zentner, trumpeter Neal Hefti, and saxophonist/vocalist Butch Stone. While Van was with Webb, girl singer Ella Fitzgerald had a notion about converting a child's nursery rhyme into a song:

VAN ALEXANDER

"I started my career with Chick Webb, Richard. The song was 'A - Tisket, A - Tasket,' a nursery rhyme in the public domain, and was Ella's idea. I was arranging for the band and she asked me to help her, but I had no time. After nagging a bit, she threatened to take it to (arranger) Edgar Sampson, so I said, 'Hold it, hold it! I'll do it,' and we worked it out, adding things like -Was it Blue...No, no, no, no (he sings it out), and instead of 'Walkin' on down the avenue'...she changed it to 'Truckin' on down'...you know the rest.

"Les and I both got married in the same year, 1938. When my band broke up, I had a guy in the band named Butch Stone. I did a thing (arrangement) with Butch called 'A Good Man is Hard to Find,' and, when the band broke up I allowed Butch to

To Richard Grudens —
"Thanks For the Memories"!
all the best.
Van Alexander (1998)

take the arrangement to Larry Clinton's Band and then to Jack Teagarden and finally to Les' Band, where he still performs that song right up to today. It was a smash everywhere he went. Les was the only one that recorded it, and it sold a half-million records. And, Rich, the point of the story," he chuckles aloud, "is that...I never got paid a dime for it." We both laughed.

Butch Stone, who first joined Les in 1944, remains with the band today. Although he no longer plays his baritone sax, Butch handles the novelty number vocals "My Feet's Too Big, Robin Hood," and, of course, "A Good Man is Hard to Find!" Remember the silly novelty recording "Frim Fram Sauce" by Butch? "They're just words made up by songwriters," explained Les, "They're just nonsense words for novelty songs."

VAN ALEXANDER

"I have been arranging for the Les Brown Band for many, many years, up until just last year, and even did a few things for Doris Day along the way. I also worked as an arranger for nine years with Les on the 'Dean Martin Television Show.'"

Over the years, Van and fellow arranger Frank Comstock were the major arrangers for the Les Brown Band. Frank and Van have preserved their personal friendship with both Les and Doris Day. A former president of the American Society of Music Arrangers and Composers, that includes arranger Pete Rugolo and arranger/bandleader Billy May, Van Alexander is a most respected and well-loved musical figure in what Artie Shaw once described as "a cottage industry."

Van was also instrumental in arranging a good part of the album produced by Les Brown for the King of Thailand. Along the way Van turned to Hollywood for additional work, where he scored and arranged music for twenty-two feature films, including the last Mickey Rooney-Andy Hardy film, and hundreds of television shows. For a time Van arranged and conducted for Capitol Records, including five Kay Starr albums and a number of Gordon MacRae recordings.

VAN ALEXANDER

"The younger generation is still interested in the big bands, and Les Brown is the best example of a quality and successful Big Band. Les and I have been friends for many years. We used to play golf together, but, he doesn't play any longer. Les lost his wife of over fifty years, Clare, a couple of years ago, and he just recently married a lovely lady, Evie, and he once again seems very happy."

According to Van, he and Les used to play a silly private game when they worked at NBC: *"We called it a celebrity game, where we would say things like Claudette C-O-L-D — bare, or look very sad and say Donald MEEK, or put a finger in our nose and say Mary PICK-ford...or Les would bend over and say...Les B-R-O-W-N. But, don't put that in your book, Richard."*

The selection process when joining Les' band was simple. "We usually knew a little about them beforehand, you know - from reputation, or having heard them with another band," said Les, "As I explained earlier, we looked carefully into their reputation— if they were clean with drugs, and not drinking too much liquor. I wouldn't hire any guy who had a bad reputation, no matter how well he played."

The band was actually called the Milk Shake Band, a sobriquet leveled on them by bandleader Stan Kenton, and first revealed by Big Band author George Simon: "Stan wryly opined, 'You know - my guys make it on *weed*... Woody's (Herman) band makes it on *booze*, and Les Brown's band makes it on milkshakes.'"

Although an arranger, Les' greatest instrumental hit "I've Got My Love to Keep Me Warm" was actually arranged just perfectly by another arranger in the band, Skip Martin. "Over the years it has been our second best selling record - next to 'Sentimental Journey' with Doris.

"Funny thing about that recording, Richard," Les further explained, "We recorded that song in 1943, or about then...then one night in '48, we played it on one of Hope's radio shows. We received a great reaction and Columbia Records wired us to come back into the studio to record it the next day, because they thought it was a great arrangement. They had forgotten that we actually recorded it back three years, but for some crazy reason they never released it. I wired them back to look into their files. They did. They released it. It became a hit."

That Irving Berlin composition along with Artie Shaw's "Frenesi," Stan Kenton's "Artistry in Rhythm," and Glenn's immortal gem "Moonlight Serenade" are my four favorite instrumental recordings of the era.

"Well, Les," I said, "We have a mutual friend in Bob Hope. I have written about him for many years and you have traveled and played for him for much longer- especially on those USO Christmas shows. How did you manage the risky traveling during those wartime days?"

"Oh, it was very rewarding. We were entertaining the troops. They were a great audience. It was wonderful doing it. My band members got to see parts of the world they wouldn't otherwise have seen. We had people fighting one another to go on those tours. Everyone who went was enthusiastic. They would say, 'If so and so can't make it, I'll go, just let me know.'"

Les spent eighteen continuous years overseas with Bob Hope and his USO troupe between each December 15 and December 30th, becoming an important part of the legendary Christmas Tours.

"Bob always brought along the greatest talents and prettiest girls for the GIs to enjoy. He took a lot of criticism from some folks. The GIs liked it, so it was okay with Bob. And he was never afraid of the possible danger we faced in those days. Once, when we flew into Tokyo during the Korean War, I got the news that the Chinese crossed the Yalu River immediately after we left. So I called Bob to tell him, 'Hey, the Chinese have come across.' He said, 'You're kiddin'!' I said, 'No, I'm not kiddin', Bob, that's not a joking matter. We could have been killed.' As usual, Bob laughed. Bob is number one in radio, television, films, everything. We have never had a written contract between us all those years. As far as I'm concerned, he's number one - a prince."

BOB HOPE

"Once, when we were headed for Iceland, I learned that a second plane had to turn back to Prestwick to pick up a drummer from Les' band who had dallied too long in the snack bar. After the plane was back in the air again, the drummer remembered the sax player wasn't on board, so the plane had to turn back and make a second landing. The pilot insisted that anoth-

er nose count be made before the plane took off again. 'That won't be necessary,' Les said. 'Get out your instruments, fellows, and strike a chord. I'll know then if anyone's missing!' I love, and will always appreciate my friend Les Brown."

Almost everywhere the band performs since those days, someone will approach Les Brown and say they saw him with Bob Hope here or there, almost anywhere on Earth: "They want to thank us for being there and making their lives a little happier during those tough times. We also did a lot of stateside shows at all the big places during the war. We did many a free concert at nearby camps wherever we traveled. Sometimes we would stop off at a camp or installation and do an impromptu show for servicemen; then we'd go on to our next regular stop... like the Meadowbrook in New Jersey or the Cafe' Rouge in the Pennsylvania Hotel in New York, and other places.

"Richard, the best band I've ever had was my 1954-55 group. The personnel was outstanding. We had Abe Most. After I found him, I gave up playing the clarinet myself.

"We had Tony Rizzi on guitar; Don Paladino on first trumpet; my brother Stumpy playing bass trombone; Don Fagerquist played some wonderful things on trumpet; Jack Sperling was a genius on drums; Butch Stone on vocal and on baritone; Dick Noel played trombone; Ray Sims also managed a great trombone - he was a good soloist, - it was my best band, Richard. This is the group who made the album Concert at the Palladium." It was my best band and that album was the best thing we have ever done.The Palladium was by far the best place we ever played in—ever."

ABE MOST

Clarinetist Abe Most first joined the Les Brown Band in 1939 when Les stepped into Kelley's Stable nightclub on New York's famed 52nd Street where Abe was playing with a small group. Typical of Les Brown, he simply invited Abe to join his band:

> *"He didn't say I would be taking his spot, but before I knew it, I was. I took all of the solos except sometimes on*

47

Les Brown's Band at Disneyland. Vocalists Les Brown Jr. and Lucy Ann Polk on left. Butch Stone on extreme right. Late 1980's. (*Les Brown Collection*)

'Sentimental Journey' when the crowd expected him to solo and Doris (Day) to sing. The band was a harmonious group of nice people including those in management, like Don Kramer, the manager, who always treated me very well. I don't remember ever having an argument about money or anything. It always felt like home. My many years with the band were interrupted just a few times (once playing for one year with Tommy Dorsey in 1946, just after returning from war service), but I always returned and finally stayed for over twenty-two continuous years starting in 1950. I even took a few tours with the first Bob Hope USO traveling shows.

"Today, I play various venues, usually highlighting my own group with the music of Benny Goodman in the form of a tribute or salute. I still play, and as long as my health holds up, even though I am seventy-eight, I will continue to play.

"To me, Les Brown is a good musician, a good arranger, and most importantly, an even better man."

We talked about Les' brothers:

Curious, I asked, "Why do they call your brother Clyde *Stumpy*?"

"Well, he's only five feet tall. Does that answer your question? All kidding aside, he prefers the name *Stumpy*, and hardly uses *Clyde*. He is the band's manager and keeps us all well-organized." Les' two younger brothers, Warren and Stumpy, both learned the trombone, later participating in their brother's band. Stumpy, who provided me with lots of assistance and photographs for this chapter, told me he joined the band at the age of eighteen, after graduating from the New York Military Academy. "He came out to the coast to try out for the band at my father's firm suggestion, and he's been with us ever since," said Les.

"Since we don't travel too much, we are able to keep the same players. Today we mostly do private parties for affluent people who followed us when they, and we, were young. Successful in their own life, they can now afford these parties." The band plays only about four gigs a month these days.

"Leap Frog," a composition written by Joe Garland, once a tenor sax player for Louis Armstrong and who also composed "In The Mood," Glenn Miller's signature recording, is the band's longtime theme. "But we don't always play it at these recent parties. We some-times play it at the end of an evening, after dinner. And we keep it down until they have had enough to drink and they've finished their speech-es, and then — let it go."

DORIS DAY

"I still see Les quite often, as a matter of fact. Not too long ago, we did a fundraiser up here for the animals (Doris Day Pet Foundation, Carmel, California) and he brought his whole band up and it was a swinging night. It was really wonderful of him to do that. He always enjoyed coming to Carmel, and he and his wife Clare used to come up a lot. I haven't seen him lately, but you never know when he will pop in. We always talk about the good old days and the fun we had and how we laughed a lot. The memories...Richard...of those long ago days are still fresh in my heart liked it happened yesterday. Isn't that something?"

Les Brown has accomplished it all, as they say. A guest conductor of the Los Angeles Philharmonic and the United States Air Force Band, he has been the musical director for the television shows of Bob Hope, Steve Allen, Dean Martin, Jackie Cooper, Mel Torme', and many Hollywood Palace Shows, as well as Marineland Specials on PBS. Two Presidents have had Les Brown personally direct their Inaugural Ball, and Frank Sinatra engaged Les to perform for the Queen Elizabeth II Gala in 1984. His new CD, "Live at the Hollywood Palladium," is doing quite well. Like our mutual friend Bob Hope, Les Brown is also a true American institution.

Even at age eighty-six, Les Brown's pleasant and genial manner is evident as it has always been. I believe that players remained so long with Les because, as Doris said earlier, of Les himself, and not because he was just too easy. Swiss radio disc jockey Max Wirz attended the BBC event at Birmingham, photographing Les at a fan autograph ses-sion. "He signed for hours and became soaked in sweat before he was done." His committment to his craft has never waivered.

50

Les Brown and The Band of Renown has not yet seen the end of the musical road. "If Les ever calls it quits, Les Brown, Jr. will take over as he occasionally does today," Stumpy Brown said, "Although Les Jr. is also involved with other things, he is the band's current male vocalist, and our wonderful Jo Ann Greer is still the girl singer."

"You know, there are more Big Bands playing now than ever, Richard," Les summed up, "Colleges play the charts of the great bands, like Miller, Goodman, and Woody Herman. They play great, better than ever. And the musicians are very, very talented and disciplined. Unfortunately there is no outlet for them. Television doesn't want them. Radio either. So where will they work? Where are the ballrooms? Rock has knocked them out. So they play for themselves. But, all that may change again one day."

Thank you, Les Brown and the Band of Renown. Thank you Doris Day, Van Alexander, Abe Most, and, of course, Bob Hope.

(L-R) Max Wirz, Ray Anthony and Les Brown at Ronnie Scott's Club, Birmingham, England in 1998, arranged by Graham Pass — BBC producer. *(Max Wirz Collection)*

STAN KENTON

The Sweet Sound of Thundering Music

(Richard Grudens Collection)

It was Roy Belcher of Big Bands International who first proposed an all-out chapter respecting jazz pioneer Stan Kenton for this book. England's Big Bands International, the world's leading Big Band Society, frequently features articles about and photos of the progressive, modern sounds of Stan Kenton, one of the premium bandleaders of the Big Band Era.

In a recent issue of their quarterly news magazine, a truly remarkable composite photo comprised of bandleaders Buddy Rich, Woody Herman, Benny Goodman, Count Bill Basie, Stan Kenton, as well as jazz vocalist Mel Torme, and Big Band booking agent Willard Alexander graced the cover. I realized I had personally interviewed everyone in the photo except the charismatic Stan Kenton, whom I had seen perform, but whom I had never met. Stan Kenton's widow Audree Kenton had furnished the photo, and, later, when I asked her about its origin, she explained, "The occasion was an anniversary party for Willard Alexander, and all those distinguished bandleaders flew into New York just to honor him." I would guess the date to be about 1977, judging by their long, full sideburns and my own research.

My only connection to the Kenton Band was a friendship I shared with bass player Eddie Safranski at the NBC studios in New York back in the 1950s when he was a studio musician and I co-managed the Broadcast Ticket Division. During lunch breaks Eddie recounted endless stories about his tenure with Stan and the strong impact the band had on music. "I never knew anyone who ever worked with Stan who didn't like him and enjoy working in his band," I recall him saying.

If you listen mindfully to the January, 1945 recording of Pete Rugolo's arrangement of Stanley's composition "Artistry In Rhythm," as I have hundreds of times, the romantic, smooth flowing Kenton piano, the punctuating brass, the thumping drums, the flowing saxes, all signature material associated with Kenton, may move you to become a Stan Kenton fan, if you are not already one. Then perhaps you might want to explore the fluent saxophone and rhythm classic "Opus in Pastels." In any case, to remain a Kenton *aficionado* you have to move musically forward as Stan Kenton did, and always would, directly into the future of the exciting and thrilling music he dreamed would some-day permeate the airwaves and concert halls, not merely sounds played to accommodate dancers who pervaded the ballrooms and dance halls. That, he once mused "Is a musical horse of a different color." With each successive recording the Kenton mystique always moves on, always changing, always growing, always different.

Stan Kenton's music was at times ridiculed by critics, even when he was leading the popularity charts. Despite their cries, he found himself playing the best venues, the premier classical concert halls and colleges. A virtual lifetime of effort affirmed his steady rise to success, thanks to showcasing a totally revolutionary repertoire, including recognizing and fostering the brilliant arrangements of Pete Rugolo.

> *Stan Kenton's early credo:*
> *"With high regard and respect for each others individuali-ty...a group of personalities can make music wide in scope...from tender, soft sounds to screaming, crashing disso-nance. This is an orchestra," Stanley declared upon the release of his 1952 Capitol LP This Is An Orchestra!*

Two years later he delivered a statement for the opening of the Festival of Modern American Jazz, at Carnegie Hall, New York on October 9, 1954:

"In spite of the hazards to which jazz has been subjected in its growth, we now can celebrate its victory. No longer does it have to suffer from an obligation to Tin-Pan Alley. Nor does it have to function in other forms. It has served its apprenticeship and is blossoming into maturity independently."

Stanley Newcomb Kenton was born in Wichita, Kansas, on December 15, 1911, a date earlier in question, but verified by birth certificate obtained by *The Network*, a long-running Stan Kenton Newsletter of which Anthony Agostinelli is editor.

Young Stanley learned piano and developed arrangements for various dance bands during the 1930's, forming his first musical group. On Memorial Day, 1940, his became the resident band at the Rendezvous Ballroom located on a narrow peninsula in Balboa, California. His music created immediate excitement, earning him a coveted booking into the famed Hollywood Palladium in 1942, a spot reserved for then big-name bands. Engagements at New York City's Roseland and Frank Dailey's Meadowbrook on the Pompton Turnpike in New Jersey followed.

His first recordings, commercial and thus unrewarding to Kenton, were cut with Decca. When composer/vocalist Johnny Mercer and former record store owner Glenn Wallichs formed Capitol Records in 1943, they signed him, allowing him musical *carte-blanche*. Then, fortunately (some say unfortunately), comedian Bob Hope hired him to replace Skinnay Ennis' orchestra on Bob's very popular network radio show, attaining for Stanley and his band important exposure and personal prestige, as they traveled to countless military bases around the country in nerve-wracking flights in every kind of weather to bring entertainment to U.S. servicemen, even though Stanley later regretted accepting the job because it diluted his musical idealism. The recording sessions with Capitol lasted through 1947 and have all been re-issued recently by Mosaic Records, which includes previously unissued masters.

In 1953 Stan Kenton and the band, with vocalist June Christy, flew to Europe in an Air Force plane, leaving Westover, Massachusetts on September 25th and played a gig the very same night in the Azores and

(Courtesy of Downbeat Magazine, 1953)

the following night in Tripoli, both shows for the U.S. Army. They opened their official tour in Frankfurt, Germany on September 28th and went on to further bookings in Denmark, Sweden, Belgium, Holland, France, Switzerland, Austria and Italy. What a terrific tour that was for the band, its popularity flying high.

On Saturday, October 9, 1954, Stanley arrived at the very realization of his dream, leading the Festival of Modern American Jazz at Carnegie Hall in New York, performing with his fresh and innovative orchestra and showcasing pianist Art Tatum and his Trio; saxophonist Charlie Ventura; trumpeter Shorty Rogers; drummer Shelley Manne; guitarist/ arranger Johnny Smith; premier trombonist Milt Bernhart; Cuban bongo drummer Candido; new stars saxophonist Lee Konitz and trombonist Frank Rosolino, and veteran trumpeters Conte Candoli and Maynard Ferguson, earning all of them well-deserving accolades in the press. It was his second trip to the landmark Carnegie Hall.

For Stan Kenton and his band of musicians, it was certainly a night to remember. It was centuries away from the embryonic days at the Rendezvous. He was now the champion of modern music, his arrangements then being practiced in music classes at major universities all over the world, for instruction at dance studios; for modern dance sequences on television; for motion picture sound tracks - and for the repertoire of the Sadler Wells Ballet Company. The early, difficult years that once made things seem hopeless were eventually conquered with perseverance and hard work.

The Kenton sound became synonymous with strength in music. A lively, enthusiastic conductor, urging his musicians on with every crescendo, Stan Kenton, lifting and thrusting his arms forward with sheer joy, propels the music onward with great artistic conviction, with every musician equally enthralled. "There was only one place on earth that was joy and happiness to Stan Kenton, and that was on the bandstand," according to band trombonist Milt Bernhart.

AUDREE COKE KENTON

Audree Coke Kenton, a public relations specialist, was married to Stan Kenton from 1975 until he passed away in 1979. She still works very hard every day to keep the Kenton music legend alive, recently through the efforts of the American Jazz Institute, first formed in 1997 under the direction of Mark Masters. This venerable jazz organization, based in Pasadena, California, celebrates with annual festivals in Redondo Beach, just a few miles from the Rendezvous Ballroom in Balboa, where Stan Kenton started, and twenty years after he played his last engagement. Audree sits on the Institute's Board of Directors.

On an exceptionally cool afternoon in September of 1998, Audree Kenton and I sat down to talk about her legendary husband:

"We have just done a jazz concert in Pasadena, California, Richard, made up largely of Kenton Band alumni, through the American Jazz Institute. I am pleased to report that we had a sold-out house. I am also happy to say with certainty that the *Kenton* name still pulls."

One week the group will present the Neophonic Orchestra, which Stanley led in the mid-60s, and the next week it will be the Mellophonium Years(1960-63). Perhaps they will be followed by a Milestones Concert featuring the chestnuts "Eager Beaver," "Intermission Riff," "Peanut Vendor," and so forth, eventually covering the work of all the orchestras he created and named for the sounds that inspired them: Chronologically, Artistry in Rhythm, Progressive Jazz, Innovations in Modern Music, New Concepts of Artistry in Rhythm and the Neophonic Orchestra.

I wondered about similar concerts that may possibly be held in the East, in the New York area one day:

"We would like to bring these concerts to the East, - but California has a nucleus of players that permit such concerts. It would be finan-cially impossible to bring to New York because of the hotel and travel-ing costs. We would need airline and other corporate sponsors to achieve that goal. That's why there are so few Big Bands on the road anymore."

Stan Kenton always wanted his band to be an instrumental band performing only concerts, rather than a dance band. "But," as Audree explained, "at one time there was only a market for dance bands. He started writing music for dancing, but then he discovered the dancers were standing in front of the bandstand anyway - not moving - not danc-ing, so he concentrated more on the listening aspect — concert music.

Stanley's music was different from what the critics were used to hearing at that time, so they panned it, labeling it empty and pretentious.

"In 1941, when I first met Stanley, I was working for a newspaper. At the time I was married to Jimmy Lyons (outstanding jazz DJ and founder of the Monterey Jazz Festival), and Stanley was married to his first wife, Violet Peters, a wonderful woman and a dear friend of mine. The four of us hung out together. Jimmy and Stanley walked the streets of Balboa soliciting funds from merchants to string radio lines into the ballroom so the broadcasts could be made over the Mutual Broadcasting System."

Jimmy got Stanley his first air time for the band when he hosted the first remotes of the broadcasts from Balboa on the Mutual Broadcasting System. In 1949 Stanley began having serious marital problems with Violet. "She was sick and tired of being left alone at home with their daughter, Leslie, while Stanley was continuously on tour. So he took some time off hoping to patch things up. He remained restlessly at home for about a year or so but he just couldn't deal with that quiet and uneventful kind of life — he had to get back to the music, and so the marriage just disintegrated. He later married Ann Richards, a singer with the band. They had two children: Dana, who is now forty-two, very tall, strongly resembling her father, and a son named Lance.

"Much later, in 1971, when he was developing Creative World Records, what he needed- and what he hired me for - was public relations. Public relations turned into marketing, publicity and advertising…and eventually marriage in 1975, I'm happy to say. By the time Stanley passed away I was his personal manager. Even then, after forty years, his whole life was still music."

"I understand that some writers and critics have characterized the personality of Stan Kenton as a 'bundle-of-nerves' type," I said.

"I can't agree. I'd say he was more an intense person, always dedicated to creating new jazz sounds in music. He looked deep within himself for those sounds. He was a great arranger and a good conductor.

"In creating that revolutionary music, Pete Rugolo and Stanley were so close — as collaborators — to one another that they would forget who had written what. They were so busy in those days, especially while doing the one-nighters, and they would have an idea and write six or eight bars and Stanley would say to Pete, 'What do you think of that?' and then they had to locate a piano, which wasn't always easy, to write those ideas down before they forgot them."

Unlike Woody Herman and some other bandleaders, Stan Kenton loved the traveling aspect of leading a band. "Stanley enjoyed traveling from one city to another, bringing his music to far-flung places. Playing the concert halls of America was part of his true dream, Richard."

To Kenton, traveling meant independence. Grounded in the studio he felt at the mercy of directors and producers. "When we are on the road we play our music the way we think it should be played, and we've absolute freedom," he once told Don Kennedy of Big Band Jump, "I think if I had to punch the same time clock every day and go to work the same way and eat the same food every day, I think I'd probably die of boredom."

Then, there were the popular and constructive clinics the band conducted on college campuses during each summer :

"We did clinics heavily for about the last ten years of his life," Audree went on, "I think we did the first clinics at the University of Indiana, the University of Michigan and in Denver, in the late 60s. And then it got to the point where we did six or seven week-long clinics each year during the summer months. Stanley really enjoyed teaching and coaching youngsters.

"We'd be on a college campus for a week at a time, and there would be classes in theory and composition, and student bands at all levels of ability. The kids loved it. There were performances every night. The individual musicians in our bands got in there and actually taught, instructing the students on their own instruments. For example, one of the band's trombone players would teach a group of maybe five or six trombone students; the band's drummer would teach drums to a dozen kids, almost one - on- one, and so forth. And it was great fun for the students to hang out with professional musicians from a famous band like the Kenton band. It was bound to impress and influence them. And, we liked it because it was a way to keep our band off the road for five or six weeks straight and still keep it together financially because the summers are traditionally poor in the band business. Every few weeks I would travel back to the office and help conduct the business of the band and the record company; then I would return to wherever the band was working. Stanley had an excellent staff in Los Angeles."

Today, Audree Kenton manages Stan Kenton's business affairs, one that states there will be no "ghost" band and that his name may not be used to front any nostalgia band.

Just before arranger Pete Rugolo joined the band, Stan Kenton had recorded their then number one hit "And Her Tears Flowed Like Wine" in May of 1944. The vocal was performed by sparkling song star Anita O'Day, becoming her signature song and a first real hit for Kenton. "Funny thing about that recording, Richard," Anita told me in 1997, while interviewing her for my book *The Song Stars*, "the first take had no Kenton piano accompaniment and was the original release. The second release on a 1952 LP featured the second take with Stanley at the piano. I love the second take with Stanley at the piano the best."

But Anita wasn't really happy in the Kenton organization. I spoke to her about it in Febuary of 1999: "I couldn't stand that *upbeat*, so I left after a year. I said, 'I'll get you a singer,' and I gave them June Christy, and I went on to sing with swing bands. We were playing at the Chicago Theater and across the street there was a place called Three Deuces, a restaurant that had a Big Band playing at lunchtime. So I went there, and after watching the singer, a little light-bulb went off in my head. I went backstage and I said to the singer - 'What's your name?' and she says, 'Shirley Luster,' and I said, 'How'd you like to be rich and famous?' and she said, 'What do you mean?' I said, 'Come across the street and meet Stan Kenton, and please take the job. I've been there a year and I just gotta change.' She said,'I'll be over.' And she came over — they liked her — and that was that!"

In May of 1945 Kenton recorded another milestone, "Tampico," June Christy's first-ever vocal recording. A followup recording for June was the popular "Shoo Fly Pie and Apple Pan Dowdy" recorded in 1946. June, a pretty blonde who sounded a lot like her predecessor, Anita O'Day, married band member, tenor saxist Bob Cooper and remained married to him for the rest of her life. Her given name, as Anita said, was Shirley Luster, but Stanley thought it sounded like a shampoo and asked her to change it.

1946 brought forth the *Artistry In Rhythm* album that characterized the band forever as the *Artistry In Rhythm* Band.

Stan Kenton with vocalist June Christy, 1945. *(Richard Grudens Collection)*

PETE RUGOLO - ARRANGER

It is November 1998. I am speaking to arranger Pete Rugolo from his California home. It was Rugolo, a modernist, progressive, and innovative arranger who, with Kenton, was able to create that revolutionary Kenton intonation. Kenton liked Pete Rugolo's work so well that he asked him to re-arrange the band's theme "Artistry In Rhythm," when he first engaged this young arranger to help develop special arrangements for the band.

Born in Sicily, Italy, Pete Rugolo and his family arrived in this country in 1921, when he was five years old. "My dad was an out-of-work stone mason, so he immigrated here to work in my uncle's shop

61

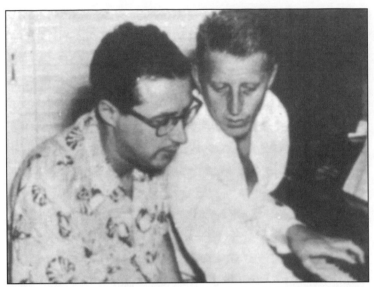

Pete Rugolo and Stan Kenton arranging for the band. *(Big Band Jump)*

as a shoemaker. He got his own place in Santa Rosa (California) where my grandfather lived. I went to school there and then attended San Francisco State College and later received my Master's studying with Darius Milhaud."

Milhaud, a French composer, developed polytonality - a simultaneous use of different keys.

"It was 1945 when I first joined the Kenton band. I first met him at the Golden Gate Theater in San Francisco. I was still in the Army; I led an Army band. Stan had a record that just came out, and I loved that style a lot and started to write like the recording. One day I went backstage to see him and brought five arrangements with me. He was very nice — and he said he would try them out, and I said for him to return them to me if he couldn't use them, as I copied them out myself and had no other copies. He got a really big kick out of that. I didn't hear from him for a month or so. Then, one day at the barracks I got an exciting call over the P.A.—'Stan Kenton calling Pete Rugolo' - much excited, I went to the post telephone and talked to him and he said he tried the arrangements, telling the band, 'that the kid from San Francisco left me.' After trying them out he said, 'My God! You do write like me, and you're even much more modern. ' I was so excited."

By that time Stan Kenton was performing regularly at the Hollywood Palladium and Rugolo brought several more arrangements to him, "...and he loved them," Pete continued, "he said 'when you get out of the Army the (arranging) job is yours. ' It was all like a fairy story to me...but, that's exactly how it happened.

"When I became discharged, I contacted Stan — he was now playing the Meadowbrook (Ballroom) in New Jersey — and he sent me the money and I went there and stayed with the band 'til he disbanded it in late '49."

"You radically changed the musical course of the Kenton band," I noted.

"Yes...I created — what they called *progressive jazz*. I promptly re-arranged "Artistry in Rhythm" at his request, and, over the course of my tenure, a couple of hundred other pieces."

Pete Rugolo actually arranged about 95% of all the band's albums up through 1950.

"I added all kinds of dissonance and incorporated some of Darius Milhaud's modernistic ideas into jazz using 5/4 material which was never used before," Pete went on to say, "I began writing compositions - more like concert pieces, for the tours. Stan really liked them."

"With Stan, well, when we were on tour, he wanted you to come over to the dance hall every night to check the arrangements. During the last set of the evening, he liked to step off the bandstand to talk to the people — the dancers, and he would leave me to play the piano, you know, taking his spot in front of the band for that short time. I was a pretty good piano player, although I played much differently than he did - I was more of a light piano player - like Teddy Wilson — he played more like Earl Hines' style, which he preferred. But, I finally gave it up. I had no time to play anymore when I started writing an awful lot. At first we got bad reviews because the critics didn't understand that kind of music. It wasn't a swing band like Woody Herman's or Benny Goodman's, you know. The people enjoyed Stan's early work too, like 'Eager Beaver' and that sort of thing."

"Pete, this relationship reminds me of the legendary Duke Ellington - Billy Strayhorn association — busy, prolific bandleader, and almost exclusive arranger, working hand in hand — a very close relationship."

"Exactly. Like Ellington, Stan stopped writing because we were doing one-nighters and he was just too busy. We had a radio show going, too. We would get together and discuss things — we'd sit at the piano and he had a few ideas about a tune or something and we would kind of write out a menu, and he would say, ' Let''s start off with a bass the first twelve bars.' It was actually like a menu. We would flesh it all out. And we wrote quite a few tunes together, in a sort of collaboration. I was such a fan of his and we were always good friends, too. Stan was an amazing guy. He looked so good in front of the band."

Their first album together was called "Artistry in Rhythm" in which Pete wrote eleven of the twelve selections. In the various album selections Rugolo projected the progressive influences of Stravinsky during "Artistry in Percussion"; Debussy in "Willow Weep for Me"; and Ravel in "Artistry in Bolero."

When Kenton gave up that band in 1949, Pete Rugolo migrated to Capitol Records for two years where he expanded his repertoire with the Capitol contract stable artists of the time: June Christy, Nat King Cole, Miles Davis, and Dizzy Gillespie as well as many other developing bebop artists.

Later on, in 1958, Pete Rugolo with Milt Bernhart and others produced an album of music under the Stan Kenton name with Stanley at the piano and undoubtedly as a consultant. The album was called "Lush Interlude" and brought Pete Rugolo back to writing and leading, overcoming a recent hiatus.

MILT BERNHART
1947 Kenton Band Supreme Trombonist

Milt Bernhart played a stellar trombone with Stan Kenton beginning with the Artistry in Rhythm band, performing on the original recording of the Kenton classic. I talked with him recently while he was stuffing envelopes to remind members to pay their dues to the The Big Band Academy of America, an institute founded 15 years ago by Big Band historian, — author Leo Walker. Milt is currently President.

"I joined Stan when I came out of the Army. I loved the sound of the band and always wanted to play with him. I was only twenty. Stan was a great front man who could face any audience, because he was very friendly. There were no formula charts like (Glenn) Miller or (Benny) Goodman."

Milt, an alumnus of Benny Goodman and other bands, felt musically secure in the Kenton organization: "I found Stan, in comparison to other famous band leaders I worked for, to be more considerate and easy to communicate with, and he was one who spoke his mind, but he allowed each member of the band to be themselves. And there was no pretense even though he allowed a pretentious title for his band — obviously someone other than Stan thought of the phrase *Artistry In Rhythm*, but it was one of the few instances where he got into the business of so-called '*packaging*.'"

Milt considered himself fortunate to be with Kenton. "His plan was that he wanted to explore music - always to be different — just like Artie Shaw — always moving forward. I knew that his music was going to come first, above everything, and it was going to be of a high standard, with music that could end up meaning something. I thought, 'If I could get on that band, it would be the best thing for me'! But, because he didn't perform exclusively as a commercial dance band, he struggled financially. He never complained right down to the bitter end. His dream was to be a concert master, not a dance band leader. That would have bored him silly."

"Perhaps his fate was likened to Artie Shaw's," I said. It was just a month ago when Artie Shaw told me the very same thing about his own career, saying, "I could have been a zillionaire if I had stayed with my early success of the 'Begin the Beguine' Band, instead of forging ahead with innovative and new material that was unaccepted at the time."

"Well, for sure, if Stan went completely commercial, and, that perhaps he would've been a millionaire may be going beyond reality. It's always been a mystery why some commercial music enterprises connect and others don't. Generally, if you are aiming to please the public, you are aiming down. Stan, from day one, couldn't do that. For him, it would have been out of the question." The musical goals of Kenton and Shaw paralleled. As true artists, both sacrificed their financial and celebrity future to play what they created, not what the bookers dictated and the public demanded of them. Milt Bernhart concurred.

As with Shaw, playing exclusively in concert halls was Kenton's goal. Stan Kenton and his 1950s Innovations in Modern Music Orchestra, a thirty-nine piece (including 16 strings) group, played only new material, omitting early hits of the band or other accepted standards. "It was thrilling to be part of that group of musicians," Milt told me, "A lot of new music was played. People listened to things they had never heard before. We played only the major concert halls coast-to-coast, like the Academy of Music in Philadelphia, the Civic Opera in Chicago, the Hollywood Bowl several times, Symphony Hall in Boston and Carnegie Hall in New York. And it didn't matter to him if there was only half a house or just a few in the audience, it would not have changed anything. His feeling of uplift coming from deep down into the soul is as real as anybody's ever was."

Of the first time Milt played in Carnegie Hall at the 1954 Festival of Modern American Jazz with Kenton, he said, "It was a thrilling night for all of us who played at Carnegie - especially with Stan — something to which I'm sure every musician aspires."

Stan Kenton personally chose each band musician. "When he was selecting who would play for the band — if there was an opening — an applicant would have to actually sit in and try out. Nobody ever got hired without playing first," Milt went on, "because that would be foolhardy. But afterwards, he would ask certain people in the band, whose opinion he respected, if they thought this person was going to work out. He would always take a consensus. And it mattered to him, as he tried very hard to make life in his band a democracy."

Because the Kenton Band had no sponsor, Stan quickly ran out of money and was forced to return to the dance hall tours in order to meet expenses. "So," Milt continued, "(drummer) Shelley Manne, (trumpeters) Maynard Ferguson and Shorty Rogers, and I all left, preferring not to play music for dancers, which meant too much weary traveling, one night stands, and playing the same charts over and over. A performer can get stale playing the same music all the time and lose interest, and then what?"

But Stan never begged any musician to stay. He felt he'd always find replacements: "He wished us good luck and with no hard feelings ever, mind you. He understood. He never gave up his dream. That's why

I respected him so much. I never knew any musician who worked for Stan who didn't adore him. Why, even during dance band dates, Stan would make an announcement that there would be a mini-concert, so anybody who wanted to hear his special brand of music would gather around the bandstand just to listen. It was fun for the musicians and the listeners as well. The selection 'Collaboration,' arranged by Rugolo, was a great favorite."

Stan Kenton's music was always exciting, especially for the musicians themselves: "Even Billy May will tell you today," Milt continued, "that it was just a job playing with Glenn Miller, and if it's just a job, what have you? Miller made no pretense, and he did very well at it, but if you looked very closely at the members in his band, they appear as if they were asleep. He made them smile, and they played, but musicians certainly didn't have the time of their life playing in bands like Glenn Miller's. That wasn't the case with Stan. The problem here is money versus art. There has never been a real meeting of the two. Benny Goodman played what he wanted to, but he always made sure it was music the dancers could dance to. All these bands, except Kenton's, made money pleasing the dancers. When Kenton played it was unlikely you were going to hear his greatest hits. If Stan could keep the band going, and keep people coming, and somehow pay the expenses every week, including the expenses of traveling, it made us all very happy, but it certainly was very difficult."

STAN KENTON:

On the future of his music:

"Well, I think nostalgia is certainly the worst commercial commodity in every way. People, somehow, are always looking back and I think there's a psychological problem there. I think they feel they've made it through one part of their life, and they're afraid of today and tomorrow, they want to go back and re-live the past again."

Audree and the rest of us lost Stanley Newcomb Kenton in 1979, but we will never lose the legacy of his original and extraordinary music.

EDWARD DUKE ELLINGTON

Ellingtonia means Belief in the Music

Many commendable books have been written depicting the life and times of Edward Kennedy Duke Ellington, including one from his own pen, *Music Is My Mistress*, so it may seem presumptuous to attempt a treatise or in-depth review of his life and career in this mostly lightweight book of biographical snapshots. Nevertheless, and especially in the centenary of the year of his birth, we will try to acknowledge the genius of Duke Ellington not only through our own anecdotal style, but also through the eyes of his sister, Ruth Ellington; nephew Michael James;

Duke Ellington, 1952. *(Courtesy Downbeat Magazine)*

Big Band Academy President Milt Bernhart; blues vocalist Joe Williams; vocalist Herb Jeffries, and drummer Louis Bellson.

Ellington has been designated the patron saint of myriad music schools, including Berklee Music School in Boston, and is invariably adored by a great number of musicians throughout the world. Duke's only sibling, his sister, Ruth Ellington James, thought all had been written about her loving brother, but, by repeating accounts of his life over and over again for the benefit of the new citizens of the world, accounts of his life and career become an appreciative celebration in itself.

The formidable Duke Ellington Band and its body of work had, over many years, survived the demise of the Big Band Era - the inroads of bebop, the rock and roll invasion, the death or desertion of its own stars and colleagues, and its own internal problems- successfully spanning the entire period of jazz. If you add it up, it counts approximately 50 years of non-stop bandleading, 800 musicians filtering through the band, over 10,000 recordings, 20,000 gigs, some 2,000 compositions, and millions of miles traveled to bring his unique category of music to fans all over the world. As an unofficial ambassador, Duke toured the world in the 1960s, sponsored by the United States Department of State.

Miles Davis, the famed trumpet player, once said of Duke Ellington: "I think all the musicians in jazz should get together on one certain day and get down on their knees to thank Duke."

In late 1998, I spoke to vocalist Herb Jeffries, the last surviving member of the 1930s- 40s orchestra, about his former boss. Herb's outstanding 1940 Duke Ellington recording "Flamingo," arranged by Billy Strayhorn, sold millions. It's in the top ten of my all-time personal favorites. You never get tired of listening to "Flamingo."

Herb said exactly this: "It was one of the highlights of my life singing with the great genius of Duke Ellington. Historically, down the road a hundred years or so, it may someday be compared to having played alongside Mozart or Beethoven- yesterday's great composers. I believe Ellington will go down as one of America's great composers. Music was everything to him. He was in love with music, more than anything in the world."

Milt Bernhart, the outstanding trombonist of the innovative 1940's Artistry In Rhythm Band of Stan Kenton, had something to say about Duke Ellington's music when we discussed the subject just a few months ago:

"While it was once dance bands, it is now big band concert music the people sit down and listen to, just like they do with symphony orchestras. With Artie Shaw, Stan Kenton, and Duke Ellington, the idea was never to play dance music. Duke Ellington made it clear that if he were in an auditorium, the music probably would be in broken tempos and not in a steady pulse from beginning to end, because that was only designed for dancing.

"Musically, Duke Ellington is our proudest possession," Milt declared, "he was ahead of his time. And the great part of it was that he didn't fight anything. He never fought — he just continued. He didn't make offensive statements, where others did, so when history draws the past, the name that will be always there will be Ellington, where others may be forgotten."

So, shall we consider Ellington the bandleader, Ellington the piano playing musician, or Ellington the composer? Let's see!

Early 1920s and 1930s musicians who became bandleaders grew out of the few bands around, so one band's intonation was not notably different from the other. There were only a few who dared to be totally unconventional. Artie Shaw tried to be one; Tommy Dorsey another, but the most outstanding was Edward Kennedy Duke Ellington. His music was certainly different from any other emerging band. You can always distinguish Duke's recordings from others without much doubt. His uniqueness was the use of precision playing instruments that seemed to talk, even when the reeds were wailing high and low. Some say it's because Duke relied on showcasing the talents of individual players, rather than composing charts at random and training his musicians to

Duke Ellington Band at the Oriental Theater, Chicago, 1932.

use them. He wrote music solely for his individual players. He actually tamed his musicians otherwise demeanor by waiting them out, never bothered by their off-stage, sometimes unruly actions. In the *New Yorker Magazine*, Whitney Balliett once wrote: "...he wrote for them, they played for him!"

"When we're all working together a guy may have an idea and he plays it on his horn. Another guy may add to it and make something out of it. Someone may play a riff and ask, 'How do you like this?' The trumpets may try something together and say, 'Listen to this.' There may be a difference of opinion of what kind of mute to use. Someone may advocate extending a note or cutting it off. The sax section may want to put an additional smear on it," said the maestro about his amazing group of musicians, and further, "We write to fit the tonal personalities of the individual instrumentalists who have the responsibility of interpreting our works." This also afforded Duke an opportunity to hear and review his every newly- written composition instantly.

"The biggest thing I do in music is listen," said Ellington, "While I'm playing I also listen ahead to what I will be playing. It may be thirty-two, or just one, or an eighth of a bar ahead but, if you're going to try to play good jazz, you've got to have a plan of what's going to happen."

In the mid- thirties it seemed like the whole country was caught up with something later identified as the Big Band Era. But, Ellington had already been playing that kind of music for almost ten years. Because the Duke's band was composed of all black players, they were not accepted in most of the fancy ballrooms and restaurants like those that featured the white swing bands of Benny Goodman, Artie Shaw, or Tommy Dorsey, although each of these leaders gradually began featuring black players and singers in their own group. However, Ellington was playing the best interracial clubs and was being reviewed and written about by important reviewers, being unanimously well received.

When Duke was asked about the racial problem, he merely stated, "I took the energy it takes to pout, and wrote some blues." And, Oh! What blues he wrote.

"There was always something different happening every night when the Duke was playing because he gave his players a great deal of freedom, freedom to learn about tempos, blending, and endurance," said one-time drummer Louis Bellson.

Ellington didn't play the hits of the day, unless it was a hit he created or unless it originated through or was composed by his own personnel. He was fearless in his quest to take unpopular musical positions. Sideman Juan Tizol's composition "Caravan" is an example. Juan wrote it and plays lead in every Ellington recording of the piece. "Caravan" is a stunning example of players in a band being featured for what they do best - from violin solo to drums - trumpet to clarinet - each piece expresssing an individual flavor, breaking like a wave on the shore of the musical stage.

Edward Kennedy Ellington was born just before the turn-of-the-century of hardworking parents James Edward and Daisy Kennedy Ellington, who fostered love and affection on their son and his younger sister, Ruth Dorothea Ellington. The nickname *Duke* began in high school, bestowed on him by a friend, Edgar McEntree, suiting his aristocratic bearing. His father provided comfortably for the family, creating income first as a butler to a prominent doctor and later as a caterer, including serving food at White House occasions and at embassies in Washington. "He raised our family like he was a millionaire," Duke declared in his book *Music Is My Mistress*. His mother instilled religion within the family, and always praised the children, fostering dignity and poise, and providing security and a powerful belief conveyed to them that they were specially blessed.

"When I was a child, my mother told me I was blessed, and I have always taken her word for it. Being born of — or reincarnated from — royalty is nothing like being blessed. Royalty is inherited from another human being, blessedness from God."

Duke took occasional piano lessons, later playing piano at church, but received motivating inspiration from observing eighteen year old Harvey Brooks playing a swinging piano in Philadelphia. So impressed, he said : "Brooks was swinging, and he had a tremendous left hand, and when I got home I had a real yearning to play. "Suddenly, jazz and ragtime music attracted his interest. In Washington, his first band, The Duke's Serenaders, was formed. Soon, Harlem's musical influence reached his senses, so he invaded New York and Tin Pan Alley as an optimistic, charming, and hungry young musician. Here he hired James "Bubber" Miley, a musician who played an exceptional muted and growling-sounding trumpet. Duke Ellington had found a catalyst in Miley and began replacing players, transforming the band into a jazz band. The growling brass became an Ellington imprint.

The early Ellington evergreens "East St.Louis Toodle-Oo," "Black and Tan Fantasie," "Creole Love Call," "Black Beauty," and "Old Man Blues," largely composed with Miley, followed. Then the Cotton Club gig came along:

"...the job called for a band of at least eleven pieces and we had been using only six, "Ellington recalled," At the time, I was playing a vaudeville show in Philadelphia. The audition was set for noon, but by the time I had scraped up eleven men it was past two o'clock. We played for them and got the job. The reason for that was the boss, Harry Block, didn't get there till late either and didn't hear the others who were auditioning earlier. That's a classic example of being at the right place at the right time with the right thing before the right people."

On December 4, 1927, a date important to jazz, Duke Ellington opened at the Cotton Club. The five year engagement as leader of the Cotton Club Orchestra was a productive time for Ellington, earning him a national reputation and financial stability. He recorded 200 sides during his tenure under the guidance of his agent, Irving Mills. The orchestra's exotic, jungle-like sound was an original attempt to apply his own rules, a technique developing his own harmonic spin. He utilized instruments differently, notably in "Mood Indigo," having the trombone working the high notes and the clarinet the low notes, the reverse of the accepted way. This introduced blends of musical color never accomplished before. The vaguely menacing number "The Mooche" fit neatly into this new wave of Ellington creations for the club's reviews. Duke Ellington's credo: "...find the logical way, and when you find it, avoid it. Let your inner self break through and guide you. Don't try to be anyone else but yourself," counciled the African American composer Will Marion Cook to the young, believing, emerging bandleader.

What followed was a lifetime of scraping, finagling, and suffering to keep his orchestra going year after year after year.

The occasion of Ellington's departure from the Cotton Club established him, alongside Louis Armstrong, as one of the two foremost figures in jazz. Dodging racial discrimination by sleeping the band in private railroad cars while on tour because hotels would not admit them, being forced to take freight elevators, and being kept from eating in some restaurants, Ellington always managed to solve the problems and keep going, his dignity and stylish projection prevailing over the more prevalent discrimination.

The great hits "Sophisticated Lady," "Caravan," "It Don't Mean a Thing (If It Ain't Got That Swing)," and "Solitude," launched during his triumphant European tour of 1933, continued his experimentation with special musical elements and forms. Later, imaginative recordings like "Ko Ko," one of the magnificent ensemble pieces with swiftly changing instrumental voices, and the striking plunger solo by Tricky Sam Nanton join forces to create a masterpiece. Then Cootie Williams original "Concerto for Cootie," later re-named "Do Nuthin' Till You Hear From Me," showcased Williams, just as Ben Webster is showcased on "Never No Lament" which was retitled "Don't Get Around Much Anymore." It added yet another standard to the book. Influences from other cultures, picturing distant and exotic places, were incorporated into his jazz repertory. The name had changed too. It was now *Duke Ellington and His Famous Orchestra.*

Inspired by various moods, Duke Ellington composed his best music. "The memory of things gone is important to jazz," he said. And his son Mercer once told me that his dad always wrote what he felt. "The happy tunes were written in happy times and the sad songs were composed when he felt sad. Isn't that sort of natural?"

The indispensable arranger and composer Billy Strayhorn entered Duke Ellington's life in 1939. He was twenty-four and stayed for 30 years. The two were a collaborative team that grew closer and closer over the years, much like the association Stan Kenton and Pete Rugolo experienced.

The year 1943 brought the Ellington Orchestra to Carnegie Hall where they performed the hour-long "Black, Brown and Beige" to a standing-room only crowd. A symbolic, historical sort of piece, it was then his most ambitious composition. Ellington had reached his personal zenith and continued composing concert pieces.

The Great Team of Duke Ellington and Billy Strayhorn at work. *(Richard Grudens Collection)*

World War II's end spelled disaster for the Big Bands. Bebop, folksinging trends, big-name vocalists, and the inflated salaries required for musicians forced bandleaders to disband. Many dance pavilions closed in deference to a more mobile population who headed for the road instead. Television had arrived, taking center stage. Radio was entering an eclipse. Times were changing for Duke Ellington. His star players were deserting to form their own combos. A crisis indeed had arrived for everyone. But, he never ever disbanded his orchestra, even though he lost some of its important players through illness and death and some through fluctuation of personnel. Even though income for the band was low, Duke Ellington paid his men with royalty checks he received for his compositions.

While Ellington recuperated in England from an operation performed in the United States, the band's sidemen performed in small

Duke Ellington and Connie Haines sign for their fans, 1943. *(Richard Grudens Collection)*

groups on their own until their boss returned. He kept the band together: "I like to keep a band so I can write and hear the (newly composed or arranged) music the next day," he said, "The only way you can do that is to pay the band and keep it on tap fifty-two weeks a year. By little twists and turns we manage to stay in business and make a musical profit. And a musical profit can put you way ahead of a financial loss." It was the music above everything for Ellington.

Maestro Arturo Toscanini commissioned Duke Ellington to compose a piece for the NBC Symphony, and it was performed in 1951. I was present during that NBC radio broadcast. The tickets I was commissioned to distribute, as co-manager of the NBC Ticket Division, were printed on a gold embossed soft oilcloth so the rustling of the program did not disturb the Maestro during the performance. The composition was entitled "Harlem." It was a miniature piece, set off by a bass simulating footsteps, and very well received by an appreciative audience and critics alike.

On New Year's Day 1999, Ruth Ellington and I had a revealing conversation about her celebrated brother: "He was practically a grown man when I was born and always a saint. Ever, overly protective of me at all times, I was his little doll. He was like a father and mother to me,

Mid-fifties Ellington Band Personnel *(Richard Grudens Collection)*

especially after our parents passing while I was attending college. Every day, going to school, he kept me locked up in the car in an effort to protect me. I meet people today who remember me in those early days, and through my years in college. They would say, 'I remember you when Duke kept you locked like a baby in the car. He felt so responsible...' they would say," she laughs — reminiscing, "...and he was always sensitive to moods." Duke was almost seventeen years older than his only sister.

"Duke was the kind of person who never acknowledged his greatness to himself," Ruth Ellington continued, "He just went on his own way of living, never thinking of himself as great... in any way whatever. He loved our mother, Daisy, more than anyone in life. Next to God, he valued his family the most; that's why he spent the last ten years of his life writing music giving thanks to God. He was a brother sent from Heaven, because he was perfect.

"He took good care of me then...and he still takes care of me today through royalties from his work." Ruth still operates Tempo Music Publishers on Park Avenue in New York, publishing mainly the music of her brother, among other material. Ruth has two sons, Stephen and Michael James, who manage the business with their mom, as well as their own Stephen James Productions. As a youngster Michael learned trumpet, and was fortunately coached by band member Clark Terry.

"We traveled around the country and in Europe with our uncle during the summers when we were kids, helping valet and performing chores for the band."

Upon Duke Ellington's passing, after the funeral, Ruth presided over the get-together of friends, acquaintances and well wishers of the family. That elegant and gracious lady made sure everyone had enough to eat and drink and someone to talk to in this otherwise dark hour. "It was exactly the way Duke would have planned it, had he been there," said author Don George, who co-wrote "I'm Beginning to See the Light" with Duke Ellington, "He loved to see people having a good time."

On January 21, 1999, legendary blues vocalist Joe Williams talked to me about Duke Ellington: "Well, I was always in awe of Duke. He had a rare musical gift that was so varied. And, Oh, man! He was such a spiritual person. His concepts — he always said he was only a messenger boy (He laughs deeply). And, he did what made him happy. He'd say wonderful things like, 'I'm not going to let you or anybody else let me lose my pretty ways.'

"We worked together several times," Joe went on, "Once at a celebration for (Billy) Strayhorn — (Metropolitan Opera star) Leontyne Price and Lena Horne were also there. And in Detroit, right after I left the Basie band, Duke and I — we worked together for a week in a show.

I think it was 1972. I didn't sing with the band; I was a separate attraction. Talk about Duke being self-effacing — I brought along a piano player named Ellis Larkins, and Duke called me into his dressing room after the first show and said rather sternly, 'Obviously you didn't read the fine print in the contract.' So, I said, 'What's that?' and he said, 'Your piano player — while playing at no time is your piano player to use his left hand.'"

We both broke out in laughter, Joe's rich in his deep, deep basso.

"He was *love*, Richard. At his funeral services his drummer Sonny Greer was crying, you know, and he said ever so proudly, 'Joe, the Duke was my *man*!'

"Duke had elegance, grace, and style, Richard," Joe said with passion, "No matter where I have performed in the world, I would say, to myself, 'Wow! God! — he was here first.' Duke's music was religious, but he called it *sacred*. Sacred music, Richard, sacred."

"My uncle's status was built on his achievement as an original musician," nephew Michael James, whose godfather was Billy Strayhorn, commented during our long conversation about his beloved uncle. "He created something new, through personal expression, and formed a new environment for musical instruments."

At the time, some musicians and composers employed European instruments and ideas to maintain American musical styles. "Duke understood that jazz - the new musical language - meaning (Sidney) Bechet and (Louis) Armstrong and the vocabulary they were bringing forth, so the sixteen piece bandstand could be turned into the new American art form." Michael said. Inadvertently, Duke had discovered a new idiom built upon jazz rhythms and harmonies.

Impresario Sol Hurok once approached Duke Ellington: "You're a great artist. I want to present you the way you should be presented, properly on the concert stages of the world. But I don't want you to play any nightclubs or dance halls. You will play strictly concerts."

"Duke was flattered by the prospect," Michael said, "but he enjoyed playing various styles and venues; a dance one night, a concert here and there, perhaps a night club the following night. He liked the diversity, to be in touch with the entire range of musical experiences. So he declined Hurok's invitation."

Ellington's "stable of stars" was important to him. They refreshed his mind and were given a backdrop they could find no other place, enabling them to be individual stars, not merely members of an ensemble as in most bands. Paul Gonsalves, who had played with Basie and Ellington, said, "You know, the difference is, Basie is a piano player with a band, but Duke is a composer. "And what kept him in Duke's band is "that Duke is always coming up with something new. It kept me stimulated." In other bands, once a musician learned the "book," they would get tired of it. The musicans held Duke Ellington in great respect because they couldn't do what he did, creating new and exciting charts for them to play almost daily.

At one point Michael and I tried to pinpoint Duke's best period with his band:

"On the whole," Michael suggeested, "the band that Duke Ellington had, particularly in the mid-fifties — up to the early sixties with Clark Terry, Paul Gonsalves and all those guys like Louis Bellson, and Johnny Hodges returning, might have been Duke's best because they could do it all. Even Johnny Hodges and Ray Nance could handle the early style of "growling" trumpets to demonstrate the old stuff of the twenties and thirties.

About the lady vocalists in the band: "The most associated with Duke was Ivie Anderson ('Stormy Weather')," said Michael, "Jazzwise, the best will be Betty Roche. Her 1952 version of 'Take the 'A' Train' is best. Classical things best belong to Kay Davis; Joya Sherill was best on swing things, along with the sweet sounding Marie (Maria) Ellington Cole (Mrs. Nat King Cole, no relation to the Duke)."

The only two events that adversely affected Duke's life was the death of his parents, particularly his mother, Daisy. "He was almost paralyzed by his mother's death. It was major trauma to him. He couldn't work or perform for a month or so. In 1959, while in Europe, they dug up the cemetery, and thus the graves where his parents were buried because the land was sold to real estate developers, so they had to dig up his parents and bury them somewhere else.

"Once, while at sea on a cruise, Duke called me into his cabin, and, although I was only sixteen, he talked to me like I was an equal: ' This is the second biggest drag of my whole life,' he said, ' I've been living an enchanted life. This is not supposed to happen. It's something you read about in story books. And I'm living this horrible story right now.'"

Duke always handled his fame well, never high, never faltering. He could step outside himself, at the same time. He said, "You know, we have been liked longer that most people who only enjoy that 15 minutes of fame they talk about. Our fame has been in overtime, having lasted for a long time."

Jazz historian, writer and producer, Leonard Feather, once described Ellington the public figure: "An inch over six feet tall, sturdily built, he had an innate grandeur that would have enabled him to step with unquenched dignity out of a mud puddle. His phrasing of an announcement, the elegance of his diction, the supreme courtesy of his bow, whether to a duchess in London or a theater audience in Des Moines, lent stature not only to his own career, but to the whole world of jazz."

"Love you madly," the Duke would always say.

Ditto and Amen!

Red Norvo and Louis Armstrong on N.Y. radio WNEW in 1943 at a Fats Waller tribute. *(Richard Grudens Collection)*

RED NORVO

Father of His Instrument

About ten years ago, singer Frankie Laine introduced me to jazz pioneer Red Norvo. Since then Red and I have held many conversations from his cozy, tree-lined home on Alta Avenue in Santa Monica, California. Those conversations centered mostly around his music, especially his unique choice of instrument, the vibraharp, (also called the vibraphone, although Red doesn't like that word) and allegories depicting the career of his first wife, Mildred Bailey, the very first girl Big Band singer featured in my recent book *The Song Stars*.

A young Red Norvo, 1936. *(Richard Grudens Collection)*

Just a week ago, in what may have been our final conversation held from a convalescent home in Santa Monica, Red Norvo and I talked about his career as a dedicated professional musician. Unfortunately, Red has serious, ongoing problems with his hearing, among other medical difficulties, and, although his recall of the old days remains sharp enough, he found it exceedingly difficult to accurately hear me; thus, he was unable to respond adequately, which forced the conversation to an early conclusion. His voice has changed from a natural deep resonance to a higher pitch. Earlier, when talking from his home, his specially equipped telephone allowed him to listen more easily than on the phone at the convalescent home. Ironically, it was Red Norvo's ultra- sensitive ear for subtle jazz that catapulted him to worldwide fame as a magnificent mallet musician. Red Norvo, one of the gentle giants of jazz, celebrated his ninty-first birthday, today, March 31, 1999, the day I finished writing this chapter. I tried to reach his daughter Portia today, for an update only to find that he had been confined to a hospital. A bleak birthday for Red.

Red (Joseph Kenneth Norville) Norvo was born on March 31, 1908, in Beardstown, Illinois, a small town built along the Illinois River. His dad played piano while a working dispatcher for the Chicago, Burlington, & Quincy Railroad. His mother, a former trumpet player, was determined to teach her children music. When Kenneth was six, he took just twelve piano lessons: "My teacher found out I was memorizing my lessons by ear. My brother Howard would play and I would listen. She nailed me." He gave up studying music for a while.

Then, while on daily excursion trips aboard touring riverboats, young Norvo observed a number of great jazzmen including jazz-trumpeter Louis Armstrong, cornetist Bix Beiderbecke, and saxophonist Frankie Trumbauer. That experience influenced him back on to the road to music.

"One year, a flood levee broke in town and flooded our house. We went to Rolla, Missouri for a while. I liked to listen to a marimba player in a pit band at the theater in that town. He let me try the thing out. I did pretty good. I liked playing it. When I got back to Beardstown, it bugged me and I thought about playing (the marimba).So my father let me work on a railroad gang for the summer and sell my pony so I could buy an instrument."

Norvo taught himself to play his brand-new, three-octave xylophone, that he purchased from a mail-order catalog, playing solo at high school dances. "I could play anything once I heard it. I learned stuff from some of those old Edison recordings. I learned harmony later. Then I went to Chicago to find work."

Norvo sought work with the traveling Chautauqua circuit, touring with a marimba octet, but, uncertain and embarrassed, he wouldn't go because he realized he couldn't read music. Back in Beardstown, his family decided he would attend the University of Illinois the following fall, his mother urging him to try working the Chautauqua tour for the summer, just for experience. The group was called the Collegians.

"I learned a lot on that tour. I worked with the other players and also took a lot of solos. I tried school again, but I split to go back on tour. We went out west to Seattle and places like that. I used to play a thing called 'Xylophone Rag.' I first heard about jazz music then."

Improving his playing skills and discovering jazz sounds, Norvo was booked as a solo into the Oriental Theater in Chicago by the booking agency. At the time, Chicago flourished with marimba and xylophone players performing on vaudeville stages. Constantly listening to recordings of Red Nichols, Earl Hines, Frankie Trumbauer, and Louis Armstrong, Norvo carefully honed his playing skills. In vaudeville he acquired the sobriquet "Red" because of his red hair and ruddy completion, and the name "Norvo" by an ever-erring announcer who could never remember his name. *Variety*, the show business chronicle, "picked it up and it stuck, so I kept it Norvo," Red explained, "It was easier."

"People liked to watch me perform. I would look at them…they would look back at me. I got to be quite an entertainer in vaudeville. That was about 1929."

Joining a band at the Eagle Ballroom, Norvo became its leader, adding jazz numbers, then emigrated to Minneapolis where he led a band at the Marigold Ballroom and worked on the staff of a radio station. The break came when conductor, composer Victor Young needed a xylophonist for his NBC radio show. Norvo filled the bill perfectly.

"I also worked part time between shows with Ben Bernie's orchestra at the College Inn (in the Sherman Hotel) in Chicago. Paul

Whiteman showed up one night. He was drunk. I didn't know who he was at first. If I had known he was there, I would've been too nervous to play. Anyway, he hired me for NBC and got me to play xylophone, marimba and vibrapharp. But, they wanted me to play vibes just for effect, not as playing an instrument. I also got on a show with (band-leader) Wingy (Manone) for a couple of afternoons every week. That's when I met Mildred (Bailey). She was singing for Whiteman. We liked each other right away. We started working together in Chicago as an act. Mildred was hot tempered, but we got along anyway." Mildred was the sister of Bing Crosby's singing partner in the Rhythm Boys, Al Rinker. She helped them get started.

THE VIBRAPHONE

Used mainly for novelty effect, "mallet instruments were a novel accoutrement of percussionists in the 1920's," according to Leonard Feather in his Book of Jazz. Norvo's instrument was the xylophone, a sort of hydrated vibraphone. Its keys were wood instead of metal; there was little resonance, and the only way to give the impression of sustaining a note was to use a half-tone tremolo or hit the same note repeatedly.

A marimba is a fuller-sounding variant in the xylophone family, fitted with resonance tubes beneath each key. The vibra-phone, like the xylophone, is an instrument with a sustaining pedal, resonating tubes under the keys, and small rotating fans, placed beneath the keys and operated electrically.

"To me, the vibraharp is a peculiar instrument because it tends to take on the characteristics of the people who play it. And it's peculiar because vibraharpists are a pretty warm fraternity. Guitarists are also like that. Certain people pick certain instruments, and vibraharpists in general are gentle, quiet people. Trumpet players and drummers, on the other hand, can be pretty argumentative. But the main thing is to play the right instrument," Red Norvo told Whitney Balliett in the 1970s for his book *Portraits in Jazz*.

When the Paul Whiteman band headed East, Red Norvo took along his xylophone and his new wife, Mildred, the couple now known as Mr.

and Mrs. Norvo." We got married when we were on tour upstate in New York."

BENNY GOODMAN

"When Red finished his routine, he would grab the bars off his instrument and throw them on the floor like he was angry. But, it was only a joke with him. The audience ate that up."

(L-R) Jimmy Raney, Red Mitchell and Red Norvo at the Chicago Preview Lounge, 1953.

The Norvos remained with the Whiteman band for a year or so. "That's when I made 'Rockin' Chair' with Mildred and Matty Malneck's band. She became known as the Rockin' Chair Lady." At this time the Norvos lived on Pilgrim Circle in Forest Hills, Queens, New York.

"We had jam sessions at our house. (Pianist) Teddy Wilson, Benny (Goodman), (jazz violinist) Joe Venuti, (trumpeter) Bunny Berigan, and (blues vocalist) Bessie Smith - they'd come over just for fun. That's where the Benny Goodman trio was born, you know - but before (Gene) Krupa went with him. (Jazz producer and "angel" John Hammond added Krupa to make the trio, along with Teddy). Mildred loved to cook

86

- and could she eat. She developed diabetes. She was supposed to be on a diet. She loved Bessie Smith. They got along just fine. Red Nichols lived just across the street. When I finally got my union card, me and Charlie Barnet would share a band — actually my first band. One time he would lead and the next time I led - depends on who booked the job first. When Charlie led for a full week at the Apollo (theater in Harlem), it turns out we were the first white band to play there. How about that!"

After that engagement, Red Norvo signed up to play in Bar Harbor, Maine. "I led a band and had Dave Barbour on guitar, Chris Griffin on trumpet, and (arranger/composer) Eddie Sauter. I had Fletcher Henderson charts. But the people up there were not used to our wild music, so they wouldn't pay us. Our little group finally gave up trying gigs in Maine. It got so bad that Mildred had to come up to pick me up. We were out of food and money by this time. It was a good, but trying experience. We had to bum food from farmers. Maine wasn't hospitable to musicians who played jazz in those days."

With an entirely new band, Red Norvo opened at the Famous Door on 52nd Street in New York. "It went just fine. We had a trumpet, clarinet, tenor sax, guitar, bass and xylophone. We had no drums or piano - that was different. We played riffs things, swinging things. We were a sensation. We played my 'Dance of the Octopus' and things like 'Gramercy Square' and 'Bix's In a Mist.' I expanded my group and played the New York City circuit of hotels."

With Eddie Sauter as the group's arranger, Red Norvo was booked into what turned out to be a very successful run at New York's Commodore Hotel, after an engagement at the Versailles, an East Side club, that didn't work out. "When the boss asked us to play a rumba, the boys didn't know how," Red said, "He shooed us out fast. We were very uncomfortable jazz musicians."

The same, happy group toured New England that fall and opened up in Syracuse, New York, for three weeks, then back to Chicago at the Blackhawk again, but this time for several months.

"That was from 1936 to 1938. Mildred came out to join us. We were called 'Mr. and Mrs. Swing.'" I love their recorded version of "Smoke Dreams" that Eddie Sauter arranged for them.

Some believe that Mildred's appearances with the band helped it commercially, since she was well-known in the area from her Whiteman band-singing days. When Mildred contracted diabetes, the band returned to the New York Commodore Hotel for a while, then disbanded. The Norvos sold their Forest Hills home for a Manhattan apartment, although they owned a country place in Kent Cliffs, New York, too, where they took occasional refuge from the big city.

The years of 1939, '40, and '41 were pivotal years for the Red Norvo group of players, who were ever-changing. It was a time for him to give up trying to maintain a big band. Small groups became the trademark for the remainder of his career.

Back on Fifty-second Street in 1942, '43, and '44, Red tried a small group, enjoying great success there and on limited East coast tours; "but the army draft grabbed too many players and I wound up playing xylophone in the Benny Goodman Quartet in 1945, doing what Lionel Hampton used to do. But I couldn't work it out with some of the passages," Norvo told me, "so I grabbed a vibraphone in a rehearsal studio, and Teddy Wilson suggested that we should mix vibraphone and clarinet with piano—and it worked out just fine." That began Red's career as strictly a vibraphone (vibraharp) player. During a special New York concert with Goodman, Red played a very delicate, sensitive solo on George Gershwin's "The Man I Love" with his first working vibraphone.

Besides working with Goodman, Red recorded with two stalwarts of bebop, Charlie "Yardbird" Parker and John Birks "Dizzy" Gillespie, fitting in with them perfectly in an all-star sextet led by Red himself.

Then: "Mildred and I got divorced. We both wanted children, but Mildred couldn't have any, so we parted - and we stayed friends till the day she died," he told me during one of our long phone conversations. He and Mildred had arranged several separations before deciding on divorce. After Red married Eve Rogers, the sister of trumpeter Shorty Rogers, they often visited Mildred on her small farm in Stormville, New York, with their two children whom Mildred adored. Mildred died on December 12, 1951, in an upstate New York hospital remaining friends with Red Norvo until the end. She was only forty-four.

From Goodman, Red joined with Woody Herman in the original First Herd, finally settling down in his long time home in Santa Monica, California. With guitarist Tal Farlow and bassist Red Kelly, Red performed for a while in Honolulu, "where the trio really got its start - without piano and drums - a very unusual deal that worked out good." Bassist Charlie Mingus soon replaced Kelly. "Funny, but Mingus was a mailman when I found him and asked him to join up with me. He gave up the music business - but I brought him back in. He had a temper like Mildred that we had to keep under control."

The trio prospered for a number of years with a few personnel changes, rehearsals taking place at the Alta Avenue, Santa Monica living room. "Everybody contributed, so it was good," Red said.

During this time the Deagan Company, who manufactured his instrument, amplified his vibes by installing a crystal mike in each resonator tube, allowing him to play with a lighter touch and even closer to the keyboard with his mallets than ever before.

While appearing in Las Vegas during the late 1950's, Frank Sinatra took a liking to Norvo's compact jazz group that first consisted of a trio, then expanded into a quintet. He enjoyed the singing freedom Red Norvo's small group offered and eventually invited him to tour with him to Australia.

"We had worked together in Vegas — at the Sands — and then at the Fountainbleau in Florida, and also in Atlantic City before — and after — we went to Australia," explained Red, "The Capitol recordings taken during that tour have just been (recently) released for the first time. Heard they are number four on the charts (1997). Isn't that sumthin'?"

FRANK SINATRA

"The higher up you get in this business the more opportunity you have to work with the people you want. Red is a man I have tremendous respect for, musically and personally. I've always wanted to work with his band."

The Australian tour remains a classic. Listening to the tracks you can tell that Sinatra was very comfortable in this jazz setting, particularly on "Just One of Those Things," "I Get a Kick Out of You," and

"I've Got You Under My Skin," Cole Porter songs all, including an album finish with a stunning "Night and Day."Unfortunately, Red and Frank never recorded a studio album together. Red, however, was the perfect backup for a loose Sinatra.

Tragedy struck Red Norvo in the early 1970's with the death of his son, Kevin, and of his wife, Eve, just two years later. "I didn't play for two years. I wouldn't play records or the radio. I just went fishing. But, I went back to playing and realized I never should have stopped. So I went back to work." During that period Red experienced medical problems with hearing disorders and underwent an operation.

Touring once again, and playing with various groups for as much as eight months at a time, Red Norvo was back on the music scene. It was a renaissance to him.

A delicate, but sophisticated musician, Kenneth "Red" (Norville) Norvo has performed on his discriminating mallet instrument with virtually every important jazz musician of the age beginning in the late 1920s right up to the '80s. I have found it difficult to find someone important who he hasn't played with over all the years either in his myriad bands or small groups, as well as in other spectacular Big Bands and small bands during his tenure in music.

Talking with his daughter Portia in February, 1999, she is hopeful that Red might come home again. "We bring him home on weekends for a few hours each day so he doesn't become too homesick. We have to return him to the *home* for special care, especially at night, for care we can't give him. We tried various nurses at home, but none worked out for us."

Not as well-known as his contemporaries, except in jazz circles, Red Norvo was nevertheless one of the best bandleaders of the Big Band Era and beyond, as I like to classify the period.

While talking with jazz singer Anita O'Day in March (1999), she simply extolled Red Norvo as a great musician and a very nice man. "I liked swinging with him," she said, "He could sure handle those vibes."

LATE NOTE: We lost Red Norvo, a great musician and a friend, in April, 1999.

Harry James and his very young vocalist, Frank Sinatra, 1939. *(Harry James Appreciation Society)*

HARRY JAMES REVISITED

You Made Me Love You with Joe Pardee and Lynn Roberts

A contortionist by age four, a drummer by seven, performing trumpet solos in a circus band by twelve. A star sideman, a consistent winner of *Metronome* and *Downbeat* Magazine Awards, a Number One bandleader, setting all-time attendance records for Big Bands. An excellent arranger, the composer of "Flash," "Back Beat Boogie," "Feet Draggin' Blues," "Tango Blues," and "Ultra." A hit maker, a movie maker, and a star virtuoso.

Simply a legend in his own lifetime.

The name is *Harry James*, perhaps the most popular bandleader ever.

JOE PARDEE

I'm a 71 year old member of the London based Harry James Appreciation Society, who really appreciates Harry. I like to refer to him simply as "Harry." I last saw Harry perform in October of 1979. At the performance, the houselights were dimmed and a spotlight focused on him. Harry raised his horn and began playing "Help Me Make It Through the Night." The audience remained very quiet as the notes floated over the auditorium, with playing so soulful, I experienced goosebumps. I left that place knowing we had been in the company of someone really special, a feeling that remained with me and still haunts me to this day.

I write this feeling the deepest respect and admiration of a man who devoted his entire life to his music and the joy of it in the hope that others might appreciate it as well.

Harry was born on March 15, 1916, in Albany, Georgia. His parents, Everett and Maybelle James, worked in the Haig Traveling Circus. Mom as an aerialist and dad as the conductor of the circus band.

"As a rule, everyone had to contribute and I was no exception," Harry explained.

Harry's first brush with music was as a drummer, a skill he retained all his professional life. However, Harry's dad determined that success for his son would be his playing of a trumpet in the band. By ten, lessons with dad as tutor began and, as Harry recalled, "with progress, I was soon doing solos with the circus band."

The circus wintered in Beaumont, Texas, where the James family settled down in 1931. Harry attended school there and took gigs with local bands Hogan Hancock, Herman Waldman, and Art Hicks. In 1935, with Hicks' in Chicago, bandleader Ben Pollack noticed Harry

Harry James with his first instrument (Circa 1922) when he played in his dad's circus band. *(Richard Grudens Collection)*

and invited him to join his band, giving him his first legitimate chance for national exposure. The Pollack band commissioned air check recordings, a sixteen- inch disc that bandleaders (and advertisers) used to check their performances on aired radio programs so they could improve their band's future performances. Sitting in with Harry at the time were trombonist Glenn Miller, clarinetist Irving Fazola, pianist Freddie Slack, trumpeter Clarence "Shorty" Sherock, and saxist Dave Mathews. Harry would spend 1935 and 1936 with Pollack, where he met, then married, the band's singer Louise Tobin. They had two sons, Tim and Jeff.

Harry was noticed by Benny Goodman's brother Irving, who heard Harry's exemplary work on a recording "Deep Elm" and advised Benny to add the young trumpeter to the band's roster, which he did Christmas week of 1936. Although Harry received like offers from Glenn Miller and Tommy Dorsey, who were forming their own organizations, Harry elected to go with Goodman. A legend was being born.

Goodman's powerhouse band was loaded with future leaders, drummer Gene Krupa, pianist Teddy Wilson, xylophonist Lionel Hampton, and pianist Jess Stacy. Sitting alongside Harry were trumpeters Ziggy Elman and Chris Griffin. This trio became the acclaimed trumpet section of the Big Band Era. Within weeks Harry elevated to first chair trumpet. His unflagging spirit and dynamic playing would propel the band to even greater prominence. There are, no doubt, readers here who may recall showing up early for the band's performances to hear Harry, Ziggy, and Chris go through their warm-ups.

Harry's exceptional works with Benny include "Ridin' High," "St.Louis Blues," and "Roll Em." Along with his magnificent work during the famed January 1938 Carnegie Hall Concert, Harry also recorded independently with members of Goodman's and Count Basie's orchestras, as well as work with Lionel Hampton, Billie Holiday, Teddy Wilson, and Red Norvo. The group used to hang out at Red Norvo and Mildred Bailey's house in Forest Hills, Queens, where they put ideas together. The Benny Goodman quartet was formed at one of the house sessions.

JOE PARDEE

If you will search out a recording Harry performed with Wilson and Norvo in 1937 called "Just a Mood," a blues number, arguably, I have heard no better trumpet playing than Harry's trumpet expressions performed on that session that day. With Gene Krupa's departure from Goodman in early 1938, Harry ran a close second to Benny as the band's main attraction. Night after night, Harry and Benny would duke it out, with Harry matching Benny note for note. With an irresistible urge to lead his own band, Harry left the comfort and security of the King of Swing's organization, borrowed $4,500.00 from Benny himself, and left him with good wishes.

94

*February 1939 saw Harry with his spanking new band open
at the Ben Franklin Hotel in Philadelphia. It was a swinging
group, heavy on the brass, but, while the critics wrote good
reviews, trouble lay ahead.*

Swing music was diminishing. The mood of the listening public
was changing. With so many excellent, established bands to compete
with, Harry found many choice locations closed to his group. This
meant less money playing lesser venues. By 1940, Harry was deep in
debt. Even the addition of girl singer Connie Haines and a boy singer, a
skinny kid named *Frank Sinatra* that Harry found performing in a New
Jersey roadhouse, failed to move the band forward.

Sinatra went over to Dorsey. "We were all starving and his wife was
pregnant and he had a chance to go with Tommy Dorsey for $ 120.00 a
week. He was only making $ 75.00 a week with me and not getting it,"
explained Harry to Richard Grudens back in 1981. "I told him, if things
don't get better with us in the next six months, get me a job with Dorsey,
too."

Harry went from Columbia to Variety Records, a less than suitable
venture. Things got so bad that Louise recalls that some weeks Harry
paid everyone but himself. Harry hung in while gradual changes were
being made. He softened the brass with strings, and Dick Haymes was
hired to replace Sinatra. Helen Forrest left Goodman, and Harry hired
her. Columbia re-signed the band. Corky Corcoran joined the band at
age seventeen, remaining with Harry for over thirty years. At one point,
Harry was appointed legal guardian of the very young man who sparked
the sax section.

JOE PARDEE

*A May, 1941 recording session featured a number on the
"B" side of a tune he admired ever since he heard Judy
Garland's recorded version. It was called "You Made Me Love
You." When it hit the markets, and with lots of help from Martin
Block, a disc jockey on New York's WNEW, who was playing it
frequently, it became an overnight sensation. When the band
arrived in New York to play the Paramount Theater, Harry*

found huge crowds gathered around the theater. At last, he had achieved fame and fortune; in his own words, "When the band eats better, they just naturally play better."

Hit followed hit. "I'll Get By" (with Dick Haymes vocal), "Sleepy Lagoon," "Velvet Moon," "I've Heard That Song Before," "I Had the Craziest Dream" (the classic Helen Forrest version), and "I Don't Want to Walk Without You." By 1943 Helen left because Harry divorced Louise and married Betty Grable. It was known that Helen and Harry were lovers. When Richard Grudens recently talked with Helen Forrest about the various bandleaders she performed with, Harry was the hands-down winner being her favorite leader, her best boss, and the nicest person in her musical life, along with her good friend and "Autolite Radio Show" singing partner, Dick Haymes.

After Helen, enter pretty Kitty Kallen with the recordings "I'm Beginning to See the Light" and "It's Been a Long, Long, Time," both very big hits for the band.

The band's reputation grew at a rapid pace, eventually reaching number one in the music polls. Harry replaced Glenn Miller on the "Chesterfield Radio Show" when Glenn joined the Army Air Force Band. Harry and the band went on to make twenty-two movies.

Harry and Betty had two daughters. Jointly, they were among the top money makers in the business.

As a show of contrast, Harry's obligation to the IRS in 1940 was nil, but his earnings in 1943 would elevate his payments to over $500,000.00. During the war years Harry was Columbia Record's biggest money-maker. The recording ban of 1942-1943 surely deprived Harry of even greater heights. It may have contributed to the rise of the individual vocalists and the demise of the bands. By 1946, most of the Big Bands had folded and Harry disbanded briefly. When he came back, a new band was formed, loaded with younger, more jazz oriented musicians. The strings were gone, and he embarked upon a more progressive

*style of playing. As Harry stated, "These talented kids make me
really want to play."*

Harry James; his wife, Betty Grable, and Harry's parents, circa 1950.
(Richard Grudens Collection)

*The 1950s and '60s were great years of artistic achievement
for Harry, with nifty arrangements from Neal Hefti and Ernie
Wilkins and tunes such as "Blues for Sale," "Bangtail," "J.
Walkin'," and revised renditions of Count Basie hits "Shiny
Stockings," "Lester Leaps In," and "April in Paris." Much was
said about Harry's taking on Basie styles, but, in fact, Harry
was too much his own man to be anyone's clone.*

The James band was the most active organization in the business
during this period, consistently playing to sell-out crowds in Las Vegas,
Reno, and Lake Tahoe, and wherever they traveled. Carnegie Hall in
1964, the annual Monterey Jazz Festival in 1965, tours to Germany in
1964, England during 1970 and '71, and South America in the '80s. The
band also appeared annually on Ed Sullivan's television show.

Harry paid his people the best salaries and naturally he hired the
best musicians. While never a strict disciplinarian, when the night's

work began, Harry expected one-hundred percent from his players. He set personal demands of his own performance, and would stand for no-less from the other musicians. The sidemen through the years reads as a *Who's Who* of the trade: alto-man Willie Smith, trombonist Ray Sims, alto saxman Joe Riggs, trombonist Ziggy Elmer, saxist Vido Musso, trumpeter Art DePew (who today fronts the Harry James Ghost Band), trombonist Ray Coniff, and pianist Jack Percival. Drumming chores were assigned to Buddy Rich, Louis Bellson, Sonny Payne, and Tony De Nicola, who would spend six years with Harry. He tells the story of when he received a new chart, and Harry would read it over just once — never to look at it again. Not only did he remember his own part, but, everyone else's in the band, as well. Of the hundreds of charts in the band's *book*, Harry knew them all by number, every one memorized. Harry also had a keen ear for vocalists, beginning with Sinatra, Haymes, Buddy DeVito, Connie Haines, Helen Forrest, Kitty Kallen, and Lynn Roberts; all would grace his bandstand down through the years. Harry's long time band manager Pee Wee Monte was loyal to Harry until the end of Harry's life.

For a nationwide celebrity tour of a 1978 show "The Big Broadcast of 1944," Harry chose Lynn Roberts to be the vocalist. Lynn had paid her dues early-on in her career singing with Goodman and both Dorsey brothers. After the tour Harry asked Lynn to stay on as the regular vocalist, which lasted until 1983. Harry held great praise for Lynn Roberts, and vice versa:

LYNN ROBERTS

"Harry was my favorite," Lynn Roberts told Richard Grudens recently during an interview, "maybe because I was older. Before the 1978 tour, I had met Harry years before when I was singing with Tommy Dorsey. Harry didn't remember the meeting, but it was in 1954 at the Last Frontier Hotel in Vegas. I don't think I need to say anything about Harry's trumpet play-ing. He was magnificent and even in '78 he was still playing great. We'd sit on the bus and talk about his life. He'd talk about his mom and always about Betty (Grable). He adored her, even though they were divorced for years. I guess it was just one

of those sad romances that just didn't seem to work. Professionally, Harry was extremely generous. He was not intimidated by anyone's talent. He loved to be surrounded by talent and gave everyone a chance to shine. He had a wonderful sense of timing and could put a show together that was perfect, for whatever was required. Harry was a showman — not just a bandleader. We were friends, and I'm grateful for that. After he died, I recorded a tribute album (with trumpeter Mel Davis) to Harry called "Harry, You Made Me Love You." I think he really would have been happy with it.

So, for whatever reason, I'm not really sure — I felt very connected to Harry James, so I would have to say that he was my favorite bandleader."

Lynn performs regularly with Doc Severinsen's band, and throughout the world with her own managed show with help from her brother, Al Raisig. If she heads your way, don't miss out on this beautiful and talented gal. A real class singing act is Lynn Roberts.

"I thought you might like this one of Harry and me in 1980." *(Lynn Roberts Collection)*

Harry blew them all away for forty-four years. By carly 1983 it was clear to all that Harry was a very sick man. So many years of touring, suffering under a poor, traveling- man's diet, and incessant smoking finally wore the Maestro down. He would play his final engagement just weeks before the end. The date July 5th held great meaning for Harry. He and Betty were married on July 5, 1943. He lost Betty Grable on July 5, 1973, and ironically, Harry passed away on July 5, 1983.

"I loved Harry James," said Frank Sinatra, Harry's first boy singer, "I loved him for a long time. I shall miss him. He is not gone. The body is, but the spirit remains."

JOE PARDEE

Well, the great trumpet man is gone, but the sound of his expressive trumpet continues on through his recordings. Richard Grudens reminds me that it was Ray Anthony describing his mentor, who coined the phrase, "The Best Damn Trumpet Player," for which Richard named his first book in 1996. Harry's legacy of music reminds us of what we possessed in his presence. I don't believe we will see or hear the likes of another trumpet player like Harry James ever again in our lifetime.

Author's note: Joe Pardee, of Ford's, New Jersey is an old friend and a senior member of The Harry James Appreciation Society, based in London, England,and handled by James archivist Jim Cutler. Joe addresssed the society in London in 1997 and will again in 1999. Any Harry James fan can join this august body of James admirers. Write to Jim Cutler, 3 Henrys Avenue, Woodford Green, Essex, England - 1G8 - 9Rb. Telephone # 0-11-44-181-504-4555. He'll be glad to hear from you.

(L-R) Jim Cutler, Tony De Nicola and Joe Pardee, Princeton, New Jersey, 1996. *(Joe Pardee Collection)*

Harry James and Jim Cutler, 1980. *(Joe Pardee Collection)*

Tommy and Jimmy

The Fabulous Dorseys with Bob Melvin

Documenting the Dorsey brothers chapter, I collaborated with Robert Melvin, a seasoned big band writer from Everett, Massachusetts, who regularly recounts similar material for "Joslin's Jazz Journal" and other periodicals. Bob and I put this piece together during the first weeks of January 1999.

Jimmy and Tommy Dorsey (Circa 1939) *(Richard Grudens Collection)*

The battling Dorsey brothers, Jimmy and Tommy, grew up in Shenandoah, Pennsylvania. Their coal miner father quit to become a music teacher and to lead a small, local band. He handed Jimmy a saxophone and Tommy a trombone and taught them to play. A disciplinarian, he kept them late at practice sessions. Jimmy was a year older than the dominant Tommy. The boys constantly argued. Jimmy had a more "take-it-easy" attitude, but when provoked, his temper was the equal of Tommy's. As their music education progressed, their father brought them into the band, thereby saving the salaries of two players. While still teenagers, the brothers left home to form the Dorsey Wild Canaries and were booked into long stays in various Baltimore hotels and ballrooms.

In those early years, before the big time, before Helen O'Connell and Bob Eberly, and well before Frank Sinatra and Connie Haines, Jimmy and Tommy Dorsey became studio musicians. Together or singularly, they appeared in the top bands of the thirties, including those of Red Nichols, Jean Goldkette, Victor Young, and Paul Whiteman's King of Jazz Orchestra with trombonist Jack Teagarden, Bing Crosby, cornetists Bix Beiderbecke and Henry Busse, pianist/ arranger Lennie Hayton, and arranger Bill Challis.

In the spring of 1934, the boys formed the Dorsey Brothers Orchestra and hired a young fellow named Glenn Miller to arrange and play trombone and Bing Crosby's brother Bob to sing. The band worked just fine, but the brothers were constantly engulfed in an adversarial relationship, to say the least; most arguments were about music, which often became violent. Glenn Miller reluctantly took on the task of peace-maker to help keep them apart.

The boys' hangout in those days was Plunkett's saloon on 53rd Street in New York City. All the city musicians (Artie Shaw and Bix Beiderbecke among them) could make their radio dates on time from that strategic location. It was a great pickup spot for studios hiring musicians. From that group they formed their first orchestra, recruiting members of other bands who were out-of-work for the moment.

The band first signed with Okeh Records and, later, Decca Records, performing regularly at New York and New Jersey hotel ballrooms. They were booked into the famed Glen Island Casino in New Rochelle, New York, staying for a long engagement. Glenn left the band partly because he could not stand the constant bickering. The arguments persisted, climaxing one night when the boys flew at each other while on the bandstand. Tommy grew violent and stormed off leaving Jimmy to carry on alone. What had been building for years finally happened, and it came as no surprise. The break-up lasted for a long eighteen years, during which time each managed to become a legend of the Big Band Era with equally successful musical organizations.

JIMMY DORSEY

Jimmy's initial dilemma was filling Tommy's chair in the trombone section. Jimmy remembered a very young sixteen year old Bobby Byrne, whom he had once heard. He sent for, auditioned and hired him. The other musicians were skeptical, but after listening their doubts were dispelled. Jimmy added vocalist Bob Eberly and drummer Ray

McKinley to beef up the rhythm section. Tutti Camarata came aboard as trumpeter and arranger.

Jimmy was well-liked by his musicians, and although he retained the infamous Dorsey temper, he kept it well under control. His fine musicianship complemented the rich, lush sound he brought forth from his saxophone. He was a true master of the sax. Jimmy's personal life never captured headlines. He preferred to keep his non-music life private. He once courted vocalist Mary Ann McCall, and it was rumored that he would marry her, but it never occurred.

His orchestra now stabilized, Jimmy appeared on the radio series "The Kraft Music Hall" for over a year, which curtailed the band's recording output. He added vocalist Kay Weber, then, near the end of the series, replaced her with vocalist Martha Tilton, who did not fit in well and was replaced by a definite asset, seasoned performer June Richmond. Martha, of course, went on to star with Benny Goodman.

Evolving from a 'sweet band' to one that combined swing and sweet sounds, and, after a few hit recordings with Bob Eberly - perfect singles like "Marie Elena," Jimmy hired precocious Helen O'Connell as his definitive girl singer.

FRANKIE LAINE

It seems that Frankie Laine had met Jimmy's secretary, Nita Moore, on Broadway one evening. Nita told him that Dorsey was looking for a girl singer.

"It happened that I saw Helen the night before at the Village Barn down on Eighth Street singing with Larry Funk and his band, so I told Nita Moore, — Jimmy's secretary, — about her and Jimmy went to see her perform and that's how he hired her," Frankie Laine told me during an interview with both he and Helen back in the mid-eighties. Helen smiled and concurred.

HELEN O'CONNELL

"It was Tutti (Camarata) who came up with the idea of the duets 'Green Eyes,' 'Amapola,' and 'Tangerine,' the great hits I recorded with Jimmy and Bob Eberly," Helen O'Connell went

*on to say, "Tutti had to come up with a closer for our weekly
radio show, so he devised a unique formula. Bob Eberly was to
sing the first chorus of a song as a ballad, then the tempo was
to pick up so the entire band would play part of the selection,
then the tempo would slow down and I would come in for a
semi-wailing finale. People loved those recordings...and they
always ask me about them."*

*"We had a unique group with Jimmy, who was a wonderful
person — never the boss. But, if anybody made trouble, I don't
care how well he played, he didn't keep him very long." Helen
told author Fred Hall in 1991.*

Always dressed in a formal-style evening gown, Helen looked pretty on the bandstand, as was expected, and Bob complimented her appearance as the good-looking boy singer in black tie. In the first months of 1941, Bob and Helen racked up gigantic record sales with "Amapola" and "Green Eyes," and in 1942 added the immensely popular "Tangerine." All three recordings still hold up today as favorites. The three tunes were number one sellers, propelling Jimmy Dorsey to the height of his popularity. The band was creating waves with the public and Jimmy could see nothing but success in his future.

In 1943, Helen left to get marrried and raise a family, so Jimmy brought in pretty Kitty Kallen, who had graduated from Jack Teagarden's band, and teamed her with Bob Eberly to record the admirable hit "Besame Mucho," utilizing the same formula as the Eberly-O'Connell duets. With World War II in full course, Bob joined the army in December, 1944. No vocalist attained the success with Jimmy that Bob had, and his loss was a negative blow to the band.

Kitty Kallen departed shortly thereafter, again diminishing the success the band had enjoyed with Helen, Bob, and Kitty. With vocalists' fortunes on the rise, the Big Bands were losing their draw. At the end of the war, veterans returned from military life with images of jobs, marriage, and homes. This left little time for personal entertainment, attendance at night clubs and dance halls. In December 1946, eight of the top bands folded due to lack of bookings. Jimmy struggled on with his band for a few more years. By 1950, television was flickering brightly in living rooms featuring wrestling, Ed Sullivan's variety show, and Roller

Derby action, capturing an important share of entertainment time. New automobiles found their way onto the nation's newly constructed highways. Times were changing for the Big Bands. Jimmy Dorsey inevitably gave up his band in 1950.

TOMMY DORSEY

After the breakup at the Glen Island Casino, in contrast to Jimmy's slow rise to stardom, Tommy promptly contacted an old friend, Joe Haymes. Haymes was leading a hotel-style band with less than great success, so Tommy hired twelve of Haymes' musicians and formed the Tommy Dorsey Orchestra. Tommy wasted little time in whipping his band into top shape. A driven man who demanded the best from himself and expected the same from his players, his temperament was explosive, yet he possessed a tender side and was caring towards those men who were as dedicated to the music as was he.

A recording deal with RCA Victor Records produced the recording "On Treasure Island," with vocalist Edythe Wright, soon reaching number one on the charts. Tommy constantly changed band personnel. He brought in classy Jack Leonard to handle the vocals, drummer Davey Tough and clarinet/saxist Bud Freeman. Trombonist Axel Stordahl was signed, eventually becoming the band's arranger. He hired Bunny Berigan for the trumpet section and produced "Marie" with Leonard doing the vocal and Berigan creating a timeless solo for this hit recording. The release of the "Song of India" catapulted Tommy Dorsey into a top rated band leader and from then on amassed over two-hundred records in both the sweet and swing category.

Although famous as a bandleader, it must be realized that Tommy was a superb trombone player and, in all respects, the equal of contemporary Jack Teagarden. Just listen carefully to his original recording of "I'm Getting Sentimental Over You" or "Once In a While" to appreciate the extent of his talent.

The years 1935 through 1938 were flourishing years for Tommy Dorsey, although his personal life did not mirror his public success. Experiencing ongoing marital troubles, a divorce became inevitable. Then, Edythe Wright and Jack Leonard left the band; drummer Davey Tough was replaced with Buddy Rich, and Ziggy Elman joined the trumpet section. Tommy hit pay dirt when he managed to hire Frank Sinatra away from Harry James in the spring of 1940, and a very young Connie Haines, who had also sung with James, joined him too. Frank, Connie, the Pied Pipers singing group (including Jo Stafford) immediately clicked with the million seller "I'll Never Smile Again."

Tommy Dorsey with *(clockwise)* Connie Haines, Pied Pipers' Chuck Lowrey, Jo Stafford, Clark Yocum, John Huddleston, and Frank Sinatra. (Circa 1940) *(Connie Haines Collection)*

JO STAFFORD

Jo Stafford remembered Frank Sinatra when he first joined the band and the Pipers, "As he came up to the mike, I just thought, Hmmm - kinda thin. But by the end of eight bars I was thinking, 'This is the greatest sound I've ever heard,' But he had more. Call it talent. You knew he couldn't do a number badly," Jo told me back in 1997.

The Sinatra tenure with the band were glory days for both Sinatra and Dorsey. Sinatra became *The Voice* and Tommy, *The Sentimental Gentleman of Swing*. The list of musicians was outstanding. Among them clarinetists Johnny Mince and Buddy De Franco; arrangers Deane Kincaide and Sy Oliver; pianist Joe Bushkin; trombonists Nelson Riddle and Earle Hagen.

The band turned out a remarkable string of hits: "Snootie Little Cutie" and "Let's Get Away From It All"; "Oh,Look At Me Now"; "There Are Such Things"; "Street of Dreams"; "Everything Happens to Me"; "East of the Sun" (with that great Bunny Berigan solo); "Will You Still Be Mine" (Connie Haines is perfection phrasing this one, the first recording Tommy allowed her to sing in her own key); "On the Sunny Side of the Street"; "Yes, Indeed"; "Deep Night"; all these recordings were made with Sinatra, Connie Haines, and the Pipers with Jo Stafford, alone or collectively.

Connie Haines and Frank Sinatra, 1940.
(Connie Haines Collection)

"Boogie Woogie," "Song of India," and "Opus No. 1" were great instrumentals, too.

In 1940, the opulent Hollywood Palladium opened, and the Dorsey band, being the most popular dance band in the nation at the time, was chosen to appear as its star attraction on opening night.

CONNIE HAINES

"It was wonderful, and you could feel the excitement. Actress Dorothy Lamour cut the big red satin ribbon, revealing a mountain of orchids and then the band. The place was packed. The dance floor was filled — they had room to swing and sway together," according to Connie Haines in her forthcoming biography 'Snootie Little Cutie.' "We spent eight exciting weeks there each year."

World War II caused drastic problems for the Big Band business. Gasoline and tires were rationed, curtailing travel for the touring bands. The draft claimed many of their players. Buddy Rich and Ziggy Elman were soon wearing uniforms. In late 1942, Sinatra decided to go it alone. However, the business man in Tommy Dorsey surfaced when he negotiated a percentage of Frank's future earnings in exchange for letting him out of his contract. The rich baritone of Dick Haymes replaced Sinatra and the band struggled on until the end of the war.

DICK HAYMES

"The actual Tiffany's of the orchestra world in those days was Tommy Dorsey's orchestra," Dick Haymes told author Fred Hall in 1978, "because he gave you a showcase. He was a star maker. He carried the arrangers — Axel Stordahl, Paul Weston, and Sy Oliver; I mean we had the cream of everything — this huge, wonderful orchestra. Tommy would say, 'Okay, here's your spot — do your song.' I learned great lessons in performing as well as singing and breath control with Tommy."

Dick sang with the band for its nine week appearance at the Hollywood Palladium that year. His own version of "Marie Elena" rivaled Bob Eberly's a year or so earlier with Jimmy Dorsey.

Tommy Dorsey was now entering a phase of his life where he became quite a business man. His band booking business *Tomdor Enterprises* was thriving, and he began a music magazine titled *The Bandstand* to compete with *Metronome* and *Downbeat*. Unfortunately, only six issues were printed before it folded, a distinct financial loss for Tommy Dorsey the businessman. Undaunted, he demanded more money for his band's performances at the Hollywood Palladium and didn't receive it. Searching for another ballroom, he purchased the Casino Gardens in near-by Ocean Park, California. Bandleader Harry James and his brother Jimmy were also partners in the deal. Evidently the brothers were able to work together in an enterprise where the sparks didn't fly. Casino Gardens proved to be a money-maker, competing with the Palladium for the services of all the other important name bands, but Tommy found himself stretched between the band and his other ventures, so the band suffered. He took on an added position as director of popular music for Mutual Radio. By 1946, bookings for the major bands slowed to a mere trickle, and in December, Tommy and seven other top bands quit.

Tommy Dorsey took a breather from the bandstand and devoted time between his record companies, his new job, and his almost defunct booking agency to get married again, this time to actress Pat Dane. In 1948 he reformed the band and claimed that he would revitalize the Big Band business. His named carried some weight, but he struggled until 1950, when he and brother Jimmy buried their differences to form the Dorsey Brothers Orchestra, their first collaboration since the infamous breakup.

Tommy assumed the role of leader of this new enterprise and Jimmy seemed content to simply take a seat in the saxophone section. The band was known as The Dorsey Brothers Orchestra or The Tommy Dorsey Orchestra, featuring Jimmy Dorsey. Both were used depending on the booking. Appearances were widely spaced, but the boys were back in business and working peacefully with one-another. In 1955, Jackie Gleason, a big fan of the Dorseys, asked them to appear on television as a summer replacement for his popular CBS show, which they did for two seasons.

LYNN ROBERTS

"I was seventeen when I joined the band," Dorsey vocalist Lynn Roberts said when I talked to her in January, 1999: "When I first saw him in the coffee shop of a hotel in Fayetteville, North Carolina, he appeared larger than life. He had a very gruff voice and was terribly intimidating. I had no arrangements of my own, so I had to sing the things that were already in the book, written for someone else — most of them not in my key. In spite of all that, he was pleased with my work. I learned to sing by listening to T.D. — as we called him. Listening to him play was an education, like going to music school every night for four hours. He was a musician who knew the lyrics to the songs he played. He thought about them while he was playing and that, in my opinion, is the reason that so many singers latched on to his incredible phrasing. Tommy was my mentor — my teacher — he taught me how to sing. Thank you, Tommy Dorsey. Jimmy Dorsey joined T.D. in 1953, so that was how I came to work with both of them. He was a sweet, almost shy guy. And — yes, - they did fight."

Times were good for the band once again, but Tommy was involved in a divorce with his third wife Jane New Dorsey, a one time Copacabana showgirl. This weighed heavily on Tommy, and on November 26, 1956, after a very heavy meal, Tommy took some sleeping pills and went to bed. During the night he became ill, vomited, suffocated on his regurgitated food and died while he was asleep.

LYNN ROBERTS

"When Tommy suddenly died in 1956, we were appearing at the Café Rouge'," Lynn Roberts said, "It was our day off and we all learned of his tragic death on the TV or in the morning paper. He was only fifty-one years old. I often wonder how the music business would have been different had Tommy lived. We, the fabulous Dorsey Brothers Band, were doing better than

110

ever. We had a five day a week radio show on NBC plus lots of bookings into the following year. Tommy was a wonderful business man and a great trombonist. I still miss him."

ROBERT MELVIN

"Jimmy was badly shaken by his brother's death but rallied and took over as leader of the orchestra and tried to carry on. This was not to be and Jimmy fell ill and died of cancer a few short months later.

"In six months, two luminaries of the Big Band Era passed away. As a final starburst for the Dorseys, a recording of 'So Rare' recorded earlier, became a hit record in March 1957. Both bands have been active as ghost bands even to this day. A Jimmy or Tommy Dorsey Orchestra ' under the direction of' is surely playing somewhere on Earth today. A fitting tribute to the musical excellence of the Dorsey Brothers."

Tommy, Frank, and Jimmy, 1955. *(Richard Grudens Collection)*

GLENN MILLER

Perspective with Band Leader Larry O'Brien

The very mention of the name Glenn Miller conjures up visions of a brilliantly lit-up Wurlitzer jukebox and peppy jitter-bugs in zoot- suits swinging and hurling one another across a dance floor to the swinging sounds of "In the Mood," "Chattanooga Choo-Choo," or perhaps "Jukebox Saturday Night"

Glenn Miller, 1939. *(Richard Grudens Collection)*

"...making one Coke last us 'til it's time to scram."

Major Glenn Miller disappeared on December 15, 1944, while on a wartime plane trip that was to take him across the English Channel, although neither his body or the plane has never been recovered; his music plays on to this day, some 56 years later. His music charts remain as timeless as ever.

Since Glenn's disappearance the band has been led by a number of worthy musi-cians. Tex Beneke, the band's original sax player and vocalist on the numbers "Chattanooga Choo-Choo" (which earned the world's first Gold Record) and "I've Got a Gal in Kalamazoo," led the band for a while, followed by former member, drum-mer Ray McKinley (1956 to 1966), as well

Larry O'Brien.

as member/saxist Peanuts Hucko; clarinetist Buddy De Franco in the seventies; then Jimmy Henderson, Larry O'Brien; and, from 1983 to 1988, Dick Gearhart; and, once again, current leader Larry O'Brien. In Branson, Missouri, vocalist Bobby Vinton, whose hit recordings of the sixties are legendary, operates and plays trumpet for an official Glenn Miller Orchestra.

In 1982 I spoke with Larry O'Brien during a Glenn Miller band get-together I covered for Long Island PM Magazine with famed WNEW

Larry O'Brien and Richard Grudens 1986
Westbury Music Fair *(Photo: Camille Smith)*

New York disc jockey William B. Williams, vocalists Margaret Whiting and Billy Eckstine. Present, too, was the man who booked the show, Willard Alexander, foremost head of the prestigious Willard Alexander Big Band Booking Agency: "Larry was working at the Dunes in Las Vegas and I had my people approach him to lead the Miller band," Willard explained, "He was working for the Dorsey organization led by Sam Donohue and a house band in Vegas. I forgot who brought Larry to my attention. Anyway, we recommended him. We felt he would keep in tune, so to speak, with the Miller sound, and he looked darn good, too."

When Larry played with the Glenn Miller Orchestra while Ray McKinley was directing back in 1961, he didn't believe the band would last. "The band is not only still around, but it's flourishing," Larry said. "There are a lot of people who still love the original sound of Glenn's immortal charts."

In 1996, Larry talked about the future of the Miller band once again, saying: "It's amazing. The applause is still tremendous today. Those tunes bring back a lot of memories. For example, we do 'That Old Black Magic' and 'People Like You and Me,' in addition to the regular stuff." But, even today, as Larry confirms, "In the Mood" and "Moonlight Serenade" are the top requested tunes.

Larry had just signed a contract as leader for an additional two years and expected to easily complete it. "At one time I was concerned about our audience, but you know," he told mutual friend *Big Band Jump Newsletter* Editor Don Kennedy, "continually we're getting more and more young people at our concerts, and that gladdens my heart because they are our audience of the future. It also means that young people are opening their ears to something besides their own frenetic music."

Every Big Band buff knows the Glenn Miller story. In its heyday Glenn's was the most popular band of the late thirties and early forties, its world-famous, lyrical theme, Glenn's beautiful "Moonlight Serenade," a Big Band masterpiece. Clarinetist Johnny Mince described Glenn's success to me one afternoon during a conversation at the Three Village Inn in Stony Brook, New York in 1983. It was Johnny Mince, the catalyst, who with Glenn "discovered" the unique, elusive Glenn Miller sound.

"The truth is that we were rehearsing with the Ray Noble Orchestra at the Rainbow Room in Rockefeller Center. Trumpet player Pee Wee Erwin called in sick, so Glenn asked me to play the trumpet part with my clarinet. 'I want to hear what it sounds like,' said Glenn. He never, ever used the clarinet on top before - playing a double with the tenor below. We went through the first eight bars and suddenly everyone knew that was the sound Glenn had been searching for all those years. It was written all over his face. The rest is history."

Glenn decided to form his own band, which he did in 1937, but he struggled to keep the band going. The band finally caught on, but only after Glenn had mortgaged both his and his in-laws homes to keep the band going. Woody Herman told me that in 1981 when we were discussing Glenn.

Glenn disbanded and tried again with a new manager and a new group of musicians. He chose an unusual, new clarinet player named Wilbur Schwartz, whose tone was exceptional. He found a saxophone player named Gordon "Tex" Beneke, whose story you can read in my last book *The Music Men*. Tex, of course, was the band's personality performer. Though he could not sing well, he nevertheless became the vocalist on those great tunes "Jukebox Saturday Night," "I've Got a Girl in Kalamazoo," and "Chattanooga Choo Choo," all accomplished with the help of the Modernaires, Chuck Goldstein, Hal Dickenson, Ralph Brewster, Bill Conway, and Dorothy Claire, or Marion Hutton.

Glenn hired vocalist Ray Eberle, Bob Eberley's brother. Bob was singing with Jimmy Dorsey and alerted Glenn to his brother's availability. Their names were spelled differently to avoid confusion.

Then, the band was booked into the famed Glen Island Casino, in New Rochelle, New York. Glenn appeared at Frank Dailey's Meadowbrook in New Jersey for a short gig before his Glen Island opening. The band was heard over the radio from the Meadowbrook, and success was just around the corner after appearances that summer at the Glen Island Casino.

Glenn recorded prolifically during that period. Bill Finnegan arranged the swinging "Little Brown Jug"; Kay Starr, temporarily replacing Marion Hutton, recorded "Love With a Capital You" and "Baby Me, "two of Glenn's best lady vocal recordings; Tex Beneke and Al Klink recorded their tenor sax duel on "In the Mood", Joe Garland's catchy tune originally offered to Artie Shaw; Billy May wrote a great opening for "Serenade in Blue"; and tunes like "Tuxedo Junction" and "Moonlight Serenade," Glenn's theme, became huge successes for the band.

Engagements in the Café Rouge in the Hotel Pennsylvania with players like Ray Anthony, Johnny Best, Hal McIntyre, and Billy May increased the band's popularity. Glenn made two successful movies with the band, *Sun Valley Serenade* with Sonja Henie and *Orchestra Wives* with Jackie Gleason.

In 1942, with the war in full swing, Glenn disbanded his immensely popular band to join the Army Air Force. In a few months he formed the Glenn Miller Army Air Force Band. The all-soldier band, except for vocalist Beryl Davis, played for American fighting men and was heard on radio broadcasts from coast-to-coast and throughout Europe.

It is now 1999, more than a half-a-century later, and the Glenn Miller band itinerary is booked far into the new Millennium. Today I spoke at length to Larry O'Brien about his life as a musician, his accidental benefactor Glenn Miller, and the destiny of today's Glenn Miller Orchestra.

The Glenn Miller Orchestra 1999. *(Larry O'Brien Collection)*

Larry's introduction to the world of music occurred the day his dad, a craftsman who could make anything with his hands, fashioned him a pretty good home-made violin in the kitchen of their Ozone Park, New York home. Larry was just ten.

"He placed it on the kitchen table. But, the violin was not for me. I wanted to play the trombone, especially when I heard a friend practicing on one in the rear of his dad's dry-cleaning shop. My dad obviously could not make one for me, so I had to get one. It had to wait until I got into John Adams High School where I borrowed one, while taking lessons at school."

Larry later received advanced lessons from a technically excellent teacher named Eddie Collier, an older, fellow high school alumni who was playing in Broadway shows. At sixteen, Larry won the New York Philharmonic Scholarship and "made" the prestigious All-City School Orchestra.

Larry O'Brien began his Big Band career playing a very smooth trombone in the house band at the Frontier Hotel in Las Vegas, backing various big-name acts who were performing as part of the Vegas star policy of the time. Along the road to his Glenn Miller success, he played in the bands of Buddy Morrow, Sammy Kaye, Art Mooney, Billy May, Ralph Marterie, Ray McKinley's Glenn Miller Orchestra, Urbie Green, Les Elgart, and the Tommy Dorsey Orchestra with Sam Donohue — quite a compendium.

"I've had a checkered past, you could say."

How did Larry O'Brien capture the coveted Glenn Miller appointment?

"As far as I know, they invited me to lead the Glenn Miller band probably because of my experience with the Tommy Dorsey Orchestra and maybe conducting for Frank Sinatra, Jr., that lit up a lamp in somebody's head. So I was called and offered the job. I said, 'Yeah! I'll take it.' and then David MacKay called me, talked further, then came out to Vegas to watch me perform, and sealed the deal. David, who was Glenn's close friend, attorney, and executor of his estate, owns the worldwide rights to license the use of the Glenn Miller name and music book, or charts, as they are referred to in the business."

Besides his skill as a leader who drives a sparkling band, Larry O'Brien is a brilliant trombonist. His version of "Danny Boy" regularly captivates the crowd. His Dorsey breath-control style playing is dominated by those long *legato* phrases. His own musicians admire him greatly.

"I keep the band in an upbeat condition. Tonight's concert in Chicago will start with 'The Volga Boatmen' chart. It will wake them up and get them started on an up-beat."

It appears as though Larry O'Brien will lead the band well into the next Millennium. The purity and nostalgic value of Glenn Miller's music remains a mystery. Of all the famous Big Bands, Glenn Miller's music is the most recognizable and the most performed worldwide. Was it because he featured great soloists? No! Great vocalists? Not a chance! Then what was it? It was a composite of everything accomplished in middle-of-the-road perfection. It wasn't hot Artie Shaw or loud Charlie Barnet swing, nor was it Guy Lombardo sweet, Lawrence Welk corny, or Basie or Red Norvo jazz- influenced music.

The definitive Glenn Miller music we are talking about was the artfully arranged material by people like Jerry Gray, Bill Finegan, and

Billy May. Their prolific charts, now preserved eternally in their 1940s style, remain timeless. More smash hits were "Pennsylvania 6-5000," "American Patrol," "Song of the Volga Boatmen," "Sun Valley Serenade," "Don't Sit Under the Apple Tree," "Blue Evening," "String of Pearls," "At Last," and countless others.

Neophyte or staunch outright fan, those Glenn Miller evergreens never fail to satisfy.

Listen, it's Paul Douglas on one of those radio airchecks announcing from the Hotel Pennsylvania in New York on NBC: *"Ladies and Gentlemen, may I introduce Glenn Miller, bandleader, arranger, leading exponent of the swing trombone, direct from the Café Rouge in the Hotel Pennsylvania.*

"Now, here's Glenn Miller's music!"

GLENN MILLER and his Orchestra Back Row- L-R - on Trumpet: Johnny Best, Billy May. On Drum: Maurice Purtill. On Bass: Trigger Alpert. On Guitar: Jack Lathropo. Second Row - also on Trumpet: Ray Anthony, Wade McMickle. On far right on Saxophone: Tex Beneke, Albert Klink. Front Row - On Trombone: Paul Tanner, Jimmy Priddy, Frank D'Annolfo. Vocal: Ralph Brewster, Hal Dickinson, Ray Eberle, Chuck Goldstein, Billy Conway. On Piano: Chummy MacGregor. On Saxophone: Ernie Caceres, Hal McIntyre, Willie Schwartz. Front and Center: Glenn Miller *(Richard Grudens Collection)*

BEN GRISAFI'S BIG BAND

Alumni's Hideaway

Ben Grisafi leads his Big Alumni Band with vocalist Denise Richards *(Ben Grisafi Collection)*

In a never-ending search for musicians who have scattered themselves throughout Big Band oblivion, except those who live in and around Los Angeles, California, where so many have settled down to a life of either casual retirement or taking gigs as studio musicians to augment the music of Hollywood, I have, at last, found a cache — a pot of gold at the end of the musical rainbow — right here in the East. Here, a major group of alumni musicians are still playing their instruments smack in the middle of composer, arranger, and saxophonist Ben Grisafi's Alumni Big Band on Long Island.

Here I found **Chuck Genduso**, the trumpet player who blew beautifully with Harry James, Tommy Dorsey, and Ray McKinley, and **Dan Repole**, a great trombonist who honed his notes with Guy Lombardo, and also produced for Tommy Tucker, and Les and Larry Elgart - Larry being Best Man at Dan's Atlantic City wedding.

Pete Chively was once modernist Stan Kenton's and Billy May's bassist; **Ed Matson** tinkled piano smoothly for trumpeter Billy Butterfield's band; and **Al Miller** rolled his drumsticks for Xavier Cugat and played with Buddy Rich and Louis Bellson's band; **Bobby Nelson** blew tenor sax with Louis Prima, Lee Castle's Jimmy Dorsey Ghost Band, and Tommy Dorsey's orchestra. Featured alto sax player **Chacey Dean** wailed with Charlie Barnet, upbeat Stan Kenton, and the much tamer Mitchell Ayres. **Tom Alfano** employed his lead alto with Les and Larry Elgart and Johnny Long's band. Tito Puente's jazz oriented band had **Schep Pullman** managing baritone sax chores for nine years. **Charlie Henry** worked with the Johnny Long and Ralph Flanagan bands, and **Jack Carman** performed on trombone in the swinging bands of Buddy Rich, Boyd Raeburn, and Georgie Auld. Trumpeter **Mike Lewis** has performed with the bands of Tex Beneke and Harry James and backed music luminaries Tony Bennett, Sammy Davis Jr., Mel Torme, Andy Williams, Gladys Knight, and Sarah Vaughan, as well as Joe Williams and Vic Damone. Vocalist **Denise Richards** performed with the Dorsey Brothers and Glenn Miller Orchestras. Whew!

Now that's a Big Band full of veteran players. It's no wonder Ben Grisafi's two CDs, *Talk of the Town* and *But Beautiful* are selling well in England through Frank Touhey's Montpellier Records and in the U.S. through Ray Anthony's Big Band Record Library catalogs. And, when you listen, you will think about Les Brown and Larry Elgart playing Grisafi charts.

Younger musicians, who complete the band's roster, hold great respect for the seasoned alumni, and, in contrast, the alumni members are amazed with the fine, talented players who comprise today's music scene. There are very few non-school bands of this size available for young, upcoming musicians who prefer playing the band's '40s style music.

Ben Grisafi has played tenor sax with Billy Butterfield, Randy Brooks, and Cab Calloway and led a band opening at Carnegie Hall for our mutual friend, vocalist Jerry Vale, with his arrangement of "My

Buddy." He has appeared with, among others, Al Martino, Julius La Rosa, and Margaret Whiting. WLIM and other New York radio stations dubbed *But Beautiful* as the best compact disc of 1995 and 1996. With the timbre of the Les Brown and Larry Elgart band, Ben effects all the arrangements, and he has since arranged over forty selections for his next CD, which will be performed by those very players.

Ben Grisafi with Billy Butterfield Band, 1950. *(Ben Grisafi Collection)*

Ben Grisafi and I first met at a luncheon last October at the old Three Village Inn in Stony Brook, Long Island. Upon learning of Ben's activities through vocalist Roberto Tirado (Ben backed and arranged Roberto's own CD *Prisoner of Love* album), who was profiled in my book *The Music Men*, I invited Ben to meet Max Wirz, a European disc jockey and author from Switzerland who was visiting me and whose radio shows, *Showtime* and *Light and Breezy*, dominate Swiss Big Band American style radio, reaching into France and other adjoining countries. Ben and I hit it off as old friends, and, later, in November 1998, he joined me and songwriter Ervin Drake and actor, vocalist John Gabriel in a tribute to Ervin at nearby Five Towns College at the invi-

121

tation of College President Dr. Stanley Cohen. Ervin Drake composed Frank Sinatra's "It Was a Very Good Year" and Frankie Laine's "I Believe."

Maybe we get along so well because Ben and I grew up just a few blocks from one another in the Bensonhurst section of Brooklyn. For as far back as he can remember: "There was constant music played in our home. My dad, although not a musician, loved classical and symphonic music. I would help wind-up the old *Victrola*."

Similarly, it was my own brother Ted who played piano and kept the live music going while I would try to sing. My mother cherished the baritone of Bing Crosby, and all you heard was "Where the Blue of the Night Meets the Gold of the Day" or "I Found a Million Dollar Baby (In a Five and Ten Cents Store)."

"I began taking sax lessons at thirteen," said Ben. "I kept it from my parents because they could not afford it. I got a job setting bowling pins at nearby Benson Lanes. Lessons were one dollar and the instrument rental was also one dollar. Because of my very young age, I had to practice more to qualify for playing in the local band. When my teacher, Carl Pinto, recommended advance studies, I subwayed to Manhattan to study under another fine teacher, Louis Arfine."

Lafayette High School music studies provided excellent musical training for Ben Grisafi. In the school band were future Big Band musicians Al Stewart, who played with Benny Goodman; saxist Buzz Brauner who played with the Dorseys, (while still in school Buzz participated in the hit recording "Four Leaf Clover" with Art Mooney's orchestra), and Dave Dweck, a trombone player who scored with Tex Beneke's band. All this professional quality activity influenced Ben.

Upon graduating, he began playing in local bands. "I began going to Nola Studios in Manhattan where many big bands rehearsed and recorded. I recall Gene Krupa rehearsing with sidemen Gerry Mulligan and Charlie Ventura. I trecked to see live bands play at the famous Metropole on Broadway. On famous 52nd Street, between 5th and 6th Avenue, I could hear the sound of developing jazz and bebop reaching the street from the Onyx Club or The Three Deuces where Coleman Hawkins, Ben Webster, or Georgie Auld would be playing. "

By the age of seventeen, Ben played with Randy Brooks and Billy Butterfield, whose solo on Artie Shaw's "Stardust" recording is classic. Ben was drafted into the Korean conflict and was placed in the Army Band, playing out his time in service clubs and in parades and uniformed dance parties.

Upon discharge, Ben Grisafi married and became a jeweler, finding work at New York's Diamond Center, but continued playing gigs weekends on the then very lean music scene. With other jeweler musicians, Ben helped form a band, naming it the Gem Tones, playing steady weekends at places like the Picture Lounge in Huntington, on Long Island.

"One summer I sat in a band in the Catskills, headed by drummer, and later record promoter and director Pete Bennett. I was excited about my first professional arrangements, "Ferryboat Cha Cha" and "Woodpecker Cha Cha," which were recorded on the Cupid

Ben Grisafi with Jerry Vale at Carnegie Hall *(Yvette Grisafi Collection)*

label. I also performed in rock and roll shows with stars like Bobby Rydell, Fats Domino, and the Supremes. I resisted leaving the jewelry business to accept an invitation to join Bob Hope's tours with Pete, but continued playing weekend gigs."

Ben's musical direction was starving his needs, as the bands and combos of the day were not suited to his playing style. Then, in 1993, Ben met an important person that changed his direction; "Bob Rosen became the one major force in my life. A record producer, Bob has engaged important jazz players like (pianists) Billy Taylor and Marty Napoleon. His vast recording experience guided me through the myriad levels of recording, studio mixing, evaluating, and editing. He spent many hours teaching me and has become a dear friend and confidant. Without Bob Rosen, there would be no Ben Grisafi band, recordings, or arrangements for you to hear."

In 1993, Ben organized a 40th reunion with the original Dixie Division dance band of his early fifties Army days. He surprised them with an eighteen piece impromptu band, arranging a dozen songs including "Dixie" and "Back Home in Indiana," where the group was last stationed before disbanding. Members arrived from everywhere, urging and encouraging Ben to continue with the band after the party had ended.

"I began running dances, which were musically successful, but not financially. Slowly, bookings grew and I continued writing arrangements at a rapid pace. I did not want to copy other's arrangements. In 1995 my first CD *Talk of the Town* was released, followed by *But Beautiful*, with my wife Yvette gracing the cover and the terrific Denise Richards performing the vocals on both, with all original arrangements." The band had backed vocalist Roberto Tirado, on his CD entitled *Prisoner of Love*. Roberto is a well-known New York area television personality and a very fine singer in the style of Sergio Franchi. Radio station WLIM's Jack Ellsworth engaged Ben Grisafi's Alumni Big Band for Jack's 50th Anniversary as a disc jockey and 75th birthday. Jack has always been impressed with Ben's band, citing his work over the air and in his weekly newspaper column. With 40 new charts completed, Ben Grisafi is now planning his newest CD album, which may become a double-album.

"When most men my age have retired to warm weather, I choose to run a band, which, of course, includes writing, planning, recording, booking, and even baking cakes for the guys to enjoy with coffee at rehearsal. I sometimes wonder if they come to play or just to eat," he jokes, "It's monumental work and I am enjoying every minute."

Over the last fifteen years Ben and Yvette have migrated to their favorite vacation place, Aruba, in the Caribbean, where he finds rest, relaxation, and musical inspiration. The island's aura has inspired him to dedicate several arrangements to Aruba. Wisely, Ben brings along his sax and makes appearances at local concerts.

"Aruba has a certain raw beauty. The cactus, the water...all of it provides inspiration," Ben swears. "It is an emotional experience for me, an experience that relaxes my mind and allows me to create my best work."

Yvette Grisafi clearly supports her enthusiastic husband, even allowing the band to rehearse in their home, permitting permanent clearance of her living room furniture to create room for all those musicians and their instruments. Apparently, the room's high ceiling is acoustically beneficial to the Grisafi Alumni Big Band sounds. It takes all those great players' combined intonations to fill that room with all that beautiful music. I wonder what the neighbors are thinking?

Ben Grisafi and his illustrious alumni musicians already have bookings into the new Millennium, especially one during this coming summer at nearby Eisenhower Park. That's when Ben and Yvette bring along their twelve grandchildren, two of whom are studying music. Young Elizabeth Grisafi, who is six, takes piano lessons in her Peterborough, New Hampshire home, and twelve-year old grandson Johnny, who plays sax on Staten Island, can't wait until he can one day sit in the band's sax section.

Who said the Big Bands are gone?

Keep tuned!

Ben Grisafi on the beach in Aruba, 1997. *(Yvette Grisafi Collection)*

125

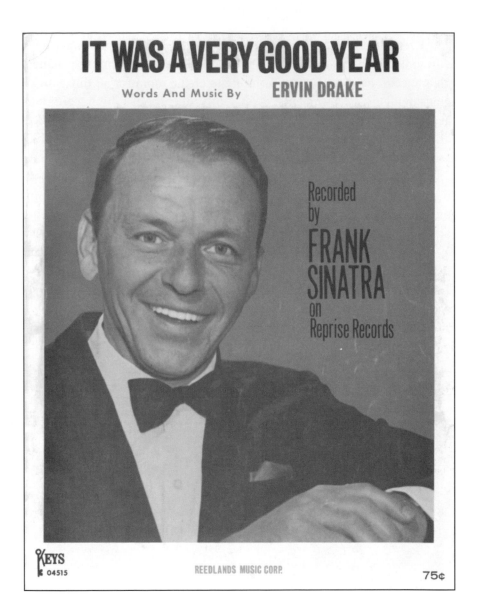

PART THREE

Three Unsung Songwriters of Tin Pan Alley

I Like New York In June,
How About You?
I Like a Gershwin tune
How about you?

Once during an interview, composer Harold Arlen said, "A good lyric is the composer's best friend." According to Arlen, a close bond between composer and lyricist is essential to the success of a song. Normally, a song is created when the usual thirty-two bar melody is written, and lyrics (words) are added and then arranged for interpretation by a musician, a group of musicians (band or orchestra), or a vocalist or group of vocalists. To become a *song*, a composition *must* include words. Reversing that role, a song may be defined as poetry set to music. A question may be: What came first, the chicken or the egg? The lyric or the melody? To which George Gershwin once glibly replied, it's "…the contract."

A notable composer is distinctive in melodic line and construction. A distinguished lyricist is able to formulate words for already written music which is extremely difficult to accomplish by any stretch of the imagination. Is it easier to write music to words, or words to music?

During the course of my career, I've known three songwriters. When I helped manage the NBC radio and television Ticket Division in New York back in the 1950's, I befriended a songwriter named J. Fred Coots who had written the legendary, perennial song "Santa Claus is Coming to Town" and another standard "For All We Know." I exchanged available complimentary broadcast tickets, which he distributed among his friends for personal prestige, in exchange for personally inscribed song sheets. We always wound up talking about music and

127

how his life consisted of an unending effort to "plug" his songs in order to maintain them in public use in order to earn royalties.

A songwriter named Joe Howard, who also wrote tunes for entertainer Beatrice Kay (mostly about the Gay Nineties), would keep me company on some days. He was down and out, and aging, so what available broadcast tickets I could spare he would give to friends in an effort to restore his importance in a world that seemed to have forgotten him. (Late in 1952, comedian Milton Berle, known then as Mr. Television, honored Joe Howard on his "Texaco Star Theater" television show).

During the same period I spent many a lunch hour with a young piano-player who fronted an instrumental trio who performed gigs at local New York Hotels, as well as on Steve Allen's daytime, pre-"Tonight Show" television program, "Date in Manhattan." His now familiar name is Cy Coleman. In one of the unused third floor radio studios, I would sit alongside Cy on his piano bench while he practiced his craft. I would woefully sing along. Stan Kenton sideman Eddie Safranski played bass. We all became lunch-time buddies. I often attended those gigs at the Park Lane Hotel on weekend evenings with my friends. Cy was experimenting writing songs even then. "Witchcraft" remains one of his best.

In my last three books, *The Best Damn Trumpet Player*, *The Song Stars*, and *The Music Men*, I wrote about many of the musicians, vocalists, and arrangers of the Big Band Era and beyond. None of these books could have been written unless somebody first wrote the songs these musicians played, the vocalists sang, and the arrangers orchestrated.

Some of the subjects of those three books also composed music or wrote lyrics at one point or another in their career : Mel Torme'("The Christmas Song"), Peggy Lee ("Mañana"), Paul Weston ("I Should Care"), Ella Fitzgerald ("A Tisket, A Tasket"), Lee Hale ("The Ladies Who Sang with the Bands"), Frankie Laine ("We'll Be Together Again"), Al Jolson ("My Mammy"), Bing Crosby ("Where The Blue of the Night"), Duke Ellington ("Sophisticated Lady"), Larry Elgart (The theme of "American Bandstand," "Bandstand Boogie"), and others, although they are not generally known as song writers.

Today, Tin Pan Alley is essentially The Brill Building and immediate vicinity in New York City, the singular place where music publishing offices are located and where songwriters and song pluggers congregate. The fourteen story Brill is located on the Northwest corner of Forty-ninth street and Broadway, once having housed the Zanzibar nightclub.

The original Tin Pan Alley first centered around West 28th Street in New York City at the turn-of-the century and up to World War I, where many of the music hall singers and vaudevillian actors once lived. There many song publishing offices, like the old Jerome Remick Company, employed piano players to demonstrate their newly published songs for vaudeville performers who may have been searching for new musical material and for the general public at large.

The location later moved uptown to Forty-Sixth Street, between Broadway and Sixth Avenue, and, when sound of radio dominated the music business, Tin Pan Alley re-located into lush office suites beneath the shadow of NBC's Rockefeller Center, extending up to Fifty-second Street where CBS radio was located.

The designation *Tin Pan Alley*, actually a sobriquet for the sheet-music publishing industry, was adopted from the tinkling, sometimes out-of-tune pianos being intensely exercised, sounding to a passerby like tin pans being drummed upon as groups of songwriters simultaneously demonstrated their craft at the offices of various publishers through sometimes open windows. Tin Pan Alley was the place where sheet music was written, demonstrated, packaged, and vigorously peddled. Remember, with no radio or television, sheet music had to thrive and survive on the strength of song sheet demonstrators playing a new tune in those store-front offices of publishers who also relied upon the illustrated sheet music covers that artfully portrayed the allegory of a tune, sometimes featuring photos of a popular musician or vocalist who had successfully performed it on stage or on recordings. To create a hit song, the axiom of the time was, "You gotta say *I love you* in thirty-two bars," and "keep the title short and memorable."

The participants called themselves *Alleymen*. The Alleymen, faced with radio companies refusal to pay songwriters for airing songs, and restaurants blatantly playing songs without compensating their authors, organized ASCAP, the American Society of Composers, Authors and Publishers, which still solidly and securely represents the song writing community in all its aspects.

Some composers collaborated with a single lyricist or maybe just a few, and some with many. Irving Berlin and Cole Porter were noted to write both the music and lyrics to almost all their compositions. Richard Rodgers collaborated first with Lorenz (Larry) Hart and later with Oscar Hammerstein II. Composer Harry Warren, noted mostly for songs composed for Hollywood musicals, collaborated with lyricists Al Dubin, Mack Gordon, Ralph Blane, Arthur Freed, Ira Gershwin, Leo Robin, Billy Rose, and others. Like Warren, Harold Arlen acquired many additional lyricists when he first split with Tin Pan Alley and Broadway and went to California to work for the movies. After all, being work for hire, composers were not always able to select their lyricists. Lyricist Ted Koehler was Harold Arlen's early, principal collaborator especially during their two shows-a-year job at Harlem, New York's famous Cotton Club. Along the way Arlen linked up with E.Y. "Yip" Harburg (who wrote the lyrics for Arlen's *Wizard of Oz* music), Johnny Mercer, Leo Robin, Ralph Blane, Dorothy Fields, Ira Gershwin, and even author Truman Capote, back on Broadway for their show *House of Flowers.*

Although most of us are more familiar with the names of Irving Berlin, Richard Rodgers, Cole Porter, or George Gershwin, it must be realized that the names of Harold Arlen and some others surely belong among this unique group of musical geniuses. No one can say why the name of Harold Arlen, who wrote the great standards "Come Rain or Come Shine," "Over the Rainbow," "That Old Black Magic," "Stormy Weather," and my favorite, "My Shining Hour," among many others, seems to be relatively unknown compared to the other greats. It may be argued that Arlen had perhaps too many collaborators, thus his name was somewhat diluted. This was due partially to the lyricist selection process when he composed for the Hollywood studios, known then as the "composer's haven."

Nevertheless, this chapter will portray, however short and imperfect, the careers of three great, not-so-great composers and lyricists who, with their well-turned torrents of verse and eight bar melodic phrases, helped create the wonderful music of our lifetime that Tony Bennett once described to me as "America's classical music!"

Collectively, they have written and composed : "It Was a Very Good Year," "What a Wonderful World," "Come to the Mardi Gras," "I Believe," "Good Morning Heartache," "Linda," "Tenderly," "Perdido," "Lullaby of Birdland," "Mr. Wonderful," "Rumors Are Flying," "All or Nothing at All," "Too Close for Comfort," and "Wheel of Fortune." Now, you have to admit that's a true treasure-trove of musical literature.

Ervin Drake, Jack Lawrence, and George David Weiss are the three sensitive poets who wrote those beautiful songs. Most of these tune-smiths names are probably unfamiliar to you. All three are members of The New York Sheet Music Society. I'm a rookie, supporting member.

Society members, dedicated to the preservation of classic popular music, meet in New York City once a month. Sam Teicher is the current president; Anthony Di Florio III is secretary and newsletter editor; song star and a subject of my 1997 book *The Song Stars*, Dolly Dawn is meeting hostess; Dan Singer of BMI (Broadcast Music Inc.) is membership director; former WNEW, New York radio disc jockey (current-ly on WVNJ, New Jersey), and songwriter/vocalist ("Behind the Green Door") Jim Lowe, is on the program committee; Steve Allen, another songwriter in his own right, and song star Margaret Whiting are also members, as am I.

The newsletter reviews appropriate books and CDs, and announces the performance whereabouts of members and associates, punctuating the songs they perform and the songwriters who authored them. Members conduct fund-raising luncheons, gather together to share memories, and produce programs for one-another to participate in and enjoy, at the same time honoring their peers and past colleagues. They are a warm, happy, and dedicated bunch.

Let me introduce you to:

ERVIN DRAKE

Yesterday, I was telling Ervin Drake that Frankie Laine recently proclaimed his best and most favorite recording as Ervin's own "I Believe," a song written in 1948 for the TV musical series "USO Canteen," starring vocalist Jane Froman. It was introduced on

Thanksgiving Day 1952, and sung one month later on her nationally broadcast Christmas Show. However, Frankie, who *owns* the definitive version, recorded it in 1953, and it carried on "The Hit Parade" for 23 weeks.

"Shortly after writing it I showed it to Mitch Miller when he was in charge at Columbia, and Mitch said,'This is for Frankie Laine!' He just knew."

Songwriter Ervin Drake. He believes. *(Richard Grudens Collection)*

Ervin Drake and I were talking songs and singers at his Great Neck, New York home on a sultry August afternoon in 1998. Ervin is a trim, robust, soon to be octogenarian, who has a bell-clear voice like that of a radio announcer and an enthusiasm for music, his own songs included, which, he sometime likes to sing himself. He is a good singer.

In early '98, a CD by teen-age country song star LeAnn Rimes, featuring his song "I Believe," remained number-one on the *Billboard* charts for over 10 weeks. And a few months later, Barbra Streisand recorded an album featuring that inspirational composition, selling over three million copies. The song's universal appeal has made it a worldwide hit.

FRANKIE LAINE

"I first heard 'I Believe' when Mitch Miller came out to see me in California. He sang four bars of Ervin Drake's song for me(and he is a terrible singer), but even his voice made sense of it. The lyrics were a simple but moving declaration of faith, and seldom had words touched me so deeply. It was almost more of a prayer than a song. In my life I've often turned to Him for comfort and guidance. He's always come through, so the song didn't only speak to me, it spoke for me."

I Believe for every drop of rain that falls,
A flower grows,
I Believe that somewhere in the darkest night,
A candle glows.
I Believe for everyone who goes astray,
Someone will come to show the way.
I Believe, I Believe
I Believe above the storm the smallest prayer,
Will still be heard,
I Believe that someone in the great somewhere, hears every word.
Every time I hear a newborn baby cry,
Or touch a leaf,
Or see the sky,
Then I know why,
I Believe!

Funny, Ervin Drake originally studied drawing, painting, and lithography at the College of The City of New York, but music and lyrics captivated his interest.

"But, Richard, while at school, I contributed songs and some sketches to school productions, and even sold a couple of songs to a publisher. I also helped my dad in the wholesale furniture business. But, I used to cheat on my dad by sort of moonlighting in a place we call Tin Pan Alley, where I tried to sell my songs. It was the place where song publishers convened their business. All the songwriters gathered there."

A songwriter-lyricist, Ervin Drake is also a prolific TV producer, writer, and composer. From 1948 to 1962 he was involved with some 700 telecasts, most of them weekly programs, involving, among others, Steve and Eydie, Yves Montand, Gene Kelly, Carol Haney, Jayne Mansfield, and Johnny Carson.

Ervin Drake finally sold his first tune "I Like It" for three-hundred dollars in 1941. "An impressive amount for the times," he recalled. His song "Good Morning Heartache," with music by Irene Higginbotham and Dan Fisher, was originally turned down by music publishers as being *non-commercial*, until recordings by Billie Holiday, Joe Williams, Ella Fitzgerald, and Tony Bennett — along with winning an ASCAP (American Society of Composers, Authors, and Publishers) Award — proved otherwise.

Ervin's first success was called *"Tico-Tico,"* earned by composing words for a popular Brazilian melody by Zeqfuinha Abreu that was featured in the Walt Disney film *Saludos Amigos* in 1942. A year later my friend Patty Andrews sang it with her sisters, Maxine and Laverne, and Xavier Cugat's Orchestra performed it in the film *Bathing Beauty*. Ervin wrote words and music to another hit "Rickety Rickshaw Man," recorded by Eddie Howard in 1945. It became a million-seller.

Ervin's contribution of lyrics to "Perdido," an instrumental piece composed by valve trombonist Juan Tizol, a member of the great 1944 Duke Ellington Band, converted that song into a solid classic. "I was honored to be linked with Tizol and consider him one of my best collaborators." he said.

JUAN TIZOL

"We were traveling," Tizol recalled in 1978 for Time-Life Records, "and I was sitting in a railroad coach tapping the window and the melody came to me. I thought that's pretty good and I better write it down before I forget it. I gave it to the Duke that evening and he liked it."

"I was in Washington with the band," Ervin continued, "and one night Juan was playing an interesting tune and I asked him — 'What is that?' and he said, 'Perdido.' I said, 'You think it needs words?' and he

134

said, 'If you come up with the right one's—sure!' So I wrote the words to his nifty tune."

I reminded Ervin of June Christy's solid version of that song recorded a little later with Stan Kenton's band, as the best version I have heard. "Yes, but don't forget Cleo Laine, who also did it beautifully — and Sarah Vaughan…and how about Ella's," he recalled. "They are all good!"

Along the way, Ervin composed: "Castle Rock" (Frank Sinatra swings gracefully with it!); both words and music for "It Was a Very Good Year," composed for the use of the Kingston Trio during the 1950s, and, of course, one of Frank Sinatra's most important signature recordings after he discovered the song in 1965 when he heard the Kingston Trio performing it on radio while driving in his car one evening, and included it on his album "September of My Years;" "Across the Wide Missouri" (for Hollywood's film of the same name), "A Room Without Windows" from *What Makes Sammy Run*, (Steve Lawrence excels on this one), and one of my personal favorites "Come To the Mardi Gras" — recorded by Freddy Martin's Orchestra.

"I became very excited when I first heard Frank Sinatra's recording of "It Was a Very Good Year." I was in London where publisher David Platz first told me about it. He played it for me over the phone. I listened and then asked to hear it again. I loved it. When I got back home, the first thing I did was to buy the LP and played it thirty times the first day. I was ecstatic. To this day I get a real charge whenever that recording is played.

"Frank Sinatra and I became friends because of that song, "Ervin said, "It brought him a Grammy. Over the years he would call me at least twice a year -'Hi! Ervin,' He would say. 'How are you, Ervin?' and, 'do you need anything?' Frank was always caring and concerned about his friends and people who have helped him."

Ervin's tune "The Father of Girls" has also brought him acclaim, having been recorded by Paul Anka, Pat Boone, Jerry Vale, Perry Como, and Mike Douglas — all of them fathers of girls.

We talked about songwriters being present at a great recording of their song. "You're rarely there at recordings, Richard. I could tell you about the few times in my life when I have actually been there."

1964 Playbill cover. *(L-R)* Robert Alda, Steve Lawrence, Sally Ann Howes. *(Courtesy Playbill)*

One of those events was when Billie Holiday recorded his song "Good Morning Heartache" in New York's Decca Recording Studio: "I was in the room. I didn't even have the guts to say 'How do you do?' or even utter my name. I was too intimidated — being just twenty-six and very scared and excited," he recalled. "I remember all the details about the date and what Billie did right after first singing it — where she demanded a drink — from a bottle wrapped in a paper bag — and got it — then continued to drink from it throughout the session, much to the dismay of arranger Sy Oliver, who was also conducting."

Like many other composers, Ervin has worked the Great White Way. "I composed both words and music for Budd Shulberg's play *What Makes Sammy Run?* which starred a young Steve Lawrence, as well as Sally Ann Howes and Robert Alda— Alan's dad. It had the longest run in the history of the Adelphi-54th Street theater."

STEVE LAWRENCE:

"I spent two years of my life in that show. I auditioned for the part three times, until they finally gave it to me—in Philly. Abe Burrows directed, Ervin Drake did the words and music, and Bob Alda and Barry Newman were also in it. It won the Drama Critics Award in New York."

Ervin also composed the music, lyrics, and wrote the book for the George Bernard Shaw musical *Caesar and Cleopatra*, that co-starred Richard Kiley and Leslie Uggams. His song "Perdido" — composed of his words and Juan Tizol's music — became part of the music in the 1981 Broadway production "Sophisticated Lady," a show about Duke Ellington's famous orchestra.

"You know, Richard, I actually went back to school after all those years, to study composition at Julliard in 1963." From 1965 to '68, Ervin extended his studies, perfecting orchestration and piano techniques.

Ervin Drake's works are showcased lately on the Hollywood big screen. Woody Allen's *Radio Days* featured *"Tico Tico,"* Spike Lee's *Jungle Fever* featured "It Was a Very Good Year;" and *Lady Sings the*

Blues had Diana Ross, portraying Billie Holiday, singing his bluesy "Good Morning Heartache."

Ervin Drake sits comfortably within the distinguished circle of songwriters:

"Harold Arlen and I used to dine together at Lindy's Restaurant in New York, usually at a table that was reserved for press agents, songwriters, TV producers, and so forth. It was quite a table. Everybody came in. I remember when the show *Gypsy* opened; it was such a smash hit. One night, when we were talking about it, in walks Jule Styne, its composer. He had been split up with his songwriting collaborator Sammy Cahn for quite a few years. When he walked in, we all stood up as one and applauded his entrance. So he came over to the table and said, 'You know, every time a show of mine opens up on Broadway, Sammy Cahn builds another wing to his house in Beverly Hills.'"

Ervin Drake, Richard Grudens, and Dr. Stanley Cohen, Five Towns Music College, 1999. *(Photo Robert DeBetta)*

Like many noted artists in entertainment, Ervin has received his share of accolades. "Good Morning Heartache" won the ASCAP Award. "I Believe" has won The Christopher Award, and there is the Grammy nomination for the score of *What Makes Sammy Run*, and an Honorary Doctorate in Music from the prestigious Five Towns Music College in Dix Hills, New York, where my friend Dr. Stanley Cohen is president.

On November 9, 1998 Ervin Drake was honored at Five Towns Music College in a retrospective of his works. As honored guests, bandleader Ben Grisafi and I happily witnessed John Gabriel's performance of "Good Morning Heartache," "It Was a Very Good Year," "A Room Without Windows," and "Father of Girls." John is a film and television actor, as well as a Broadway performer, appearing in productions of *Brigadoon* and *On a Clear Day You Can See Forever* "But, Richard, singing is my very first love," he said to Ben and me that night.

In a surprisingly strong and rich voice, Ervin vocalized his songs "The Rickety Richshaw Man," "Al Di La" (a song actually done just a little bit better by Jerry Vale), and "Come To The Mardi Gras." An absolutely wonderful four-man *a cappella* group called the Future Four performed the best version of "I Believe" that I have ever heard, besides Frankie Laine's. The college's Festival Chorus vocal group performed a

Five Towns College's A Cappella quartet Future Four sings Ervin Drake's "I Believe"
(Photo Robert DeBetta)

thrilling version of "Across the Wide Missouri" and closed with a ful-filling reprise of "I Believe."

It was an evening to be remembered. College President Dr. Stanley Cohen has skillfully directed the course of this young music school into a living, working, thriving endeavor consistently promoting the works of the Big Bands, the great composers and lyricists, the important arrangers and conductors, and the vocalists and individual musicians who have proliferated throughout popular music over the last sixty years.

Later that month, Ervin participated in Hofstra University's Frank Sinatra seminar, The Man and His Music. And, in London, on October 4th at the historic Drury Lane Theatre, Ervin Drake proudly performed his song "It Was a Very Good Year" in a stirring Frank Sinatra tribute to benefit the Princess Diana Charities.

It was his shining hour.

JACK LAWRENCE

Today I talked with the man who wrote the lyrics to the song "All or Nothing At All," Frank Sinatra's first solo hit recording; Rosemary Clooney's blockbuster hit "Tenderly"; Don Cornell's come back success "Hold My Hand"; words and music to Buddy Clark's charming performance of "Linda"; Harry James' signature solo, "Sleepy Lagoon";Dinah Shore's "Yes, My Darling Daughter"; and both words and music to the Ink Spots' famous theme "If I Didn't Care." What a pleasant conversation it was:

"I really owe Rosemary," Jack Lawrence was explaining to me at his West Redding, Connecticut home. "' Tenderly' was an important song for Rosey, and her success with it became important to me."

Rosemary Clooney was honored in the fall of 1998 by the Society of Singers in L.A., and Jack was there to honor her." "I also took a full-page ad in the journal to let her know just how I feel," Jack said. My friend Lee Hale, author of the book *Backstage with the Dean Martin Show*, who produced the video of the party, sent me a copy of the Clooney party. Rosemary sang Jack's song "Tenderly."

Jack was also very friendly with bandleader Harry James back in the forties when Frank Sinatra was James' vocalist. "I showed him *'All Or Nothing At All.'* They both loved the song; so they recorded it." Jack said, "The original recording label read *All Or Nothing At All, HARRY JAMES AND HIS ORCHESTRA* in large print—then in very small letters underneath — *Vocal by Frank Sinatra*. The record bombed. When Frank later auditioned for Tommy Dorsey, he sang 'All Or Nothing At All,' and that earned him the job with Dorsey. After leaving Tommy, going out on his own, and starring at the Paramount as a single, the musicians went on strike. Columbia couldn't take advantage of this great prize they had in Sinatra, trying to make *a cappella* records with

Jack Lawrence writes so "Tenderly." *(Richard Grudens Collection)*

singing groups. But it didn't work. Lou Levy, who had published 'All Or Nothing At All,' reminded Columbia to pull the earlier recording of the song and re-release it with Frank Sinatra's name on top. Now, with Frank hot, it will probably do well. It was Frank's first record success on his own."

Jack is still a vital, busy man in his mid-eighties who never retired and doesn't intend to: "I work when it strikes me and I rest otherwise. Many of my friends are gone, but I've been fortunate, being in good health, I'm still around to put some words on paper and hope they turn out pretty good."

Jack Lawrence started picking out tunes back in the East New York section of Brooklyn, New York, when he was just a lad of twelve.

"My first big hit was 'Play Fiddle, Play' which was featured in a 1933 movie they still show on television once-in-a-while *Dinner At Eight*, with John Barrymore, Marie Dressler, and Wallace Beery."

It was quite a thrill for the twenty-year-old songwriter: "Richard, that song opened the doors for me in the music business. I became very friendly with Jack Kapp of Decca Records, and Decca had what they called an R & B Label that featured all the black bands of the time, so

I got to know Andy Kirk and his Clouds of Joy, and the Mills Brothers — and Ella." This unique access enabled Jack to bring his songs up to Decca and they would record them even before they were formally published.

"I wrote the melody 'What's Your Story, Morning Glory?' for Mary Lou Williams," he sings it out loud for me, "and others for Andy Kirk, too." Jack has written both words and music for some songs, having collaborated on others with composers Burton Lane, Hoagy Carmichael, and Victor Young, although he prefers writing his own complete songs.

Jack loves to tell the story about the origin of his legendary song "Linda":

"I wrote that song for a three-year-old little girl named Linda Eastman. Her father, Lee Eastman, was an attorney for some big bandleaders and some writers, like me. I was visiting Lee at his Scarsdale (New York) home. His wife Louise, and another daughter Laura both had songs after their name, as did their son Johnny, but, Linda did not. So he asked me to write a song for Linda. So I did. Linda was not a popular name at the time, so I found it hard to get it published. Of course, it was later recorded by Buddy Clark and it became a number one hit."

There is an interesting epilogue to this story. Linda turns out to be Linda McCartney. When Linda suddenly passed away in 1998, Jack was invited to New York's Riverside Church by her husband, ex-Beatle Paul McCartney:

"It was a very touching ceremony, and the last speaker was Paul. He said, 'When Linda was forty-five, I wanted to surprise her, so I got together a big band, and made a recording of me singing Jack Lawrence's song "Linda." Oh, she loved it,' he went on, 'and I think we end on a high note tonight, so I'm going to play that recording.'

"And when he was finished, he started walking up the aisle, and when he saw me, he stopped for a moment to hug me, saying 'Thanks, Jack.'"

To Jack's overflowing cornucopia, you can add "Poor People of Paris," "No One But You," "Beyond The Sea," "Sunrise Serenade," and "With the Wind and the Rain in My Hair" among others. How happy has he made you over the years with his songs?

And now,
GEORGE DAVID WEISS

Another one of our remarkable songwriters is Califon, New Jersey resident George David Weiss. Look over this treasury of pure evergreens: The Ames Brothers' "Can Anyone Explain," Patti Page successes "Confess" and "Cross Over the Bridge," Gordon Jenkins' "I Don't See Me In Your Eyes Anymore," Sammy Davis' hits "Mr. Wonderful" and "Too Close for Comfort," The Andrews Sisters popular recording of "Rumors Are Flying," and that special song by Louis Armstrong "What A Wonderful World."

"I wrote that song especially for Louis at his personal request," said this former arranger for both Stan Kenton and Vincent Lopez, whose extensive musical education at the Julliard Conservatory of Music in New York has sure paid him off handsomely.

Back in high school — 1948 — I remember Frank Sinatra's recording of Weiss' "Oh! What It Seemed To Be" being played at the weekly dance in the gym, and the dancers floating to Frank's version of that seemingly perfect love song — so poignant — in the right place for young romantics. Frank made perfect use of his phrasing techniques on this beautiful song.

My first book, *The Best Damn Trumpet Player*, described Weiss' song "Rumors Are Flying" in a chapter about the Andrews Sisters: "When they recorded my favorite "Rumors Are Flying," and Patty did that doubling-up-jive patter with such melodic perfection, *Whatta-ya-do-do-do that keeps 'em buzzing...* I couldn't wait until the record was over so I could lift the recording arm and play it again and again, waiting for those passages to enter my brain once more. The Andrews Sisters really had me hooked."

And, how about Kay Starr's great version of Weiss' marvelous tune "Wheel of Fortune," a song that Kay told me she never gets tired of singing:

"Richard, when I think I'm wearied of singing it, and I wonder Oh, maybe people are also tired of it. But what happens is, every time I start to sing it, somebody reaches over and touches somebody next to them, or they just smile, and you can just feel the memories starting, you know, and you can't deny that's what it's all about."

"Wheel of Fortune" sold over five million copies of Weiss' song worldwide.

George David Weiss' compositions have helped make stars of people like Frank Sinatra, Sammy Davis Jr, Kay Starr, and The Andrews Sisters. "Yes, that's true," he said, "but it's funny — no one has ever heard of me," as we both laughed. When he composed "What a Wonderful World" for Louis Armstrong at the request of Teresa Brewer's record producer husband, Bob Thiele, the record bombed, as they say. It took a revival of Louis' recording featured in the film *Good Morning, Vietnam* with Robin Williams to at last turn that song into a million-selling hit.

Kay Starr sings "Wheel of Fortune." 1985 *(Courtesy Camille Smith)*

George David Weiss cooperated closely with Jack Rael in producing two important first songs for Patti Page — "Confess" and "Cross Over the Bridge," which were originally two-part songs. Jack Rael was Patti's manager for 50 years. When he first discovered her, searching for something special to showcase her talents, he was responsible for the "overdubbing" process first used on the song "Confess," which produced that famous echoing sound that sounded like a group singing different harmonic parts.

For the Broadway hit *Mr. Wonderful*, George Weiss and Larry Holofcener composed the lyrics to Jerry Bock's music. Sammy Davis Jr. became a star as a result of this show. Not bad, Mr. Weiss.

Well, that's the short story of three wonderful poets of Tin Pan Alley: Ervin Drake, Jack Lawrence, and George David Weiss. Can you count how many hours you may have spent enjoying, maybe singing along with, or even dancing to their splendid lush, lyrical words and music?

CARMEL QUINN

A FAIRYTALE STORY

This is a pleasant story about a very lovable and revered Irish singer named Carmel Quinn. Carmel is a premier Irish singer in a class with Kate Smith, Frank Parker, and actress Maureen O'Hara. Carmel enjoyed a very long season singing with Arthur Godfrey on his radio and television shows during the mid-'50s. Her story is classic, rising from total obscurity to total fame virtually overnight.

Carmel Quinn's singing career actually began in Ireland when she was a mere pretty wisp of a lass. I talked with Carmel from her cozy home in New Jersey. Even when speaking, she retains that clear, crisp, but sweet homespun voice. Surely, she is the quintessential Irish beauty in face, voice, and spirit.

"Growing up in Dublin, you know — everyone sang, especially in my house. My father sang and played the violin; my sister and I — my two brothers — people everywhere in Ireland sang. It was part of your life. People sang in the streets. The mailman would come to the door singing. Everyone sang!"

"So, what were they singing?" I asked.

"Anything! The chimney cleaner would come up the street singing. We were so used to it. We would say, 'that is a nice song.' I liked all sorts of songs. Irish songs and American songs, too. There was an American radio program sponsored by the Irish Sweepstakes. We all listened to it. Patti Page would sing (she sings) "How much is that doggy in the window?"

"Did you get to sing professionally?"

"Well, when I was in school, in college — in Ireland you go to college when you are fifteen. I was in a teacher's college, and I heard of a dance band that was looking for a singer. I went and auditioned — without music. I actually went to make an appointment for some other time.

"In Dublin, everyone sang," says Carmel Quinn. *(Richard Grudens Collection)*

But they said, 'Do you want to sing now?' And it was a lovely band. They played in a ballroom in Dublin. So I sang for them."

Carmel Quinn sang "Wheel of Fortune," and got the job.

The Wheel of Fortune
Goes Spinning Round
Will the Arrow Point My Way?
Will This Be The Day?

"Wheel of Fortune" gave Kay Starr her career and Carmel Quinn her start.

"I copied everyone, including Kay Starr."

Every singer copied singers before them. Jerry Vale copied Sinatra. Sinatra copied Bing Crosby. Bing Crosby started singing by emulating Al Jolson. That's exactly how it works. One singer influences another.

"So they took me on, even though I really didn't sound that good. With this band — Johnny Devlin and his Orchestra- it was called — I was to sing on Saturday nights. They were very good — very advanced."

This was in 1950 — the success cycle of vocalists Frankie Laine, Perry Como, Tony Bennett, Rosemary Clooney, Pat Boone, Patti Page, and Dean Martin, among others.

"Johnny was a Stan Kenton fan. Later, I married the man I worked for who owned the ballroom, Bill Fuller, and he brought the Kenton band over to Ireland. June Christy was the singer then. So we all got to meet them. I was very excited. It was such an advanced band, musically."

Carmel began singing around Dublin, and later married Bill Fuller, who wanted to go to America. Although very happy just where she was, she went along with him to America, anyway.

"I came to America with Bill, who was going to open ballrooms. And he did. He opened the City Center on West 55th Street in New York City for the Irish immigrants coming over. Pat Boone opened the first night. Then he opened one in Boston and one in Chicago and one in San Francisco."

The big bands were touring these ballrooms that Bill and Carmel Fuller were opening like McDonald Restaurants. But Carmel did not sing.

"No one was looking at me, you know, at all. But I didn't mind. I was happy and caught up in things. We had an apartment in Washington Heights and people would hear me singing in the next door apartment. They would say, 'Do something.' And I didn't think — I thought what went well in Ireland wouldn't be good enough here."

However, her friends convinced her to try to get a job singing. They went to CBS on 52nd Street to see what they could do about procuring a singing spot for her somewhere with someone. What do you do?

"I found out they would let you audition for *Arthur Godfrey's Talent Scouts* program, but that you had to wait six months for an audition. And then, if you win, there's another six months wait to get on the show."

Carmel was aghast at the six month wait rule, CBS claiming they were backed up with requests for auditions.

"Six months? We might be all dead in six months, I told the secretary. And she began to laugh and said, 'Hold on,' and went back to another room and came back again within a few minutes and said, 'They'd like to hear you now.'"

So, as luck would have it, an important door opened.

"Always pure luck again. No music — totally unprepared. The pianist was sitting there in a huff — she was waiting on the music — and there was no music and I was singing. I sang everything. I sang seven songs *a capella* (without musical accompaniment)."

The panel listening to Carmel singing came out — "and one man Jack Carney — he was Art Carney's brother — I didn't know that — I didn't know anyone, and he said 'We are going to put you on Monday night.'"

Now, there's your six month wait. The luck of the Irish prevailed for one of its daughters Carmel Quinn. That Monday night, on this big, big show, *Arthur Godfrey's Talent Scouts*, Carmel Quinn sang her heart out.

"Monday night came and they picked a song they liked, an Irish song, 'How Can You Buy Killarney.' They rushed in the musicians, the arranger — you know — they sat him down at the piano and got a key — no one knew the song. So this huge twenty-piece orchestra of Archie Bleyer played the introduction. And I couldn't believe it."

The young singer became very nervous. There was a rock and roll group appearing on the show who had a record high on the charts. Their manager apparently wanted them to have exposure. This intimidated Carmel even further. She recalls them saying, while looking out from the stage, "It's cold turkey out there." She had never heard that expression before and did not understand its impact.

"I thought, 'that's nice. They serve cold turkey out there after the show.' Anyway, I don't know how I won. Apparently, they did well. It was a machine, you know; I came on last, and he said, 'the winner is the young girl from Ireland,' and the place broke up."

She just stood there, and Godfrey said, "Looks like you're the winner."

"He said, 'Come on over here,' and I walked off instead. I was cryin'. I just was so touched by these people that I didn' t know. They all said to me backstage, 'Go on out, he wants you.' But, I didn't. I was so touched. I was still cryin'."

Carmel Quinn was just twenty years old. The next morning Carmel appeared on the daily morning radio and television simulcast show with Godfrey. "Oh, my God!" said I.

"Oh, my God, is right. And there were other prizes. And I was making five-hundred dollars a week. Oh, my God, again. And we would get an extra seven hundred and fifty for the Wednesday night show. That would be like making ten thousand now."

The young singer was simply flabbergasted. The otherwise elusive world of show business had opened up for her in a matter of days. From obscurity to fame in hours. *Instant success*, as it's sometimes labeled. Suddenly, Carmel Quinn's singing became in demand. On weekends for guest shots on other shows, or on specials or variety shows on television and radio, Carmel Quinn had arrived. There were jammed concerts at venues like Carnegie Hall. During that period in television annals, being associated with Arthur Godfrey meant an extension of power for those aboard his ascending star.

The musicians performing on Godfrey's radio show were guitarist Remo Palmieri; the great clarinetist, and my friend, Johnny Mince, and premier trombonist Tyree Glenn, great players all. Carmel Quinn had the good fortune to sing to these great players, hand chosen by Godfrey himself for his *Arthur Godfrey Time* daily show.

Godfrey allowed Carmel to select the song she would sing on each show. She would go over each tune with a pianist and arranger before performing. They generally liked her choices. She remained with Godfrey for six happy years. It ended with Godfrey's illness. They became and remained very good friends for the rest of Godfrey's life.

Being so well-known by this time, life after Godfrey meant recording and regular guest appearances on shows like Jack Paar's, and also appearing in light comedic roles recounting her homespun, Irish-laced stories.

"I was working just about everywhere; the Copa (Copacabana nightclub in New York); the Waldorf (Waldorf Astoria Hotel); and in all the good clubs that unfortunately exist no more. During this period I made about eight albums that still sell pretty well, thank God."

Carmel performs an annual concert in Carnegie Hall and has for 25 years. And, I'm sure you have caught her on *The Today Show*, *The Tonight Show*, *Regis and Kathie Lee* show, now and then over the years, singing her songs and telling wonderful anecdotes of her early life in Dublin.

Along the way Carmel had four children, one of whom she lost; Michael was her eldest son. Today there is Jane, Terry, and Sean. Jane (Fuller), after her mother, is a singer who has played many clubs in New York, like the Eighty-Eights. A pretty and rather witty gal, she is well liked and well received on the cabaret circuit.

"Jane likes the old songs, Richard, like Irving Berlin's 'What'll I Do,' (Carmel sings the first four bars), and, of course, we all go to see and support her. She does very little in the pop rock stuff. I'd say, 'Jane, you were marvelous tonight,' and she says, 'Mom, let me tell you something. I know the show went well, and I'm glad. But when you all go home, and I pay the sound man, my pianist, the light man, my bass player, I don't have one penny left.'"

Sometimes Jane would have to visit the ATM machine to pay up everything. "I can't live like this," she explained to her mom.

"The cabaret business is difficult at best as a business," Carmel went on, "I used to be booked by the Copa for a fee. At any of the old venues, you were paid and you had a suite upstairs. Now, you get the room, but you have to pay all those people, and you have to gather the crowd. You see, you get the 'cover' and if it's a tiny room, then what?" Choosing otherwise, Jane Fuller went back to law school and passed the bar. She is now an attorney, but will perhaps take up her heart's desire, singing, sometime in the future. It's her first love, but at least she is now independent.

Carmel Quinn still works, singing and recounting her very funny and endearing stories, being booked regularly all over the map, and she intends to continue her work, "Some people say if you're over thirty-five you should shoot yourself, but I've come up with an idea or two which I am working on and will put to work."

On a recent Sony CD album of Irish songs titled *They Call It Ireland* she sings the traditional ballad "Galway Bay" so beautifully. And, best of all, is her rendition of "Isle of Innisfree," a Dublin police-man's song (Dick Farrelly) that was used as the theme music for the classic John Wayne and Maureen O'Hara film *The Quiet Man*, the quintessential Irish-American film.

No wonder Arthur Godfrey wasted no time in hiring her on the spot for his program back in 1955. The luck of the Irish prevails.

"How High the Moon?" Les Paul and Mary Ford in 1952. *(Courtesy Downbeat Magazine)*

LES PAUL

The Wizard of Waukesha

During the 1950s, the multiple voice of Mary Ford accompanied by her husband, pioneer guitarist Les Paul, introduced a new method of recording called multi-tracking, employing multiple vocal lines. With multi-track hits "How High the Moon," "Vaya Con Dios," "The World Is Waiting for the Sunrise," "Bye Bye Blues," and "Mockin' Bird Hill," the talented and inventive couple rode, in a phrase, to the top of the charts. And, even earlier, Waukesha (Wah-keesh-aw), Wisconsin's Les Paul had introduced his novel idea with a series of multi-track guitar instrumentals, "Lover," "Nola," and "Brazil," while Jack Rael's protégé, popular singer Patti Page, produced a number one hit with "Tennessee Waltz," followed by other hits, employing the same technique, but only after consulting with Les Paul himself about how to do it.

Legendary, fascinating and engaging guitarist Les Paul and I sat down in his cozy mountainside, Mahwah, New Jersey home of 45 years, and talked about his phenomenal inventions and the rest of his career, and about his wife Colleen Summers, who changed her name to Mary Ford, and of mutual friends and acquaintances: arranger and bandleader Billy May, Frankie Laine, Mitch Miller, Artie Shaw, Patti Page, Jo Stafford, arranger Frank De Vol, Connie Haines, and vibraphonist Red Norvo. He had been long out of touch and was glad to be updated on the health and activities of some of his old -time friends and collaborators.

Les Paul's career as a guitarist and inventor began a long time ago in the age of bath tub gin and vaudeville shows. While still a teenager Les was already broadcasting on the radio playing his Sears & Roebuck mail-order guitar and Hohner harmonica; he formed the Les Paul Trio by the time he was twenty-one.

"Eddie Lang (jazz's first guitar virtuoso) was my idol and mentor, and he was the first person I would learn by. I would get some Paul Whiteman King of Jazz Orchestra records and listen to Eddie and (jazz violinist) Joe Venuti. That's when I decided to get serious. They made a lot of great records together that totally influenced me. Eddie could play all the great stuff, harmonics, hammering on, pulling strings, and great vibrato, too."

Les performed first on radio station WRJN in Racine, Wisconsin. "I was only ten years old, playing my guitar and harmonica in vaudeville style shows. My Sears & Roebuck guitar came with a set of chord instructions called the E Z method. That's how I learned my chords. The rest of it I got off the piano rolls. I watched the keys go down on our player piano and I started poking holes in and then put band aids on them to correct errors. (he laughs) Oh, man! A little tape and an ice pick and I could do all kinds of things. The first multiples were there, but I had a problem getting my voice in that hole…my harmonica. I could get another note on the piano, but I wanted to get my voice on there — and other instruments in that hole. So I went to a recording device, different than the piano. The piano was digital, so I had to figure it out on analog, so I went over and built a recording glade."

Eager to experiment, Les built a primitive studio in his parents' living room in Waukesha. "I had a telephone, a player piano, my father's Kolster radio and Victor Victrola phonograph machine, my guitar, my harmonica — I didn't have to leave the living room, because the telephone was the receiver — the microphone was my transmitter, and my transducer — everything was there."

Jack Rael and Patti Page would visit Les when he worked out of his garage in Hollywood years later and observed him working on a new sound-recording innovation. "Patti got the idea to record with multi-tracking later when I was out in California, and they came over to visit and saw what I was doing, and what they claim, and it's partially true, is that they were the first one to come out with a hit record with the multi-track vocal. I only had a few things out with Mary (Ford), and they knew that."

The first multi-track with Mary Ford was "Until I Hold You Again." "It didn't go anywhere," Les said,"it may have only sold five records, (he laughs again), but, it was on the back of one of my things way back in the early days going back to '37, prior to Patti and Mary. Mary was on there (the recording) but she wasn't listed as Mary Ford. It was just called 'a vocal group.' It was actually some neighbors of ours on the recording with her."

Later, Les played his recordings for his friend Mitch Miller, A & R man first for Mercury Records and later for Columbia, who was the starmaker, selecting recordings for many vocalists including Frankie Laine, Tony Bennett, Guy Mitchell, and Rosemary Clooney. Les lent the idea of multi-track voice recordings to Miller who later used them on successful record albums produced under his own name.

Meanwhile, in-between all the inventiveness, Les became a regular on Fred Waring's NBC radio show to earn a living and remained with Waring's Pennsylvanians orchestra for over five years. During that time Les doubled as a well-sought-out studio musician.

In 1942, after being drafted, Les Paul backed Bing Crosby, the Andrews Sisters, Rudy Vallee, Johnny Mercer, Kate Smith, and others as part of his job with the Armed Forces Radio Service during World War II.

"Then, I broke my right arm in an automobile accident (1948), and when the doctor set my arm, I had him reset it at an angle so I could still play the guitar."

Besides pioneering recording techniques, like the electronic echo, Les also invented the solid body guitar, an important staple of yesterday's and today's guitar-playing world, and a device important to the development of rock and roll music. In the early '50s, I purchased a Gibson solid body electric guitar. It was a Les Paul model finished in a very high cherrywood gloss. Teaching beginning guitar students at a neighborhood music store in Flushing, New York, I simultaneously received lessons from an advanced fellow-teacher, Gus Coletti, an accomplished player himself, but soon gave it up for ten-finger style classical instruction, selling my solid body Gibson to him. Les Paul fashioned that instrument for Gibson Guitars, who first did not believe in it, but later employed all his ideas.

"Back in the '20s, when I was just a kid, I was playing this barbecue stand and I rigged up a telephone and I was singing into it through my mother's radio, playing the harmonica and guitar at a road house — a juke joint — near Milwaukee. It was a drive-in place that served barbecued hamburgers and root beer. This one guy sends a note up with the bar-hop saying, 'tell Red' — that's me — 'that his guitar isn't loud enough.'" He called himself Hot Rod Red or Rhubarb Red in those days.

"So I went home and said, 'Ma —— I gotta make the guitar louder for this guy in the rear who made a helluva point.' (His mother always encouraged her budding genius,) And she says, 'Well, I know you'll figure it out, ' and so I come up with the idea of taking a phonograph pickup and jabbing it into the guitar and turning it on. Instead of playing a record, it would pick the vibration up off the top of the guitar. It was a crystal and it's the same thing — and I did, and that was the answer. It played for ten minutes and then it fed back. When it started to feed back, I stuffed it with rags, then I filled it up with plaster-of-Paris, and everything and anything I could try to fill the hole up in this guitar to prevent feedback."

It was a prototype of the very first solid body guitar.

Filling the body "solid'"would prevent the feedback noise. Les contemplated whether the new body should be constructed of wood, steel, or even another untried substance. So, with help from friends, he gathered up a piece of steel about a yard long, a remnant from a nearby railroad track.

"It took six of us kids to put it on a wagon to bring it home. We got it into the backyard and we strung a string on it and I said, 'I'll try that' — and tried a piece of the softest wood I could find to hold the strings so I could see which way I am going to go — soft wood or hard wood. So I come running to my mother and said, 'hands down — it's steel — that's the best, the railroad track.'

"So my mother said to me, 'The day you see Gene Autry on a horse with a.......,' and I said, 'Don't even finish......' Gene Autry was one of the people from who I learned my craft. He came to our town when I was a kid, and here he is on the stage, and I was in the front row with a flashlight. Every chord that he played that I didn't know, I was trying to write down. Noticing the light, he stopped the show and said, 'Every time I hit this chord, and he hit it again, there's a light going on,' so he called me up on the stage, and that's how we met. I played for him and he encouraged me to go on — isn't that a wonderful story? And, about three years ago, I spent a day with my hero Gene Autry, just before his sidekick Pat Buttram died. I videoed a whole day with him, and it's just absolutely priceless. I have it here and haven't done anything with it or even edited it."

Continuing about the solid body guitar invention, Les recounted how he strung up the strings on the solid piece of wood and produced the very first electric guitar that he expects one day will be placed in the Smithsonian Institution in Washington, D.C.

"This electric guitar is the very first," he holds up a crude, primitive first-stage instrument that simulates a four-foot wooden board with a door hinge, strings and a tailpiece, "and it's just God-awful." It was a beginning, however, not unlike some of the early -stage inventions of Thomas Edison. He calls his "experiment" *The Log*.

"No one has seen this one…it's just like it was the day I finished it a hundred years ago. It was stored in a neighbor's garage, and the guy, a boyhood friend — one day when I was back home visiting, he said to me, 'Hey, I found something in the garage that belongs to you.' I had given it to him to keep for me, but forgotten all about it, and he gave it back to me, and with my mother's writing on it that read, *This is Lester's*. My real name is Lester Polfus. Oh, my God, I had found it intact. Here was the very first wood solid body guitar ever, and, of course, the other one was there with the steel railroad track, too."

In 1974, Les returned to active playing, recording a hit LP with "Chester and Lester" (Chester being famous country icon guitarist Chet Atkins) which won a Grammy. You must get a copy of that album. Distinctly, Chet is Chet, and Les is Les, meaning it's two completely different musicians with one mike. They are on different roads, but blend beautifully anyway. In 1980, an in-depth television documentary told the world about Les' life and work.

Les Paul admires all the other leading guitarists. "There are so many, many great ones, Oh, my goodness! Chet Atkins, for one…but let me start from the top. You admire different pickers for different reasons, each being individually great in their own style. Chet and Merle Travis in the world of country are among the best. I've played and recorded country with them for years. For a guy with a clean technique, there's Al Damiola. Same goes for Eric Johnson. And Bucky Pizzerelli, Tony Mottola, Charlie Christian, Jeff Beck and George Barnes are also great pickers. There are so many, Richard. Of course, as I said earlier, my mentor was Eddie Lang, who played so beautifully for Bing Crosby, and who unfortunately passed away very young, (because of a medical error during a simple tonsillectomy). It's ironic, I took Eddie's place backing Bing later on. It's where I always wanted to be."

The Wizard of Waukesha is not laid back these days, as you would think an 83 year old would be. Like our friend Frankie Laine, Les will never retire.

"Retirement for me is nil. When I had my bypass operation, the doctor told me to keep working like I was. He said I would have a better and longer life if I kept up the activity. I'm not the kind of guy to retire, anyway. I love working every day at one thing or another."

A television documentary in 1980 helped revive his career for a while. In 1992, at the age of seventy-seven he performed at the Seville, Spain Guitar Festival.

Today, Les Paul plays Monday nights at Iridium in New York City, backed with a bass and rhythm guitar. Fat Tuesday's was his home on the same night for a number of years until the place closed, when he moved to Iridium.

"Everyone knows it's me, when they hear just one note. It's an identifying thing from me to them and back again. Count Basie had only one note, but it was the best note of all. The whole band is like a locomotive, and he plays only one note. But he was Basie, and that was enough. I am Les Paul and I play *this* way."

Les likes the ease of playing in a small club, even more than an important gig at a place like Carnegie Hall. He said that Mary had liked the recording studio, but not the personal appearances."

For each of us, there was no pressure doing what we liked and where we liked. I just don't like being nailed down."

I hope Les gets back on the phone with all those friends we talked about this momentous day, those survivors of the Big Band era and beyond whom he and I revere so much.

BERYL DAVIS

I'll Be Seeing You—Major Glenn Miller's Last Vocalist

On November 2, 1944, a communiqué from Lieutenant General Jimmy Doolittle at Eighth Air Force Headquarters outlined invitational travel orders to a pretty young British singer as an authority for providing entertainment at Air Force installations in England. The excited young lady was London born Beryl Davis. Beryl was the only British civilian ever attached to the 8th Air Force.

Late last year, Beryl Davis and I had first sat down to talk about her friend, Big Band vocalist Connie Haines, for Connie's forthcoming autobiography, *Snootie Little Cutie*. Connie, Beryl, and actresses Rhonda Fleming and Jane Russell are very close friends. Today, from her Palm Springs, California home, Beryl and I once again got together to talk about her own illustrious singing career that has spanned over 50 years.

This is her story:

"My father was a bandleader, and we lived in the center of London. I started my career as a dancer. I would sing one chorus and dance two, then I gradually sang two choruses and danced one, and then finally left out the dancing part altogether. I was just three, and became the girl vocalist when I was merely eight."

This auspicious beginning was performed in notable music halls all over England, Ireland, Scotland, and Wales, as Beryl's dad, at the time, was an orchestra pit leader, and she, on cue, would hop up on stage and sing a rousing chorus of "Constantinople," collect a box of chocolates and then run offstage to smiles and applause.

Her guitarist father had inherited the popular, Stan Kenton-style, Oscar Rabin dance band when ill-health forced Rabin to delegate more of the band leader work to him. And, like their American counterparts, the new Harry Davis orchestra fulfilled endless one-nighters. Beryl traveled with the band much like Doris Day did with Les Brown and her friend Connie Haines with Harry James and Tommy Dorsey.

"All the American singers were my musical heroes, Richard. I listened to the Big Bands all the time because it was the only way I could learn the songs, particularly when the war came. We were really isolated, and perhaps would get just one record a month, and everybody would run to the music store to find a new song. We did all the Glenn Miller, Benny Goodman, and Tommy Dorsey stuff. I would listen on my

160

little wind-up phonograph to Ella Fitzgerald, Helen O'Connell, Helen Forrest, Maxine Sullivan, and someone who would become my life-long friend, Connie Haines. I tried very hard to emulate Ella the most, trying to learn that special, clear Ella sound."

Beryl's career blossomed throughout the war and she became England's prominent vocalist.

"From my father's band, I freelanced with all the important British bands. I sang with Mantovani, Syd Lawrence, and Ted Heath, all the great bands of England, and wherever I was needed. When they wanted a vocalist, they simply called me. I was a very quick learner. Before the war came I was in Paris singing with Stephane Grappelli and Django Reinhardt, and, when we arrived back in England to go on tour, England declared war. I continued on tour with Stephane in a small group that included (pianist) George Shearing, and it was a wonderful time of my life — Richard — musically speaking."

In the early days of the war, Beryl was one of the group's resident players at famous Hatchett's Restaurant, featuring the hot jazz violin of Stephane Grappelli, Arthur Young at the piano, and "Chappie" D'Amato and Belgian gypsy Django Reinhardt playing swing guitar.

The little group toured all the theaters with the bombs regularly falling all around them. "We just learned to handle the pressure. I was working the entire time and there I am running from door to door in an air raid. I would have to be down at the BBC, who had me under contract, at odd hours of the night, over there on Portland Place to do a broadcast to the Armed Forces or the BBC World Service. Bombs would be dropping, and you just did your best to dodge them. Well, if you didn't dodge them, well, that was that, you know."

Beryl was not terrified, as you would expect her to be under such circumstances. For her and other brave Britons, the daily bombings became a way of life. She would find herself in the bomb shelters or subway entertaining people who were nervous and could not sleep.

Then Glenn Miller came to town. "I was very excited about that, because, for me, that was the *creme-de-la-creme* of bands. Glenn wanted to be part of the overseas entertainment force — and he had (vocalist) Johnny Desmond and the Crew Chiefs (singing group with Artie Malvin, Lynn Allison, Ray McKinley, Gene Steck, Murray Kane, and

Steve Steck); and I was invited to join because I had an American style, and an American sound, accent, and knew all those Miller charts. Glenn was quiet, elegant and very much a leader."

Beryl Davis became the number one favorite girl singer of American Forces overseas. The very last show that Beryl performed with the Glenn Miller Band was at the Queensbury Club, on Lower Regent Street in the heart of London, on December 12, 1944. She sang the haunting war song "I'll Be Seeing You."

"As he left, he patted me on the shoulder, and he said, 'Good show, kid. I'll be seeing yuh.' That was the last time that I saw him."

After Glenn Miller was lost on that fateful plane trip over the English Channel, Beryl decided to expand her career and emigrate to America.

"I always wanted to go to America — for the music — and for no other reason. I wanted to meet Nat King Cole, Frank Sinatra, Helen Forrest, Benny Goodman, — ever since I was a little girl, I wanted to meet them in person. I love my home country, but all of the music I loved came from America. So I had to go there to see things first hand." Beryl by this time was singing regularly with the BBC doing ten shows a week.

America took to Big Band singer Beryl Davis, and Beryl Davis took well to America.

"I was booked into the Commodore Hotel. I woke up on my first day in New York and looked down the Avenue of Americas and saw so many people and taxis. I ran out the door and walked around the city for hours, just absorbing everything. Growing up in London, I had the impression it was a huge city; when I went back, I realized how small it really was."

Bob Hope heard her recording of "I'll Be Seeing You," and, through my old friend, band booker supreme Willard Alexander, brought her to Hollywood to debut on his radio show. Chosen by Frank Sinatra himself to be his partner for one year on *Your Hit Parade* radio show, Beryl replaced Doris Day, who went to Hollywood for her first movie, *Romance on the High Seas.*

"Frank was very kind and supportive, and always a perfect gentlemen. He always included me, as after each show we would go out to dinner." Beryl's singing reputation expanded, leading to featured engagements with the Benny Goodman, Vaughn Monroe and David Rose orchestras.

In California, Beryl met and married Peter Potter, a well-known Hollywood disc jockey. They had three children and remained married for seventeen years in their Taluca Lake home.

"One of the most exciting times of my life was when I joined with my new friends, Connie Haines, Jane Russell, and Rhonda Fleming, and recorded 'Do, Lord,' a record that went gold. We were all members of the same church, the Hollywood Presbyterian Church, which you can read about in depth in Connie Haines' new autobiography, *Snootie Little Cutie*, due out this fall."

Good friends Jane Russell, Connie Haines and Beryl Davis charm comedian Red Skelton. *(Connie Haines Collection)*

CONNIE HAINES

I asked Connie Haines about "Do, Lord's" success.

"How did June, Beryl, and I get together as a singing group? It happened back in 1954 at Beryl's St. Stephen Episcopal Church. I agreed to sing at a fund-raising event

there. Della Russell was there to sing with her husband (singer) Andy Russell. Jane Russell was also there. In the basement, we dressed and practiced before the event. 'Connie, what am I going to do, just stand there with egg on my face?' Jane complained. We can all sing an old church spiritual called 'Do, Lord,' I told her.

"Beryl was from London and never heard of the song. But we worked on it, rehearsed and perfected it in no time, and we sang it for the church group and later picked up another friend, Rhonda Fleming, when Della had to leave, and recorded it for our Four Girls tour."

The girls sold a million records and performed the song on the Bob Hope, Red Skelton and Ed Sullivan shows, and on shows featuring Milton Berle, Abbott and Costello, Arthur Murray and Hedda Hopper. They went on to record a dozen more uplifting spiritual songs. The royalties from "Do, Lord" were divided up and donated to the girls' separate church or charity.

Beryl continued on, singing with Mel Tormé, the Gene Krupa Orchestra, Kay Kyser's Band, and, over the years, on many salutes to Glenn Miller.

Beryl is married to drummer Buck Stapleton, ironically a member of the Glenn Miller Air Force Band and a later Promotions Manager for Capitol Records. They have been married for thirty-four years. They lost the Taluca Lake home in an earthquake and now live in a Palm Springs condo.

Beryl is still a dynamic performer in the Big Band world of today. Her rendition of "I'll Be Seeing You" has become her vocal trademark and is always dedicated to the memory of Major Glenn Miller.

"I'm honored to still be working part of the music scene. Sure, it's not the good old days anymore, but I notice that young musicians are taking a good look at the charts of the Big Bands, and I want to work with those kids and pass along the Big Band legacy. One of the things that makes me doubly happy is that I'm not just an observer. I'm still part of the scene."

As *Jukebox* goes to press, Beryl Davis is performing on a cruise ship, singing her heart out with Tommy Dorsey's Bill Tole and Les Brown's premier clarinetist Abe Most, while sailing from Florida to Acapulco with a show appropriately called *The Glenn Miller Hit Parade*.

As Yogi Berra aptly noted: "It's *deja vu* all over again."

SALLY BENNETT

Magic Moments with the Big Bands

Sally Bennett is an amazing, enthusiastic lady. Perle Mesta- like, maybe. Dinah Shore-ish, definitely. She has talked with and has entertained and been photographed with more celebrities than Oprah Winfrey.

She is a composer, musician, playwright, model, actress, poet, radio and TV personality, and author of the book *Sugar & Spice*, "a composite of most of the lyrics I've written...over 100 songs," she says. Sally, who was born in Pennsylvania with an ancestry of "sugar and spice," has hosted President Eisenhower's Inaugural Ball, walked the White House Rose Garden with President and Mrs. Johnson, and has been a companion of the young Grace Kelly and Jackie Kennedy. Most of Sally Bennett's life has been overflowing with what she calls "magic moments." So much, that she actually composed the song "Magic Moments" to celebrate them. The song was recorded

by Buddy De Franco's Glenn Miller Orchestra in London, England, and was featured at Tricia Nixon Cox's wedding and at Nelson Rockefeller's grandiose party for Henry Kissinger. Many of those "moments" have been spent promoting the Big Bands; in fact, Sally is the founder of the Big Band Hall of Fame which, at long last, officially opened their doors at the Palm Beach, Florida Community College on March 22, 1999, just before publication of this book. It was a fitting tribute for the Big Bands, and everyone was there.

The *Palm Beach* (Florida) *Post* headlined the event: *"Doors swing open for big band museum, as Sally Bennett's dream becomes reality as her music-world artifacts are put on display in Palm Beach,"* they cried. *"The opening fulfills a 3-decade old dream for Sally Bennett, who collected most of the memorabilia from big band leaders and musicians she interviewed on her shows in Atlanta, Georgia and Cleveland, Ohio.*

"Over the years, many people tried to discourage me, but I never gave up." Sally comes from a long line of classical musicians, but she always wanted to sing with big name bands and write their songs. Her musical circle of friends included Frank Sinatra, Sammy Kaye, Guy Lombardo, and Tommy Dorsey, drawn from her days as an Atlanta, Georgia disc jockey on radio station WBGS, and those in Cleveland, Ohio in 1966. "A few years later, my show in Cleveland was canceled when I refused to play rock n' roll," Sally explained, "Our Big Band music is still sorely needed today."

Back in 1967, bandleader Sammy Kaye honored Sally with an hour concert featuring all her own original songs — both words and music. The idea was to launch a crusade to revive interest in the Big Bands, which eventually led to the founding of the *Big Band Hall of Fame*. That first ball was held at the Sheraton Cleveland Ballroom and became an annual event, featuring the bands of Glenn Miller, Guy Lombardo and Harry James.

"She's done a wonderful job with it," said Xavier Cugat band director Bob Kasha, who also secured the bands that played at the Big Band's early balls and now manages the new Xavier Cugat band. "It's been a long labor of love for her."

Sally has very strong feelings for the museum:

"To not commemorate this era of music is like hiding a Picasso or a Rembrandt in a cellar," she told me during a long and pleasant conversation in March 1999. She has consistently and actively promoted her ideas to help keep Big Band music alive. Through the years she organized many annual Big Band balls which eventually evolved into charity events to support her dream museum.

Sally began collecting items when she interviewed Big Band people during the 1950s in Atlanta. "When I interviewed these people, I would kid them, 'Give me something to remember you by,'" she said. "Liberace took his tie off that very minute and gave it to me.

"The museum's aim is three-fold: to honor big-band composers, vocalists and musicians. For 16 years the museum has existed only as money-raising events at which many Hall-of-Famers have been inducted. I have gathered an extensive collection of Big Band artifacts for the museum, including copies of your last three books, Richard, and much memorabilia collected while I was conducting radio and television interviews of Big Band personalities back in the good old days," she chuckles.

Among them are many rare photos, bandleader Russ Morgan's trombone, Billy Butterfield's and Harry James' trumpets, Glenn Miller's bandstand jacket, a mirrored ball that hung over the famous Aragon Ballroom in Chicago, an autographed baton from bandleader Guy Lombardo, and an Xavier Cugat Orchestra bandstand.

In 1995, The Big Band Hall of Fame charity, which was held at the famous Breaker's in Palm Beach, inducted bandleader Jack Morgan and composer Claire Rothrock Graham, with music by the Russ Morgan Orchestra, conducted by his son, Jack.

In 1996 the Hall of Fame held a special tribute to Sammy Kaye for his assistance, belief, and dedication to establishing the first Big Band Hall of Fame. Sally was presented with *The Music of Your Life Award* in the same year by mutual friend Al Ham, President and Founder of Music of Your Life which syndicates Big Band musical formats to radio stations throughout the country. Only Frank Sinatra, Tony Bennett, Rosemary Clooney and Dinah Shore have received it before her.

In 1997, the Big Band Hall of Fame Ball featured the Glenn Miller Orchestra, directed by Larry O'Brien, and honored music man, vocalist Don Cornell. Over the years, especially in the formative stages, Sally Bennett has enlisted many famous names of the 20th Century to help her along with her project: Dinah Shore, Count Basie, Bob Hope, Alan Jay Lerner, Guy Lombardo, Douglas Fairbanks, Jr., Ray McKinley, Pat

Boone, Robert Merrill, Roberta Peters, Richard Tucker, Tammy Grimes, Buddy De Franco, Jonah Jones, Buddy Rogers, George Hamilton, Alan Jay Lerner, Joni James, Frances Langford, Hoagy Carmichael, Mitchell Parrish, Mitch Miller, Bob Crosby, Bob Crosby, Mike Douglas, Don Dunphy, Nelson Riddle, Count Bill Basie, George Murphy, Marla Trump, Joe Franklin, Arthur Godfrey, Harry James, and former Vice President Hubert Humphrey. Today, it's people like Don Cornell, inducted in 1998, and song star Dolly Dawn, who is a veteran Big Band vocalist and featured in my book *The Song Stars*, who are the current subjects.

If it seems like we are high on celebrities, the above list is merely a drop-in-the bucket, to coin a phrase. To learn more about Sally Bennett, you will have to read her book due out in the year 2000. Naturally, Sally is going to name it *Magic Moments*.

Sally Bennett and Sammy Kaye, 1996. *(Courtesy Bert and Richard Morgan)*

Pepe Lienhard leading the Swinging Swiss Army Big Band *(Courtesy Thomas Gerber)*

Top: Syd Lawrence and Orchestra. *Bottom:* Bryan Pendleton leads Syd Lawrence Orchestra *(Courtesy Big Bands International)*

170

PART FOUR

THE BIG BANDS OVER THERE

Europe and England
BY MAX WIRZ

Introduction by Richard Grudens

It's more than exciting to collaborate with fellow-author, Big Band radio host Max Wirz, who communicates enthusiastically from the other side of the world by phone, fax, and post, who even flew over to meet with me last fall to map out his unique contribution to *Jukebox Saturday Night*. Vocalist, newsman Roberto Tirado; bandleader Ben Grisafi; Max and his wife, Nelly, and I polished off a superb sauerbraten lunch during our historic meeting at the Three Village Inn in Stony Brook, New York, as we worked over various ideas for the book and exchanged notes and photos.

The historic meeting of the Stony Brook five organizing *Jukebox* at Long Island's Three Village Inn. January, 1999.

Max Wirz, Switzerland's and, thus, one of Europe's premium dispensers of American music; photographer *extraordinaire*; and now, productive interviewer and author, searched throughout Europe and England to report accurately about the Big Band activities of the old bands and new bands. As you will remember, Max was responsible for the splendid Hazy Osterwald profile in the book *The Music Men* in 1998.

For *Jukebox*, Max committed to covering the Big Bands of England and Europe of yesterday and today. He braved ice, snow, and blocked highways to reach the young, popular German bandleader Thilo Wolf to recount Thilo's experiences. He traveled to England for the sensational BBC Graham Pass production of the Les Brown/Ray Anthony/Billy May/BBC historic tribute held at Ronnie Scott's in Birmingham, garnering interviews and snapping photos; and, at Pontin's Ballroom near London, he attended concerts by the legendary Syd Lawrence Orchestra (now directed by Chris Dean and arranger, pianist Bryan Pendleton) where he caught Bryan between concerts. From Bryan, Max learned about the legendary Ted Heath Orchestra and other Big Bands which continue their musical activities throughout the United Kingdom. He attended *The Magic of Sinatra* show starring dynamic, youthful Andy Prior and his Night Owls; achieved a connection with Glenn Miller's nephew John, who leads England's Herb Miller/ Glenn Miller Orchestra; developed direct contact with Tony Fisher, current leader of the great Bert Kaempfert organization; and interviewed the elusive Paul Kuhn, legendary German pianist, Big Band leader, and great entertainer, among some other difficult chores, all while facing a fast approaching publishing deadline.

Here are the bountiful, sumptuous rewards.

PEPE LIENHARD

In the city of Lenzburg, Switzerland, where the imposing sight of the majestic Schloss Lenzburg (Lenzburg Castle) prevails along the Autobahn between Zurich and Bern, Pepe Lienhard was born on March 23, 1946. Encouraged by his mother, and kept in bounds by his father, who wanted young Pepe to learn a "proper trade," Pepe learned to play the recorder flute and saxophone as a small child. He began playing the drums by age ten, and, at eleven, fulfilled his dream to play the saxophone. At twelve, he started a Dixieland band he named the Lenzburg College Stompers and entered the 1963 Zurich Jazz Festival with a 28 piece Big Band.

"Musically, I grew up with older musicians who came out of the Big Band Era. I learned to read music from them, and, at seventeen, I had my own first Big Band."

However, reality soon caught up forcing Pepe to build a *show band* where he featured the popular music of the period, although his heart beat strongly for the Big Band sounds.

"You see, although I had an early start as a bandleader, when I later was given the opportunity to put together the Swiss Army Big Band with the best young musicians in the country, I grabbed it. Unfortunately, that gig lasts only two weeks out of the year, although they are two wonderful weeks during which we do one-night stands throughout Switzerland. For the rest of the year my show plays anything and everything *higgledy-piggledy* (a mixture of every known band's music)."

The Swiss Army Band is a conventional Big Band with five trumpets, four trombones, five saxophones and a rhythm section, whereas the Pepe Lienhard Band is a thirteen-piece band with three trumpets, two saxes, one trombone, and a large rhythm section with two lead singers.

Pepe isn't partial to the Dixieland sounds, "I like to listen to a good Dixieland band, but I don't think I could play 'When the Saints Go Marching In' three times a night, let alone for the rest of my life.

"We are a large enough band to produce Big Band sounds, and we do it with precision and quality. We have mixed audiences from late teenagers to seniors and mostly the younger set attending jazz clubs. Years ago we played swinging Big Bands sounds all night long. If we did only that today, the folks would turn away."

In 1963, at Andy Berner's Zurich Jazz Festival, with modernist and *avant garde* Stan Kenton, and Quincy Jones as his idols, Pepe Lienhard remembers the first appearance of his band:

"I included French horns, tubas, and bass clarinets in my band. The bigger, the better, we thought. We had a twenty-eight piece group with everything but the kitchen sink in there. I was full of enthusiasm — and composed and arranged like a madman."

As a boy, Pepe attended some Stan Kenton concerts, adopting Stan as his idol. Pepe later won this Festival in 1965, and again in 1969. After giving up law studies, he turned professional by debuting the Pepe Lienhard Sextet. Club dates, the Grand Prix Eurovision 1970, recording dates and TV appearances made the Sextet a popular group throughout Europe. The year 1977 found them touring Thailand, and, together with singing star Udo Jurgens, they embarked on a lengthy concert tour throughout the U.S. and Canada.

In his early years Pepe followed the career of popular bandleader Hazy Osterwald, attending his concerts whenever his parents would allow it. "Hazy would give me arrangements and sheet music, and we became great friends and still are."

Once, in a small club in Zurich, Pepe was spontaneously visited by Sammy Davis, Jr. and Buddy Rich, who were performing locally. They could not believe that a sextet could do Woody's "Four Brothers" in a

Pepe Lienhard, Frank Sinatra and Sammy Davis, Jr. *(Max Wirz Collection)*

Big Band sound. "They stepped up and jammed with us, and, boy, what an experience."

He keep the sextet until 1980, then moved on to bigger things, a thirteen piece band that had abundant volume, was flexible, and increased in band size when working with such performers as English vocalist Shirley Bassey. At the Sporting Club in Monaco, the thirteen piece group played behind Frank Sinatra, Sammy Davis, Sarah Vaughan, Diana Ross, Shirley Bassey, Michel LeGrand, Paul Anka, Whitney Houston, and Caterina Valente.

In 1995 Pepe Lienhard was commissioned to form the Swinging Swiss Army Big Band, a Swiss edition of a Glenn Miller-style Orchestra.

"I was thrilled to accept the job of forming and leading a Big Band again. So we set up auditions to test volunteers from the many military marching bands. We wanted modern sounds, but not rock, and I was flabbergasted by the talent of the young players. Some were twenty and most younger than thirty. We had great fun. During Army Days in Frauenfeld, Switzerland, more than 100,000 visitors were treated to the band's concerts, where the favorites Glenn Miller, Benny Goodman, and the Dorseys charts command the most applause."

Just back from Freiburg, Germany, in July of 1998 the thirteen piece band played at a concert with Joan Orleans, and one-night stands and longer engagements throughout Europe during the fall and winter of 1998 and 1999.

Pepe told me he is a dinosaur who keeps coming back at every chance. He feels the swing must go on. "My heart and the hearts of my band members very much favor *our kind of music*. Eventually it will have to be First Lieutenant Gilbert Tinner and other young European bandleaders who, together with us older fellows, keep bringing back the great music of the Big Band Era, and who will find ways to add their own licks to present new melodies in the Big Band format."

The best proof was the Zuri Fascht (Festival of Zurich) where SRO crowds, including grandpas and grandmas, danced to "Moonlight Serenade," "Tuxedo Junction" and "In the Mood" for three days through rain and shine.

The Pepe Lienhard Band
Billy Todzo, percussion, singer; Tommy Geiger, baritone, tenor, soprano, clarinet; Sebastian Strempel, trumpet, flugelhorn; Rolf "Capo" Mayer, bass-guitar; Thorsten Maass, trumpet, flugelhorn; Peter Lubke, drums; Pino Gasparini, singer; Carlo Filaferro, guitar; Edgar Schmid, trombone; Georges Walther, keyboards; Pepe Lienhard, alto, tenor, flutes; Onita Boone, singer. *(Max Wirz Collection)*

"We always hear that Big Bands are dead. I don't think so. Even though it's an economic problem, the bands are still out there, like Hazy Osterwald, Ray Anthony, Les Brown, and other ghost bands with surviving leaders. Fifty years ago the whole world was dancing swing, but only a small fraction is doing it today. Don't forget, Max, the folks who used to come and listen to my band have grown older. Today it is the 17 to 25-year-olds who go out every night, but sometimes for different kinds of sounds. It is my conviction that Big Band music lives and is here to stay. No one can make it disappear from the world."

THE GLENN MILLER ORCHESTRA
of Europe

Today, Europe's only licensed Glenn Miller Orchestra, directed by Wil Salden of Holland, performs everywhere in Europe. This friendly Dutchman was born on June 14, 1950 in Obbicht, Holland. He studied

The Glenn Miller Orchestra
directed by Wil Salden
Europe's only licensed Glenn Miller Orchestra

Wil Salden's European Glenn Miller Orchestra during one of their 180 annual plus Concerts.

Wil Salden of Holland carrying on the tradition of the Swing Era with the Glenn Miller Orchestra. *(Max Wirz Collection)*

177

piano, led his own bands, and played piano for the radio and TV orchestra of Hilversum, which he later conducted.

Today, on October 16, 1998, I talked with Wil....yes only one *l* in *Wil* — prior to the concert at the 7th International Festival of Light Music in Winterthur.

The Glenn Miller Orchestra, with offices in Hammersbach, Germany, gathers musicians from Germany and Holland and does a lot of traveling throughout the year in Europe with 180 concert dates between Stockholm, Sweden, and Sicily, Italy.

"I was always inspired by the Big Band swing music of the thirties and forties. Back in 1978 and 1979 I began planning to play Glenn Miller music on a regular basis. That was not so simple. Of course, you could find arrangements of 'Moonlight Serenade' or 'In the Mood,' but these were not originals and did not sound the way Miller should sound. I did some Miller-style arranging myself, but I got in contact with David MacKay of the Glenn Miller Foundation in the USA. So, since 1990 we legally represent the Glenn Miller Foundation in most European countries."

Like Glenn Miller and other bands of the Big Band Era, this band travels by bus. One day they are in a small town near Salzburg, Austria, and the following day they arrive in Winterthur, Switzerland, then two days later they are playing Berlin. One hundred eighty performances is quite a load and there is no life for the musicians — no time for family or little things. Of the 180 shows, only 20 are dances. The musicians' and vocalists' lives revolve around a new stage, a new hotel room and the same bus every day.

"We choose from a vast repertoire. The people like the original Miller standards, so we give them five to ten every performance. We also play Glenn's arranged works of Franz Lehar, and the people are thrilled when they hear it."

Wil Salden plays mostly concerts, "because Big Bands have become too expensive for ballroom organizers, but we do have a dance repertoire. Sometimes we change the selection sequence, just to sound different."

In every concert Salden plays familiar titles by other orchestras like those of Benny Goodman and Tommy Dorsey. That night, to 650 people, the band played Goodman's "Sing, Sing, Sing" and Dorsey's "Marie," but they are careful not to overdo it because the audience came to hear and expect Glenn Miller music.

Among the band's vocalists, Miet Molnar and a vocal group called the Moonlight Serenaders, composed of Erik Hilferink, Uli Plettendorf, Wiebe Schurmans, Wil Salden and Miet, re-create vocal renditions of the Crew Chiefs, the Modernaires, and the fabulous Andrews Sisters, who sang a lot with the Glenn Miller band on radio broadcasts.

Glenn Miller is alive and well throughout Europe…and England, too, where Ray McVay now directs the official Glenn Miller Orchestra UK.

RETO PAROLARI AND THE ZSOW

Reto Parolari, a master musician, composer, arranger, conductor and founder of the ORP, Orchester Reto Parolari, a 44 piece symphonic orchestra with headquarters in Winterthur, 15 miles east of Zurich, who brought the Wil Salden Glenn Miller band to Switzerland, also maintains and conducts the ZSOW — Das Zivilschutz Show Orchester Winterthur (The Civil Defense Show Orchestra), an 18 piece Big Band.

The famous ZSOW is really a rather unique orchestra. The members are professional musicians who perform in Reto's ORP while they serve their Swiss military obligation in a civil defense service during a two week "camp tour."

"We all like to play swing and jazz, so we make the best of the time. With good arrangements we don't need formal rehearsals for public appearances. We play 'Sing, Sing, Sing' then Viennese Waltzes and go right back to Goodman, Dorsey, Ellington and Miller standards. Tonight, during the 7th International Festival of Light Music, we did George Gershwin. With the ORP, where I celebrated 25 years in 1998, and the ZSOW, we combine the great music of Vienna, Broadway, and the Big Band Era during one week a year. The audience rewards us with full houses everytime. For the 8th Festival during fall 1999, Kurt Bong and his radio Big Band Orchestra of Frankfurt, Germany, will be back. As long as the audiences desire Big Band sounds, the ZSOW and other Big Bands will be here to perform for them."

179

BRYAN PENDLETON
THE SYD LAWRENCE ORCHESTRA

I met Bryan Pendleton in 1995 when Frank Touhey of Montpellier Records introduced me to five British Big Bands at Pontin's Big Band Center in Lowestoft, on the wind-blown East coast of England. There was the Herb Miller Orchestra, conducted by Glenn's nephew John Miller; Andy Prior and His Night Owls; the Geraldo Orchestra; the 68 year old Joe Loss Orchestra directed by Todd Miller; and the great Syd Lawrence Orchestra, directed at the time by Bryan Pendleton, who is also the arranger, piano player, and part of the vocal group. Since last year, the band is fronted by Chris Dean with Bryan as musical co-director.

Bryan, a thorough gentleman, spoke to me that day about his very busy musical life:

"We have been down to the Southwest coast of England, with the band, in a place called Western Super Mare. We played three nights to a great reception. In December (1998) we played the Theatre Royal, Windsor, with vocalists Sarah Gilbertson and Tony Jacobs"

Bryan studied classical piano early in life, then he heard some remarkable jazz when he was about fifteen." It was Art Tatum, who I thought was two people playing when I first heard his recordings. I was amazed; it was only Art Tatum without any help. I knew I wanted a career in jazz piano, as my interest turned to pianists Errol Garner, Oscar Peterson, and Bud Powell."

Bryan played piano in the service on and off in the Officers Mess. In 1958 he was discharged. At that time he heard that the pianist of a quartet in a ballroom near home was leaving. He auditioned, got the job, and toured with the quartet. It was the end of the Big Band Era in America, but not so in England. It was still going strong as it is today.

"I played in some twelve-piece bands on the circuit, then got the chance to play with the BBC Northern Dance Orchestra in Manchester, my first Big Band, a twenty-one piece who played broadcasts every day of every week. It was all studio work. I met Syd Lawrence who played in the trumpet section. Syd got tired of playing Beatles and Rolling Stones' stuff and formed a band of his own, promising to play just for kicks, nothing more."

In 1967 they rented an upstairs room in a hotel and the patrons would hear them, bring up their beer and listen. The musicians would also drink a pint or two, and there was no money. After a few years the band became known around Manchester and London, and soon promoters and theater owners from London started inquiries, eventually setting up tours. It was sort of the rebirth of the Swing Era, in a local sense.

That was the beginning of the legendary Syd Lawrence Orchestra, which still has a fan club with over five thousand members, many of whom travel to Pontin's each year to the Syd Lawrence Convention for five successive nights.

"This, for me, lasted about five years. The band was very popular. We did a lot of television and radio and recorded albums — and played theater and dance halls with crowds on hand six, sometimes seven nights a week. We toured the country and were on stage, on the bus, or in a hotel room with no leisure whatsoever, a very tiring way to make a living, indeed."

Exhausted, Bryan left Syd, moved to Birmingham and played for a TV show five days a week. "The anchor man would interview guests and I played in between on the piano — right up into the eighties. I also played in piano bars, literally every night of the week, and it did get very lonely at times. You could not understand, Max, how lonely that is, when you just play solo piano. You sit there and play and nobody seems to listen. Sometime you get a request. If you had a bass or a guitarist or somebody to take some of the load it would get you more comfortable. In 1989 Syd called. He asked me to front the orchestra so he could relax a little. I accepted."

So the circle closed, Bryan was back with the great Syd Lawrence Orchestra. There are a number of British Bands working on the road today: The Andy Prior Orchestra; The Herb Miller Orchestra with John Miller; The Don Weller Big Band; The Great British Big Band with Chris Dean; The Joe Loss Orchestra with Todd Miller; The Pasadena Roof Orchestra; The Syd Lawrence Orchestra with Bryan and Chris Dean; Ted Heath's Band with Don Lusher; the Bert Kaempfert Orchestra with Tony Fisher and, of course, the (BBC) Radio Big Bands.

"But, quite simply, the finest orchestra this country ever produced, and that would include Syd's orchestra, is the great Ted Heath Orchestra. And, if Syd were here today, he would agree. Syd admired the Ted Heath band. Whenever Syd was recruiting musicians in later years, he would scout for men who had worked for Ted. We still have men in our band who were with the early Ted Heath Band, drummer Ronnie Verrell and saxist Ken Kiddier.

"The Ted Heath band still exists, fronted by Don Lusher, a wonderful trombone player," continued Bryan, "The band does not work a lot like we now do. They do maybe 15 performances a year. But, that's all these guys want to do. Don was a member since the fifties and has been fronting it since the seventies, after Ted died in 1969. Don is about seventy-two, as are a number of the band members. A few years ago Don recorded an album of hits like 'Skyliner,' 'Take the A Train,' 'Opus One,' 'Let's Dance,' all those beautiful Big Band hits. Don also runs the Don Lusher Orchestra and is an active session player doing radio and film studio work. He also works the Bond and *Star Wars* films."

The Ted Heath Orchestra was formed in 1945, the oldest member being Kenny Baker, one of the great lead trumpet players who is now seventy-seven.

Bryan Pendleton and Andy Prior are friends. On the current *Magic of Sinatra* show, Bryan did the arranging for "I've Got the World on a String," "Too Close for Comfort," "They Can't Take That Away From Me," "The Shadow of Your Smile," and "All the Way," as well as the instrumental arrangement of "In the Mood" for Andy's band.

"I transcribed the original Nelson Riddle or Billy May arrangements so that Andy can sing those in exactly the same version as Sinatra did, by putting an original song on tape, listening to it over and over, and going back until I have all the voices and notes on paper. Of course, there are differences in the inside instruments, second trombone and third trumpet for instance, but not too many."

That, dear readers, is the story of two of the great bands of England. The Syd Lawrence and Ted Heath legends are still alive. When I revisit Pontin's next May, *Jukebox Saturday Night* will be in the bookstores, even in England, through Gazelle Book Services, and I will meet Bryan Pendleton once again.

"I'll meet you at Pontin's," Bryan waves, "at the far end of that new L shaped, 45 foot bar. And the pint's on me, Max."

Pontin's — That wonderful Big Band place in England *(Courtesy Pontin's)*

PONTIN'S PAKEFIELD
EUROPE'S FOREMOST BIG BAND CENTRE

We first learned about Pontin's from Montpellier Records' Frank and Olive Touhey of Cheltenham, England. In the Spring of 1995 my wife Nelly and I visited Pontin's, and have been annual visitors since.

North of London and East of Birmingham, Pontin's Pakefield Big Band Centre, situated on the East Coast of England just south of Lowestoft, is where hundreds of Big Band aficionados may dance simultaneously across the massive Grand Ballroom floor during one of the exciting Big Band Holiday Weekends to the strains of Glenn Miller's immortal "Moonlight Serenade" or perhaps Les Brown's evergreen "I've Got My Love to Keep Me Warm."

A comfortable train ride on the Intercity will bring you to Pontin's from London's Liverpool station by way of Ipswich, to Norwich, where you may change to a two coach diesel combination for a comfortable half-hour trip to Lowestoft, on the North Sea coast.

Pontin's sponsors the "Legend of the Big Bands," and other Big Band extravagances showcasing England's foremost bands.

Pontin's is vast, with a panoramic glass-window view from the large dining room, an indoor swimming pool, a large soccer field, children's playgrounds, tennis courts, a large field with golf greens, and a sprawling motel with views of the North Sea viewed across the large, grassy field. The complex is perched seventy-five feet above a three-hundred feet wide pebbled beach accessible through a ravine for those who need to wander closer. Accommodations include welcome, enjoyable and convenient English tea-making and television facilities

Pontin's demeanor is always homespun and familiar, not like one of those compact luxury cruise ships, but more like a true dance pavilion and holiday center of the old days, and the Big Band music provided is simply deluxe, featuring England's cream of Big Bands.

Hungry is the feeling as you line up on one of the two dinner lines with all the other guests in the large dining room to enjoy home-style English food, complete with cheddar cheese on crackers, deep-dish apple pie and creamy custard, while friendly Big Band music lovers across the table prepare you for deluxe evenings in the grand ballroom.

Then those wonderful Big Bands break out and under with their fully familiar themes. Evening after evening, spreading that deluxe feeling, was the Herb Miller Orchestra (his son John has directed since Herb's passing in the late 1980s); the Joe Loss Orchestra with Todd Miller; the Geraldo Orchestra with Chris Dean; Andy Prior and his then Night Owls; and the Syd Lawrence Orchestra, as well as Sunday morning concerts by the Big Band sounds of Peter Frazer and the young musicians of the East Norfolk Youth Jazz Orchestra.

Pontin's Pakefield origins date back to 1931. Pontin's Centres were providing inexpensive holidays for middle- class families, until the war, when the site was used as first a training camp, then, a prisoner of war camp.

In 1957 Sir Fred Pontin acquired the Centre and developed it over the years. Recently, Pontin's completed a multi-million refurbishment program which included all the "Club" and "Classic" apartments, the main entertainment area, indoor pool, restaurant and leisure facilities that included the creation of the S.S. Queen Victoria Bar that provides the favorite orders of pints or halfpints of ale, bitters, and "shandy." The ambiance in the Grand Ballroom, with its great L-shaped bar, remains as elegant as ever.

The Big Band concerts began in 1983 with a Herb Miller Orchestra Weekend. Some band names have changed since that year. Now it's Big Bands like Andy Prior and his Orchestra performing the Magic of Sinatra Show and the Syd Lawrence Orchestra directed by Chris Dean and assisted by Bryan Pendleton. These fabulous British bands along with the BBC Big Band and the Passadena Roof Orchestra, among others, are regulars at Pontin's — a good reason for you to come to Pontin's when you visit England to hear those Big Bands featured right here in Jukebox Saturday Night.

THE BERT KAEMPFERT ORCHESTRA
With Tony Fisher

The unique Bert Kaempfert orchestra, now led by Tony Fisher, has been around since 1960. He's a very busy bandleader these days; I talked with Tony Fisher just before this book's closing deadline.

We reminisced about his old boss: "Bert was born in October of 1923 in Hamburg, Germany. His parents encouraged his interest in music and, by age of 16, after graduating from the Hamburg School of Music, he was an expert on the accordion, clarinet, saxophone, and piano. He played with the popular Hans Busch Orchestra. In 1939 WWII interrupted his career. He served in a German Navy band, winding up a prisoner of war in Denmark where he formed a POW band."

Marion Kaempfert and Tony Fisher
(Courtesy Roy Belcher Big Bands Int'l)

After the war Bert started a sextet and then a band he called Ace of Spades, performing regularly at US Army Officers clubs.

185

"That's where he got the chance to play those beautiful Big Band arrangements of Miller, Goodman, and Dorsey, Max. He married Hanne-Lore in 1946 and had two daughters, Marion and Doris. Marion helps with the band today."

In about 1950 Bert returned to Hamburg, working at the Esplanade Club, playing and writing arrangements for British Forces Radio. Then he worked for North West German Radio.

"It's funny, Max. Bert actually discovered the Beatles at the Top Ten Club in Hamburg. He had them do a demo single for Polydor

Bert Kaempfert Promotional *(Max Wirz Collection)*

Records, and they turned them down. Perfect story! In 1961 when Bert put his Big Band together in Hamburg, he called it by his own name and recorded "Wonderland by Night" which went to the top of the charts in America. That put him on the international map."

When I listen to "Wonderland by Night," "A Swinging Safari," or "Dankeschon," and I could go on… with many other tunes… I hear instrumentals with a distinctive sound. Unlike Dorsey, James, or Goodman, the Kaempfert sound with bass guitar, trombones, saxes setting the pace, gentle voices and strings in the background, and then, that often soft and hard again trumpet… reminds me of Glenn Miller things.

"You've got it, Max," Tony said, "You are dead right. The whole thing was based around that 'click' sound on the bass guitar. It's a weird sound because there is more 'click' than actual notes. To get it, Bert actually had his guitar player Ladi Geisler de-tune his guitar. Nowadays, I find it difficult to find a bass player who can master that technique."

Bert Kaempfert composed most of his own songs. Tony has the 600 original scores. Bert's partner, Herbert Rehbein, was a violinist and a close friend. They died one month apart: "It was June of 1980. We did a concert at Royal Albert Hall in London, and I said goodbye to Bert, 'See you in Hamburg at the recording session.' A few days later I heard the news that he had passed away at the age of not quite fifty-seven."

Tony was Bert's lead trumpet and personal friend for many years. Tony is English and born in Manchester, England in 1936.

"My music fanatic father started me on cornet and got me into brass bands. By thirteen, I graduated to the trumpet and traveled with road shows doing all the Harry James material, including the 'Carnival of Venice.' After the service, I worked for the Ted Heath, Eric Delaney, and Ken Mackintosh bands. That was the best time for the Big Bands of England."

Tony settled in London in 1965 and became a session (studio) musician. The James Bond films were being produced then, and, with his friend Don Lusher, trombonist and director of today's Ted Heath Band, he did the sound tracks for all those movies.

"I worked with — Oh, well, Max…I'm a great name-dropper…so here goes…the big guys: Harry James; Les Brown; Ella Fitzgerald;

Vicky Carr, Caterina Valente, Dean Martin, Steve Lawrence, Bing Crosby, The Beatles; Shirley Bassey; Sarah Vaughan, and everybody who came to England... Sinatra, Mathis, Bennett, Mancini, Streisand; Astaire...everybody."

Tony joined the Kaempfert band in 1970: "Let me explain! I did not really join the band because it was not a road band. He did concerts here and there, but mostly worked in recording studios. About twice a year I would fly to Hamburg and record albums. I was the lead trumpet; the solos were done by Ack van Rooyen."

Tony took over the band in 1993 in London.

"I had forgotten all about my Kaempfert days. There were Glenn Miller bands all over England, and, when I was out there, helping this or that band, people came up and asked me about my days with Bert. I thought, 'Well, if there is that much interest in Kaempfert, maybe I should do something about it.' So I rang Marion Kaempfert: 'Marion,' I said, 'It's thirteen years after your father passed away. Out of the blue, I have got a suggestion. You might hate it, you might say,' 'go jump in the lake' '...but, how about forming the band again.'"

"Yes, Tony," Marion replied, "We should do this. We were thinking about bringing it back, but for the world of it, we couldn't think who would want to stand in front."

"So, I re-formed the band out of English musicians, the cream of studio players. Marion allowed me access to all the incredible music. Everything, even the original music stands. And that's how we did it. Marion and I have been working together ever since."

The band doesn't travel much. It does mostly concert events. A full organization with four each trombones, trumpets, saxes, rhythms, Tony as leader and trumpet soloist, four strings, two female and two male singers. Up to twenty-eight people in all. They work 15-20 concerts a year, plus TV shows and short tours in England and Europe, and even Switzerland, Holland, and, of course, Germany.

"My bread and butter is working the TV and recording studios. Band leader friends call me; Barry Forgie of the BBC Big Band; Chris Dean of Syd Lawrence, and others to substitute for a player now and then. That's how I met you at Pontin's, Max, while I was playing in Chris Dean's Great British Big Band on that day."

188

In February of 1999, Tony Fisher and the Bert Kaempfert Orchestra performed two concerts. One near London and one in Chichester. Just before that it was "Music for the Millions," a nationwide TV extra in Hamburg. Freddie Quinn, who used to record vocal singles with Bert, was there too.

With no specific plans for new engagements, there are many possibilities in the near future for Tony and the band. A May TV show in Hamburg, and maybe a concert tour of Japan. Yes, Japan! And there is a chance they will perform in Florida, an ideal place to play Kaempfert music considering the retirees there were the fans who bought many of the 150 million albums Bert recorded.

"Those albums were all instrumentals. Bert never wanted solo singers, just back up singers providing another voice, with exceptions, of course," Tony carefully explained.

So, dear reader, if you have a Bert Kaempfert album, put on the selections "Dankeschon," "Bye, Bye Blues," or "Red Roses for a Blue Lady" (containing quintessential Kaempfert inflections), while you read about Tony Fisher and the great Bert Kaempfert Orchestra, another amazing band of musicians who play Big Band sounds "over there" for the millions of fans like you who enjoy them. His exciting music still belongs today, vibrant, trumpet-oriented — it is abundantly affluent in not one, but many intriguing sounds. It's the Bert Kaempfert *idiom*.

PAUL KUHN AND His Orchestra
an interview on February 12, 1999 at St. Gallen, Switzerland

It was Paul Kuhn who helped introduce swing music to post-war Germany. I have known Paul, the singer; piano player; Big Band leader; composer; arranger; radio and TV personality, since my days as a sergeant with the 273rd Infantry Battle Group at Wildflecken in 1957 and 1958, he was active on AFN radio (American Forces Network) and toured the enlisted men's NCO's and Officers Clubs with his combo. I remember hearing Paul on the radio and caught him on TV, singing American popular songs and German ditties. Later, in the seventies, Nelly and I watched Paul's regular Saturday night TV show for years.

Paul Kuhn and I met in February of 1999 for an earnest talk for this book.

189

Born in Wiesbaden in 1928, Paul achieved an education in classical music in Frankfurt through 1943, towards the end of the war at age 16: "I was part of the civilian group who entertained German frontline troops. After VE Day in 1945, I came back to Wiesbaden and became a regular piano player in a GI enlisted man's club."

Paul's mother was also musical. "It was my godfather, whose name was also Paul, who detected my musical vein and presented me with an accordion when I was quite young. I mastered it rather quickly, playing songs by heart after hearing them once or twice. The feeling for melodies, harmonies and a certain beat must be a birth gift."

That's Paul Kuhn *(center)* and Ute Mann, Paul's wife *(second from right)* of Ute Mann Singers. 1984. *(Max Wirz Collection)*

Paul's musical life parallels Thilo Wolf's, who also started with an accordion. However, Paul became aware of swing music and the legendary names of Miller, Goodman, Ellington, and Dorsey, about the time the United States entered the war.

"American music was not actually forbidden until that time. We heard the Andrews Sisters, Tommy Dorsey and the Pied Pipers, and others over a short wave radio or from recordings in friends homes. The music was a challenge to me. The music had a certain 'thing' to it. It

190

took possession of me; then, in 1944 and '45, it did become adventurous and even dangerous to listen to BBC radio and AFN stations operating from England."

Paul Kuhn began entertaining GIs in service clubs and first styled European music in an international way. When famed broadcaster Mark White was stationed at AFN Munich, Paul was on the radio show "Midnight in Munich" and became acquainted with radio and show people.

"But our American employers furnished us with American sheet music, which included the latest hits, and on the back page of these 'Hit Kits' were standards like 'Tea for Two' and 'Smoke Gets In Your Eyes.' Over the following years I established a repertoire so that the education I gained at the time became very valuable. The music went from Dixieland to Jazz and Country and Western style, right up to the Broadway musical and music of the films."

Paul played the piano and sang, sometimes finding fellow musicians to team up in small combos with vibes, guitar, bass and drums. They followed the George Shearing style. Some of them were amateurs, and others emigrated from symphony orchestras and had to struggle with the emerging styles.

"After West Germany slowly restored to normal life, a budding recording industry turned out new German popular songs. One night during a gig at the Femina Bar in Berlin, a record producer listened to me and gave me a recording contract and induced me to record a ditty *Geben Sie dem Mann am Klavier noch ein Bier* ('Give the Fellow At the Piano Another Beer'), an Arthur Godfrey — 'She's Too Fat for Me' style song.

"It made the German Hit Parade and became a million seller for me and was followed by other hits of standards."

Paul's trip to the United States fortunately placed him in the company of jazz greats Toots Thielemans and George Shearing at the Embers where he "jammed" with them. "At Basin Street East I saw and heard Ella Fitzgerald, Oscar Peterson and Matt Dennis, who wrote the beautiful ' Angel Eyes.'"

Matt Dennis offered to help Paul start an American career, but Paul was already a popular performer in Germany and hesitated starting over again. Back in Germany, with headquarters in Cologne, Paul began writing arrangements, composed band orchestrations, and led a number of bands through studio work.

"It was the beginning of rock and roll, Max. I recorded 'Blue Suede Shoes' in German, even before Elvis made it a hit. On TV I did American and German songs where we wrote our own texts and music, giving me great public exposure."

As an arranger, Paul formulated his impressions of American music by listening to those V - discs while at AFN (Armed Forces Network) and playing for American service clubs, especially on songs like Frankie Laine's "That's My Desire." In 1968 Paul Kuhn was called to take over the *SFB Tanz Orcherter*, the dance band of radio and TV Free Berlin. On a monthly Saturday night show that was kept up for 12 years, he had a wonderful time. Visiting American movie stars regularly appeared on the show.

After the interview, Paul Kuhn and Max Wirz, February, 1999. *(Courtesy Nelly Wirz)*

"We presented swing and dance numbers and beautiful tunes from Broadway and Hollywood, all during which I laid the groundwork for my work with large orchestras and Big Bands. We contracted great sidemen like Carmen Jones on trumpet, Leo Wright on alto sax, the Swedish trombonist Orker Person and Rolf Erikson on trumpet and flugelhorn, both of whom played for Duke Ellington."

Most of these musicians who played in active orchestras in Germany in the seventies became bandleaders in their own right. Sax player Mad Man Max Greger, Willy Berking, Kurt Edelhagen, Erwin Lehn, Hugo Strasser, Werner Muller, and Horst Jankowski were some of the names Paul recalled. They all led their own orchestras starting in the fifties continuously right up to the eighties.

"All those Big Bands are gone now. The orchestras became too expensive to be carried. My SFB Big Band was dissolved in 1980. Today, Kurt Bong and his Big Band of the Heissische Rundfunk in Frankfurt is one of the last regulars on radio and TV. Max Greger, like me, is still doing private and commercial appearances. Heinz Schonberger from Frankfurt and his Main Stream Power Band put out a CD recently. There is also young Herb Herbolzheimer who does a wonderful job leading young musicians into Big Bands. There's a lot of talent around, including, as you know, Max, Thilo Wolf."

Today, when Paul has an engagement to perform, he picks up sidemen from a list of the best qualified soloists. Top quality is always assured. Changes in the 1980s forced Paul to lose his recording contract. Even well-known European vocalist Catarina Valente was without a recording contract. Record producers looked in other directions for different material.

"These days, if you think you have a song or product with a chance for success, you have to produce it yourself and find a distributor for it."

Along the way, Paul met and married his wife, Ute, who was a lead singer with Gunther Kalmann's Choir. They moved to Cologne where Ute organized a four girl group, The Ute Mann Singers. They sang earlier group successes "Rum and Coca Cola," "Sincerely," "On the Sunny Side of the Street" and others.

"I put a ten piece band together with two saxes, three trumpets, two trombones, piano and keyboard, just to keep expenses down. I wrote arrangements for dances and corporate events, and, when we got the chance, three or four of us would get together and play jazz. We even put out CDs. Then I accompanied Peter Alexander, the Austrian singer/entertainer, throughout Europe with the Ute Mann Singers. We toured 120 cities. It was a great time for us. We also slipped in a few jazz gigs here and there."

This has been Paul Kuhn's life for the last 15 years or so. He has recorded a CD recently with Kurt Bong and the Band of the Hessische Rundfunk in Frankfurt; "I played piano and jazzed it up at the piano with Kurt on drums."

There are not too many other young players besides Thilo Wolf who will take up the torch playing Big Bands sounds in Europe.

"The youngest I know would be Peter Herbholzheimer, who is one generation behind me. Peter is a wonderful teacher and everyone who graduates from his orchestra is an outstanding musician."

Paul smiles disconcertingly over the plight of the Big Bands. He hopes younger generations may rediscover our kind of music. "It was popular once, and we heard of a movement in the United States, but it may not come back in the same exact way. The new generation may experiment with it and bring it back."

In March of 1999, Paul Kuhn with his orchestra flew to Leipzig to perform in the venerable Gewandhaus, Germany's version of Carnegie Hall, followed by appearances in Switzerland and a gig at the Widder Bar in Zurich. While he skis the Alps, he will ponder his immediate future in music.

For you GIs who served in Germany during the late forties and fifties, know that the piano player you met and heard in the service clubs has become one of the really big band leaders over there. Paul Kuhn, like all the heroes written about within the covers of this book, *Jukebox Saturday Night*, carries on in the best tradition of the Big Band or Swing Era, and I can assure you that, whenever and wherever these great musicians perform, they will have the folks swinging and smiling.

THE NEW GENERATION
THILO WOLF AND ANDY PRIOR

THILO WOLF and His Orchestra

On the weekend of December 5-6, the roads between Frauenfeld in Switzerland and Furth in Bavaria would be covered with snow and ice. Fortunately, the 250 mile trip was made both ways without mishap. The goal? To meet and talk with young Thilo Wolf, the grooving and swinging jazz musician, who composes, arranges, plays drums and piano, who plays in small formations, and plays in and conducts his own Thilo Wolf Big Band.

Thilo Wolf, pianist, drummer, composer, arranger and leader of his own Trio, Quartet and The Thilo Wolf Big Band. *(Foto Dreier-Press)*

Born in Nuremberg, Germany in 1967, Thilo Wolf played the accordion by age nine. While listening to his dad's old swing albums, he composed his first piece of music at age ten. At sixteen, Thilo wrote his first Big Band arrangement, and at seventeen he won a prize for composing the sound track for a film. He went on to take drum lessons from Charlie Antolini, a foremost European drummer. Thilo also managed time for classical piano lessons and studied at the Friedrich-Alexander University in Erlangen-Nuremberg, graduating with a business administration degree. Upon his father's death, Thilo gradually took over the family business, The Eduard Wolf Werbung Exclusive Advertising Agency. He has successfully combined business with the music he loves to play.

Now thirty-one, here is Thilo Wolf, a national entertainment figure of great stature, and a host to great musicians and bandleaders such as Germany's Max Greger, Hugo Strasser, and Horst Jankowski, and America's Ray Anthony, and just two hours prior he and his Quartet performed a benefit concert in a lean-to, in near freezing weather at the Christkindle's Markt on the Waagplatz in Furth.

Thilo Wolf and his Quartet with friends Norbert Nagel, saxophone, Stephan Eppinger, drums and Christian Diener, bass playing in near freezing weather at the Christkindle's Markt in Fürth, Bavaria.

It was on the day of St.Nikolaus, and Thilo Wolf and I are sitting in his comfortable apartment talking about our kind of music.

"Yes, I am a musician first. Along the way, I have played the contra bass, banjo, guitar, clarinet, saxophone, all simply because it tempted me. Today, I am glad I have this experience.

"Although I'm not an expert on every instrument, it helps to know how they function and how they can be employed to create different sounds."

Thilo was brought up in the seventies and eighties, exposed to so much rock and roll. His idols, however, were not rock stars, but his father's heroes Glenn Miller, Benny Goodman, Hugo Strasser, and Max Greger, who all influenced him greatly.

"Of course, during high school, I played in a rock band, too," he confesses, "...and we had a lot of fun. And my peers wondered why I listened to Charlie Antolini instead of Kiss or The Rolling Stones."

Along the way Thilo decided for the Big Band sound. "I believe the combination of an education in classical music, which requires technical skills, discipline and exactness, combined with the musical freedom and flexibility inherent in jazz, are good tools that take you in different musical directions."

The Thilo Wolf Big Band during TV Show in Germany. *(Foto Günter B. Kögler)*

Thilo and I agreed that a Big Band jazz arrangement is much like a symphony in that the jazz musicians must also possess the training and skills to read music, write arrangements and intone, and must be disciplined about it. In addition, however, the soloist enjoys a certain freedom to open the music and form the beauty of jazz, where musical spontaneity plays a larger role than in classical music.

Thilo Wolf is a business man, but isn't music also a business?

"Music is very important to me, being more than an occupation, or even a *calling*; it's a vocation. Half of the music business consists of administration, schedules, rehearsals, set up and signing of contracts, travel arrangements, invoices and parcels to be mailed. I have a well functioning staff behind me. With all of this off your hands, I'm allowed a wide horizon to work within without pressure and restraints. The music side is writing arrangements, engaging musicians, investing time in rehearsals, thus I move from one office to another and become the musician. So when I am not with the music, then I devote normal hours to our thriving family business. It both works well."

Later that day, Thilo Wolf and his Quartet performed live practically in the snow, in near freezing temperatures.

"Between the Bratwurst roaster and the Gluhwein brewer, when the fingers get cold, we just take a slug of Gluhwein and play a little faster."

The quartet started these benefit performances when Thilo was fifteen and have been doing them ever since. The two hour concerts have become a tradition.

Thilo Wolf will move into spring with a Big Band CD and a television concert with the Windsbach Boys Choir (Windsbacher Knabenchor), interesting and challenging for an otherwise ecclesiastical choir's adventure in jazz, a new kind of crossover. The future for Thilo Wolf and his music will continue to be inspiring and adventurous well into the New Millennium.

ANDY PRIOR and His Orchestra

I first met Andy Prior on a sunny afternoon in the Spring of 1995 at Pontin's Big Band Centre in Lowestoft, England. We sat outside our chalet, enjoying an unusual warm British sun and talked about Big Bands, our kind of music. Andy was thirty-two then and already a veteran of sixteen years as a professional musician and twelve years as an active Big Band leader. Appearing with his Night Owls that evening, Andy talked about his career as a trombone player, singer, and being the youngest bandleader touring the British Isles.

"I was born in Leigh, Lancashire, from a home filled with music. My dad was a bandleader, too, and my mother was trained as an opera singer."

Beginning in 1983 Andy formed the Night Owls.

"I was just twenty, and my boys were even younger than I. We did about 140 appearances every year, performing for dances, for radio and

TV and recording dates. I was in charge of everything for the band, even the business portion securing concerts and contracts, and even arranging for the buses."

It would have been more natural for Andy Prior to follow rock and roll, considering the time, but rock and roll offered no challenge. He would rather have conducted a large symphony orchestra, but settled down to a Big Band, which is just his size to manage and to be comfortable with.

Let us hear now, some four years later in 1999, how things have changed for Andy Prior, as he tours with his new show Andy Prior and "The Magic of Sinatra Tour."

Suffering through a series of head colds, Andy Prior and his Orchestra are still going about their business. "We have completed about 65 performances of The "Magic of Sinatra" show, with about 15 to go. Performing at Birmingham Symphony Hall was very special. We were there for two nights in a row, about 2,000 seats were filled each night. On the smaller size the crowds numbered about 500. In Glasgow, Scotland, however, one show commanded over 3,000 people. Our performance in the London Palladium was also a memorable, but strange experience."

Expecting to be a bit nervous performing at the

Andy Prior on "The Magic of Sinatra" tour, 1998. *(Max Wirz Collection)*

199

Palladium, Andy wasn't anxious at all, probably due to the momentum of the tour. But, everyone was surely excited thinking about the big names who have performed in that venerable hall.

"It's funny, at dances you expect people to shout, or to talk to us. But in the concert hall, there is a different discipline altogether."

Andy's "Magic of Sinatra Tour" received great praise from Big Bands International Magazine critic Jean Magg, writing, "Andy Prior himself is a self-assured personality with a 'sock it to em' approach and he doesn't pretend to be another Sinatra."

So how does the audience accept that precept: "It takes quite a while, about an hour into the show before they accept it. Then I just hammer it out. After twenty years, Max, I have the right to stand up there and sing his kind of music, but, as myself."

Andy probably sang more hours in front of a Big Band than most other singers. And the other fact with the Sinatra thing is, "Why do they say, 'that's it, it can't be taken any further,' when the truth is Frank Sinatra himself wanted us to take it further? He wanted us to listen to what he had done and try to do it better, not to emulate it, but to try and build on what he had given us. Very few people do that."

It turns out that Bryan Pendleton writes Andy Prior's arrangements, which include many Glenn Miller charts. His arrangements are always exciting and fresh. "There is one golden rule, Max, and that is melody. There must be a melody that everybody can hear. If they can hum it, if they can sing it, they'll like it."

Oddly, Andy never chooses music that musicians like (he laughs).

"A long time ago I asked every band member to pick their favorite. We pulled the sheets from the pad, had a look at them, took them out of our chart book, and said to them, 'If you like those, nobody else will!'" (We both laughed.)

Andy has several women in his band, including trumpeter Georgina Bromilow, who is only 22, as well as vocalist Donna Canale. Interestingly, his musicians are all younger than he.

"Yeah…and I still believe it has to be that way, so I can bully them." to more laughs.

After the Sinatra tour, Andy heads to America and Las Vegas, followed by a vacation at Disneyland in Florida. It will be all for pleasure, no business. The band will not tour America and has exhausted Britain with over 80 shows in different theaters and cities. "The national media doesn't do much to help the Big Bands in England," according to Andy, "Television will not support musical activities except for the 'Top of the Pops' show. Being a realist, I believe we may only go to Europe and into Japan, but unfortunately not the United States."

The Big Bands cannot compete with country and rock and roll there. Andy believes that Big Band music has its place, but needs marketing to succeed again. Andy is in the throes of contracts with a recording company. Bryan Pendleton, with another arranger, will experiment in new recordings, adding a French horn, an extra keyboard, and a guitar. The keyboard is used only as a bridge for new technology "pad sound," a new modern sound, like George Shearing once created with his piano, vibraphone and electric guitar back in the fifties.

"Nelson Riddle once did an arrangement of Ray Noble's 'The Very Thought of You' using vibraphone, celeste and glockenspiel. With a keyboard we have all of this at a touch of a button. We should embrace this new technology and use it to our advantage."

As to what happened to Andy's original Night Owls, he explained it this way: "Oh, it's the same band, you know. I just changed the music stands. Max, if you know anybody who wants to buy the name, I will sell it for a small fee. We now use *Andy Prior and his Orchestra*."

Andy wishes other bands would also move forward paying more attention to stage presence, production, lighting and the whole presentation of the show.

"People need to see a show," he says, "To borrow a title from Irving Berlin, we have to go back to 'Puttin' On the Ritz.'"

I see Big Bands sprouting up all over the place like dandelions in my back yard. There may be a music teacher, a marching band conductor, or a professional musician who likes swing music and goes out and recruits 16 to 18 young people, like the members in Andy Prior's band, and performs the charts of a Miller, Dorsey, or Basie band and makes the crowds go wild.

Is it happening all over again? Andy Prior is certainly a great example of such a success. Andy occupies a unique place in Big Band music. He wants to replace nostalgia with a new beginning.

"Singing and bandleading a large orchestra is like holding (back) an avalanche," Andy explains, "The hairs stand up on the back of your neck and the orchestra is like a big volcano behind you. It's raw power, but controlled power."

Keep a watch on Thilo Wolf and Andy Prior as they bring their music into the new Millennium.

Ray Anthony, Big Band Legend, and **Andy Prior**, successful young English Big Band Leader who will take "our kind of music" into and through the next century! July 26th, 1998. Swallow Hotel, Birmingham, England.

PART FIVE

Jack and Dot Ellsworth take a moment for cameraman Bob DeBetta.

ANATOMY OF A BIG BAND RADIO STATION

On the Top of the AM Dial

First there was Marconi, then crystal radio sets, followed by New York City's WNEW. Then out on Long Island a former U.S. Marine Corps Combat Correspondent, Jack Ellsworth, planted his daily ten-til-noon disc jockey show "Memories in Melody" on radio station WALK enduring for some thirty years, and, when the station went Top 40, Jack, his wife Dot, and his newscaster partner, George Drake, established WLIM radio where they have been dispensing Big Band music ever since for a total of 50 years. The first anniversary of the station was enthusiastically celebrated with an appearance of Larry Elgart and his Hooked On Swing orchestra, and the second produced the entire Glenn Miller Orchestra under its present leader, Larry O'Brien, who began leading that legendary group for the first time that very year.

During the ensuing years right up to the present, Jack has interviewed a long list of Big Band personalities on-the-air, including Bing Crosby and Frank Sinatra. Frank Sinatra wrote a letter to Jack on April 15, 1997, saying,

"We've traveled many musical miles together, my friend. I am delighted to send cheers and bravos to you on 50 marvelous years of championing our kind of music.

"As I raise a glass of bubbly, I thank you for your generous support of my career — you're a good man!"

Jack's Sunday morning Sinatra show has been on the air for over 50 years, perhaps the longest running Sinatra show on the airwaves.

When WNEW, which housed the famous, ground-breaking "Make Believe Ballroom" show first with Martin Block and ending with William B. Williams in 1986, tuned out their good music forever in 1992, radio station WQEW took over with the same personalities except William B., who earlier had suddenly passed away. On January 1, 1999, WQEW reluctantly gave way to a Walt Disney tiny-tot radio show, leaving the field wide open. WVNJ in New Jersey, *Music of Your Life* station WLUX in Farmingdale, WHLI in Hempstead, WRTN in New Rochelle, and especially the evergreen WLIM became the keepers of the flame — the survivors. WLIM is not really typical, because they strive to stick to the pure stuff and not insert too many peripheral intrusions like Glen Campbell, Pat Boone, or preferred Beach Boys, Elvis or Beatles. WLIM works closest to the original WNEW formula, and, although it's a small station whose signals reach most of Long Island, Southern Connecticut, right down to the New Jersey shore, it is certainly the purest. That is precisely why Frank Sinatra consistently endorsed Jack Ellsworth and his *Memories in Melody* program over the years with unique recorded promotionals.

With the publication of each of my books *The Best Damn Trumpet Player*, *The Song Stars*, and *The Music Men*, Jack invited me to the station to share airtime and to apprise his audience of the books and just how they developed. The response was always terrific.

Jack Ellsworth meets his hero Bing Crosby in September of 1944 at a Bob Hope USO show in California. *(Jack Ellsworth Collection)*

Here is Jack's story:

"In 1941, I received a phone call from popular jock Art Ford, who later had an all-night show on WNEW called the "Milkman's Matincc." Art was running a Bing Crosby show on station WBNX in the Bronx, and he had heard I had a great Crosby record collection. He asked me to bring them up to his studio. I was a teenager and very impressionable. I was thrilled to be a radio show guest."

Jack became a frequent visitor on Art's show, talking about all the greats. Smitten with the radio bug while at Brown University in 1947, Jack hosted a show on campus, using his Art Ford credentials. There was no monetary compensation, but he thoroughly enjoyed spinning the 78's that so influenced his life.

"I applied for a disc jockey job with a station that had a WNEW-style format and got the job. After three years of top ratings, I accepted a similar position at WVNJ in Newark, New Jersey, and in 1950 I heard about a station in Huntington, Long Island, called WGSM, and obtained a job there doing the same stuff. One year later finally I finally settled in Patchogue, on the south shore of Long Island, at WALK.

Along the way Jack appeared on many soap operas and on several other radio stations as an announcer or actor, including a TV appearance on the "Colgate Comedy Hour" on NBC's local station WNBT in New York.

"I met my wife, Dot, in 1951 and married her in November. Dot was a legal secretary in the same building as the radio station. We soon relocated to the quaint, adjacent Village of Bellport, and I began work as Program Director-Broadcaster for WALK."

In 1963 Jack was promoted to Station Manager, and in 1975 he became President, General Manager and CEO.

"I worked closely with many great people including Chet Huntley, the famous NBC commentator and news anchor, who was one of the owners of the station, and Edward J. Wood, Jr., a partner in the station who was clearly my mentor."

Jack's show was always "sold out" and received excellent ratings. During the thirty years at WALK, Jack interviewed heavyweights Bing Crosby, Frank Sinatra, Benny Goodman, Doris Day, Dick Haymes, Les Paul and Mary Ford and many other great performers. Jack's knowledge of American music, particularly the Swing era, is remarkable. The content of some of his classic, intimate interviews are considered fascinating, as well as entertaining.

"In 1980 WALK was sold. Dot and I, along with our colleague, newsman George Drake, tried to purchase the station to continue our work, but we were outbid."

Undaunted, the group purchased what was to become WLIM and took their "act" across town. Many sponsors and most of his listeners followed. That was nineteen years ago.

"There's uniqueness in radio," Jack says,"When I put on Glenn's "Moonlight Serenade," I could cry from its solemn beauty. People can close their eyes and take themselves back in their life when they first heard the classic tune, or any favorite recording that punctuated their lives. It's great therapy, and always pleasant listening, unlike the frenetic music of today."

Unlike most broadcasters who spin records on the air, Jack knows who all the performers are and everything else about any record he plays on the air. He is familiar with all the greats and the lesser-known musicians who perform on the recordings. Jack regularly writes about the participants of the Big Band Era and beyond, and reviews re-issues and current works of "our kind of music," as Sinatra described it, in a number of regional publications.

Jack Ellsworth takes a drum lesson from Gene Krupa. *(Jack Ellsworth Collection)*

As former WNEW/WQEW disc jockey Jonathan Schwartz once opined, "I think it's criminal to go on the air without an intimate knowledge of every record by each of the artists. Not only one album but every album. Every song on the albums. Every note." Jack fulfills that decree on WLIM. He expects and gets just that from his on-air employees.

I remember back in 1983 when Jack invited me to interview band-leader Ray Anthony at the station. Ray was totally impressed with Jack's music library consisting of several hundred thousand classics; those recordings directly representing all the music of the thirties, forties, fifties, and right up to the CDs of the nineties. I also participated with Jack and Dot in *Benny Goodman Day* at WLIM, when Jack was able to arrange to have the great clarinetist/bandleader come to the station and spend several hours on the air, while Jack spun Goodman records and interviewed his old friend.

"Benny, how do you feel about WLIM playing your recordings all day?" Jack asked Goodman while on-the-air.

"Well, if you can stand it, I guess I can," Goodman quipped back. We all enjoyed a good laugh.

While on-the-air Jack regularly receives calls from people like Glenn Miller's Larry O'Brien to '50s singer Julius La Rosa, who sometimes rides out to visit the station from his home above New York City.

Jack, known as the "Silver Fox" with his snow-white hair, and Dotty have two handsome sons, Gary and Glenn, and a lovely daughter Susan. The three have presented their parents with eight grandchildren. Dot and Jack feel very blessed, indeed.

Jack and George have also hired some pretty talented voices to fill their airtime, and when WGSM moved into country music, popular disc jockey Gil Ellis brought his popular show to WLIM. Gil, who counts William B. Williams and Jack Ellsworth as his mentors, does exclusive on-air interviews with both veteran and currently popular performers and features their music while they hang on the phone or hang out in the studio.

GIL ELLIS

"My parents were always associated with show business. Mom was a Ziegfeld Follies showgirl and appeared in Earl Carroll's *Vanities* on Broadway. Dad was a theatrical attorney with MGM. Thanks to Dad, I found myself spending summers at comedian Ben Blue's home in California, where Ben and I were picked up each morning by legendary comedian Red Skelton and driven to the studio where they were making the film *Panama Hattie*. Gil studied

Gil Ellis at WLIM's mike. *(Richard Grudens Collection)*

trumpet at Tulane University, had his own sextet, and briefly played with Charlie Barnet and Harry James as a pickup musician and with Stan Kenton as a band regular at the Hollywood Palladium and

Rendezvous Ballroom in Balboa, California, before heading for the broadcasting booth.

"I got my first important job in broadcasting by clipping a newspaper ad advertising for an News Anchor and landed the job, but quickly switched to disc jockey because it paid better and was more fun." A writer friend told Gil he made people feel so good while he was on the air, so he labeled him "The Medicine Man."

"I liked it, I used it, and it stuck. Friends of mine, Big Band arranger Ron Aprea and vocalist Angela De Niro, wrote and multi-track recorded my show theme, and I have used it ever since, opening every show:"

Listen to the Gil Ellis Show
Go On and Tell Everyone You Know
The Music's Just the Thing
On the Gil Ellis Show
The Medicine Man Named Gil
Can Cure Your Every Ill
He'll Harmonize Your Dreams
With Your Favorite Themes,
On the Gil Ellis Show
You Can Sing and Dance While You Listen
To Sarah, Bennett, and More
Sinatra, Basie, and Ella
All Will Guide You Cross the Floor
There's a Secret Singer's Game
With a Star That You Can Name
And His Interviews
Will Chase Your Blues Away
On The Gil Ellis Show

Gil's feature, Secret Celebrity Singer, is unique. He plays rare recordings of non-singers singing, beckoning listeners to call in to try to identify them, the winner earning a prize.

"Two of the most difficult singers for listeners to identify were Alan Ladd and Orson Welles. Sometimes we keep a Secret Celebrity Singer on for as much as two weeks before someone calls in with the right answer." Gil scans old radio shows and keeps a stash of un-aired voic-

209

es for future broadcasts, hardly ever repeating a voice. Gil's listeners surprisingly range in age from 20 to 80, with 40 year olds in lighter numbers. Reflecting, Gil says it's important to program an abundance of music that comes from shows and motion pictures, "All of those great songs that come out of the shows and movies, because it crosses all age lines. They can be played by Artie Shaw and Les Brown, and sung by Sinatra. I would never change that, but the selections should change, and all disc jockeys should be instructed to acquire detailed information about the performers and the music they feature while on the air."

Afternoon man, bearded, brilliant Bob Stern, plays Broadway material as well as Big Bands. Bob's knowledge of the songwriters and the songs are legendary. Former WNEW — and later WQEW disc jockey and songwriter (The Green Door) Jim Lowe has joined the WLIM team with a Sunday afternoon show "Jim Lowe and Friends" on which there is "live" as well as recorded material.

Around the country famous broadcasters Fred Hall, Chuck Cecil, Joe Franklin, Jonathan Schwartz, and Mike Prelee have regularly dispensed the same kind of music over the years with the same kind of success. Californian Chuck Cecil has recently celebrated 42 years with his nationally syndicated show "Swinging Years," while veteran broadcaster Fred Hall has run his show "Swing Thing" for almost the same period of time. Don Kennedy of *Big Band Jump* fame also hosts the same kind of music from Atlanta, Georgia, over a nationwide group of stations from New York to Los Angeles, including WLIM, and produces a newsletter for his many subscribers that reviews CDs and books; presents interviews of bandleaders, sidemen, and vocalists; and provides anecdotes and background stories about key personalities.

Former WNEW newsman Mike Prelee has contributed to the cause with his WVNJ show "In the Spotlight," spinning records and interviewing such greats as Mel Tormé, Margaret Whiting, and Kitty Kallen. Young host Chris Valenti takes requests on his Garden City, New York WHPC-FM "Big Band Broadcast," and interviews musical greats from Tex Beneke to Doris Day, as well. George Kalman intends to beef up WLIM type music at WNJR, Newark, New Jersey's Riverfront Plaza

210

radio station, with, I just learned, Julius La Rosa signed to host "Make Believe Ballroom."

There are now (and were then), many exemplary broadcasters out there who showcase the precious, familiar music we all know and cherish: Joe Franklin, one of the best interviewers ever; California's great Whit Whittinghill; former WNEW "Purple Grotto" caretaker, and later KSFO San Francisco disc jockey, Al "Jazzbeaux" Collins, (who is portrayed in my book *The Song Stars*); Chuck Niles, a friend of Woody Herman, who has been dispensing pure jazz in the LA area on KLON-Radio for 43 years and has a star on the Hollywood Walk of Fame; and too many more to mention here.

Still Jack Ellsworth personifies the sobriquet *disc jockey*. His station WLIM and "Memories in Melody" program endures.

The benefits are ours. So keep listening.

A modest home with a powerful voice — WLIM, Long Island radio 1580 AM. *(Courtesy Robert DeBetta)*

HONORABLE MENTIONS

JOHN HAMMOND was the quintessential jazz fan. He loved jazz and blues. He was born wealthy and used his own money to produce records and encourage musicians and vocalists. In the thirties, John worked for Columbia Records and produced recordings with Fletcher Henderson, Billie Holiday, Bessie Smith, and later Benny Goodman. Benny married John's sister, Alice. Besides shaping the careers of artists like Holiday, Basie, and Goodman, he also later uncovered the talents of Pete Seeger, Aretha Franklin, Bob Dylan, and Bruce Springsteen.

John Hammond was important to jazz, and thus to popular music. He traveled endlessly all over the world to sell Big Band music.

FRANKIE CARLE started his career with **Mal Hallett's** band from New England with members **Gene Krupa** and **Jack Teagarden**. He credits his mother for his success, "She made me practice two to three hours a day ——even at lunch time and after school, for a total of sixteen years." **Horace Heidt** featured Frankie with top billing for four years and even suggested that he form his own band. "My first theater date with my own band was in April, the same year I opened at the Pennsylvania Hotel playing my top hit 'Sunrise Serenade' which I wrote.

"A fellow named **Bill Lackenbaugh** asked me to write something different, so I composed 'Sunrise Serenade' for him to publish. He became my lifelong friend. You see, no publisher in New York, including **Jack Mills** of Mills Music, wanted it because it was different."

His song, that became his famous theme, was originally introduced by the Casa Loma Orchestra at New York's Waldorf-Astoria Hotel. You can find it on the original 78, with "Moonlight Serenade" on the "A" side. "So many people have recorded that tune of mine, even from foreign countries. Why, even **Ray Charles** recorded it," Frankie said with pride.

Frankie Carle's piano has been a musical institution for many years. "I'm going to play until the man upstairs says it's time to quit. I still get mail every day, even more than I did when I had my band going. I still practice an hour or so each day, because I like to keep playing to keep my ear tuned."

Frankie Carle is well over 90 and living in Phoenix, Arizona, from where we talked to him.

KEN PATTERSON'S PITTSBURGH MUSICIANS

An old friend **Ken Patterson** brought me up-to-speed on a group of musicians he circulates with in his Pittsburgh, Pennsylvania neighborhood. "Pittsburgh has contributed many musicians to the Big Bands, such as **Billy May**, **Earl 'Fatha' Hines**, **Dodo Marmarosa**, and **Billy Eckstine**." How about this roster of Big Band alumni: **Bob Boswell**, acoustic bass with Louis Jordan; **Bob Cardillo** played piano with Ina Ray Hutton; **Ray Crummie** did his piano tricks with Ray Anthony's Navy band. **Danny Conn** blew trumpet with Clyde McCoy, Hal McIntyre, and Claude Thornhill; **Dave LaRocca**, acoustic bass with Woody Herman and Buddy Rich; and **Vince Lascheid** hammered his ivories with my friend Tex Beneke; **Joe Negri** strummed guitar with Shep Fields; **Dave Pew** blew trumpet with Raymond Scott and Henry Busse's orchestras, and **Rodger Ryan** played drums with Woodie's Herds. All these guys are still active in radio and TV and with local symphonies. And Dave Pew's wife sang with some bands as **Marcy Lynn**.

"With the exception of a 100 piece symphony orchestra, there is nothing to compare to the enormous precision of a 17 piece Big Band," according to Ken, "We are fortunate to have lived through that wonderful time." **Benny Goodman** labeled today's music "amplified junk." Thanks, Ken, for all you do for the Big Bands.

BILLY MAY

As I write this, I learned from Stan Kenton trombonist and Big Band Academy President **Milt Bernhart** last month that **Billy May** was in the hospital. We talked with Billy for my recent book, *The Music Men*, but mostly concerning his arranging career. Billy May also led a terrific Big Band. He's the guy that arranged "Cherokee" for **Charlie Barnet** and that beautiful opening, that I love so much, for **Glenn**

Billy May and his orchestra at the Pennsylvania Hotel, New York, 1952.

Miller's recording of "Serenade in Blue." For those two gems alone, Billy would deserve honors in the Big Band Hall of Fame.

Billy's band turned out the massive Time-Life re-creations of Big Band recordings, utilizing original arrangements and leading the band itself. Billy May organized his first band in 1952, late for Big Bands. Earlier, he spent a lot of time with Charlie Barnet. "I worked for Charlie for two years. That was in 1939 in New York. On the day Roosevelt was elected President, I joined Glenn Miller. I was in the trumpet section, but I also played solos that Glenn asked me to do. I did lots of arranging for him, too, with **Jerry Gray** and **Bill Finegan**."

After two years on the road, Billy tired of bandleading, and the band, financed by **Ray Anthony**, was turned over to **Sam Donohue**. Billy May settled in Hollywood and worked for films and television, where he was in great demand. Billy recently traveled to London with **Les Brown** and Ray Anthony for a BBC re-union of sorts. Our own **Max Wirz** went along to interview Billy and Les, and snapped some great photos, too.

214

GENE KRUPA

The **Gene Krupa** story began in Chicago on January 15, 1909. The youngest of nine children reared in the Polish section of town, Gene attended Catholic school and worked in a music store on weekends, arousing his early interest in music.

His second job was in a dance hall where he gained his first experience playing saxophone in a junior band called The Frivolians; he soon developed an interest in playing drums. Like a plot in a movie, the drummer called in sick one night and Gene took over. At St. Joseph's College, a preparatory seminary in Indiana, Gene was encouraged by a priest, a professor of music who liked jazz. Instead of becoming a priest, Gene turned to music, and sought the help of percussion instructor Roy Knapp, who helped him improve his playing.

Impressed with other jazz musicians of the era, Gene Krupa gathered momentum: "I learned from **Zutty Singleton** and **Baby Dodds**, who taught me the difference between starting a roll or sequence of beats with the left or right hand and how the tone and inflection changed entirely when you shifted hands."

Taking a hint from what he heard, Gene worked out on tom-toms to get them in tune and learned when to implement them. "I punched holes in them with an ice-pick," he said.

Gene worked the local bands, making his first recording in 1927, impressing those who hired him so much that they acknowledged it marked the arrival of a new force in jazz drumming. Gene emigrated to New York City and found work in Broadway pit-bands, where **George Gershwin** applauded his percussion efforts in two of his musicals, *Girl Crazy* and *Strike Up the Band.*

Working in **Red Nichols'** Five Pennies band, Gene played in recording sessions alongside jazz artists **Jack Teagarden**, **Benny Goodman**, **Jimmy Dorsey** and **Glenn Miller**. Trecking uptown, Gene would jam with drummers **Chick Webb** and **Big Sid Catlett** in Harlem jazz clubs.

His most important career move was joining up with Benny Goodman, replacing **Stan King**. At **Red Norvo's** house in Forest Hills, Queens, Goodman; Krupa; **Bessie Smith**; Red's wife, **Mildred Bailey**; and neighbor Red Nichols would all get together and play. This was where Benny got the idea for his small groups. In both the small and large Goodman bands, Gene contributed heavily with his personality, good-looks, drive and exuberance, becoming a super star under the Goodman umbrella of success.

The immensely successful Benny Goodman Carnegie Hall concert in 1938 was the highlight of Gene's career. Gene formed his own band after leaving Benny, making his debut in Atlantic City in 1938 on the Steel Pier.

Anita O'Day, who recorded regularly when she sang with Krupa, told me in early 1999 that her happiest and best years with a band were with Gene Krupa.

"He allowed me to sing things my way. Gene was a groovy guy and didn't like flat ballads or heavy upbeat things. He was smooth as jazz." Anita's recorded some hip ballads like "Skylark," swing things like "Stompin' At the Savoy," and with **Roy Eldridge**, a tune called "Let Me Off Uptown," the band's biggest hit and biggest moment.

Anita, one of the best jazz vocalists ever, will be singing it at Lincoln Center in New York in June, 1999, when she appears with the **Manhattan Transfer** singing group, among others.

Gene Krupa was one of the brightest and most popular personalities of the Big Band Era, enjoying fame as a movie star, appearing is The Glenn Miller Story and The Benny Goodman Story as himself. After spending some time in jail for drug-related problems, he continued on to become one of the most beloved bandleaders. Actor **Sal Mineo** played the role of Gene Krupa in the 1959 movie *Drum Crazy, The Gene Krupa Story.*

We lost Gene Krupa in 1973.

SAMMY KAYE
The Swing and Sway Band.

In 1945, the top three *Billboard* artists were Number 1 — **Bing Crosby** with 1,428 votes, Number 2 — **Sammy Kaye** with 855 votes, Number 3 — **Harry James** with 785 votes. **Frank Sinatra** came in 4th with 731 votes. In 1946 **Sammy Kaye** was Number 4, and was back in the Number 3 spot once again in 1947. In the later world of music, that would be equal to a Madonna, Beatles, Rolling Stones, or Elvis Presley. No easy task for a Big Band in any era.

Did you know that Sammy Kaye had more hit records than any other Big Band in history? Well, neither did I until I contacted Robert De Mars and Timothy Pierce of West Palm Beach, Florida, who are keeping the Sammy Kaye legacy of music going through The Sammy Kaye & Big Band Archives. Remember his beloved renditions of "My Blue Heaven," "Sometimes I'm Happy," "Carolina Moon," "Stardust," "On the Street of Regret," "Chickery Chick," "I'm a Big Girl Now," "I Left My Heart At the Stage Door Canteen," "The Old Lamp Lighter," "Harbor Lights," "Laughing On The Inside," "It Isn't Fair "(sung by music man Don Cornell), and his ensemble hit, Bobby Troup's "Daddy," plus too many more to list here.

The fact is, jazz fans not withstanding, that Sammy Kaye was the number one band from 1945 to 1949. Kaye's was a "sweet band" — a gentle, rhythmic, danceable Big Band. Sammy could play the clarinet, violin, trumpet, saxophone, banjo and guitar. He led a dance band in college called Sammy's Hot Peppers, circa 1932. His later band was compared to **Guy Lombardo's**, and earned him gigs at New York's Essex House and the Commodore Hotel, providing plenty of visibility for the band. Appearances at the Paramount Theater followed, then a national tour, which broke cross-country records wherever they played. The band broke attendance records at Frank Dailey's Meadowbrook in the days of their hit recordings of "Rosalie" and "Love Walked In."

Influenced by the **Kay Kyser** and **Gus Arnheim** Bands, Sammy Kaye featured song titles at the start of each record. On the "Old Gold Program," "The Chesterfield Supper Club" radio show, and "So You Want To Lead a Band" show, Sammy devised a novel innovation. He would allow eager members of the audience the chance to become the bandleader. At the conclusion of each session, Sammy would autograph the participants baton and present it as a gift to the "leader" of the moment. The show graduated to television in the 1950s, paving the way for **Lawrence Welk's** great success.

Among some other tunes, Sammy Kaye composed the wartime hit "Remember Pearl Harbor" and "Kaye's Melody." And, remember his excellent vocalist, Song Star **Nancy Norman**? Some of her hits were

"Walkin' With My Baby," "As Time Goes By," "There Goes That Song Again," "I'll Buy That Dream," "Chickery Chick," "Gotta Be This or That," and "There Will Never Be Another You," a treasure trove of wonderful, listenable recordings performed as well as any lady vocalist of the era.

Over the years of the Big Band Era, millions listened and danced to Sammy Kaye's Swing and Sway Orchestra. Were you one of them?

BILL ELLIOT SWING ORCHESTRA

One of the new bands around is the **Bill Elliot** Swing Orchestra from California with featured singer **Amy Weston**, **Paul Weston** and **Jo Stafford's** lovely daughter. Bill performed his charts in England at Pontin's as a guest of **Chris Dean** and his **Syd Lawrence** band. Bill's music has been featured in the films *Independence Day*, *Nixon*, *Dick Tracy*, and *Sticks*, as well as on the TV show "Northern Exposure." His band played in the Disney films *Aladdin* and *That Darn Cat*. **Michael Feinstein** has sung with the band. On Catalina Island, Bill Elliot and his band have played the famed Avalon Ballroom.

KAY KYSER

Some of you may remember the Ol' Professor **Kay Kyser** and his "Kollege of Musical Knowledge" radio program. It was a mixture of musical trivia and some great swing music and novelty tunes set in rhythm by vocalists **Harry Babbitt**, **Ginny Simms**, and **Merwyn Bogue**, known as **Ish Kabibble**, who sang most of the comedy songs.

Their top recordings were "Three Little Fishes," "Two Sleepy People," "Praise the Lord and Pass the Ammunition," "Why Don't We Do This More Often," and "Jingle, Jangle, Jingle." Kay

"Evenin' Folks! How y'all?" Kay Kyser's familiar greeting. *(Richard Grudens Collection)*

toured the USO camps and traveled to the Pacific war theater to enter-tain the troops. He appeared in two significant films *Stage Door Canteen* and *Thousands Cheer*.

The bands last two hits were one of my favorites, "Slow Boat To China," and "The Woody Woodpecker Song" both in the late forties. Kay Kyser, whose real name was James King Kern Kyser, retired in the early fifties, when he felt he was no longer wanted by the public and also needed to quit because of adverse health.

MITCH MILLER

Mitchell William Miller was eighty-eight years young on July 4, 1999. You may safely say that if it weren't for Mitch Miller, much pop-ular music of the 1950s and 60s would have taken a different course with different players.

An oboist, record producer, arranger, and himself an important, commercially successful recording artist, Mitch Miller learned to play

Mitch Miller and Frankie Laine listen to playback at recording session, 1952. *(Courtesy Downbeat Magazine)*

piano by the age of six. He studied oboe at twelve, and attended The Eastman School of Music in Rochester, New York.

By 1932, Mitch played oboe with symphony orchestras. CBS hired him to play with music director Andre Kostelanetz, one of the best light classical orchestras ever, and Percy Faith.

In the late forties, Mitch became director of Mercury Records, where he was responsible for producing Frankie Laine's "That Lucky Old Sun," "Mule Train," and "Cry of the Wild Goose," and conducted the orchestra on Laine's "Jezebel" and my favorite Laine recording, "Rose, Rose, I Love You."

Frankie Laine and I talked about Mitch Miller in late 1998.

"At Mercury, Mitch became the new kid on the block. He was a classical guy, and I figured 'What's a guy like him going to do for me?' I soon found out he was smart and eager for advice, and a great story-teller. Mitch demonstrated a talent for setting off voices in original, if not downright quirky, musical settings. Who else would've put a harpsichord on a Rosemary Clooney record, or backed Guy Mitchell with swooping French horns?

"After working with one another and getting to understand our mutual needs, Mitch came up with a song that he considered a combination of 'Old Man River' and 'Black and Blue.' We took it over to my piano accompanist and friend Carl Fischer's house and listened to it. The title was 'That Lucky Old Sun.' It was a change of pace for me, but it was a fantastic song and I decided it would be a good way to begin our association. The rest, as they say, is history."

When he moved to Columbia as A& R man, Mitch selected the songs "Singing the Blues" for Guy Mitchell, "Cold, Cold Heart" for Tony Bennett, "Half as Much" and "Come On-a-My House" for Rosemary Clooney, "Cry" for Johnnie Ray, and "Just Cryin' In the Rain", and "Two Purple Shadows" for Jerry Vale, and "American Beauty Rose" for Frank Sinatra. Not a bad list of hits. Mitch and Frank Sinatra did not get along very well, so Guy Mitchell wound up with hits that otherwise would've been Sinatra's.

Mitch Miller's own hit recordings with his Mitch Miller and the Gang begun in 1950 with his adaptation of the Israeli folk song "Tzena, Tzena, Tzena" with a choral background; it became his signature. Songs like "The Yellow Rose of Texas" and "The Children's Marching Song" from the film *The Inn of The Sixth Happiness* were great Miller successes.

I tried in vain to talk at length to Mitch Miller in January, 1999. He just wasn't interested in talking much about himself, citing that at 88, I guess, he has said it all too many times to too many interviewers over all the years. Today, Mitch Miller spends his time mainly directing George Gershwin works in symphony halls. A very noble endeavor, bringing him back to his early classical roots.

JUKEBOX SATURDAY NIGHT

BIBLIOGRAPHY

Belcher, Roy, Editor. *Big Bands International Newsletter*, Reading Berkshire, England. Various dates.

Dooner, Roger, and Maurice Dunn. *Dick Haymes Society Newsletters*. Birmingham, England, and Minneapolis, Minn: Dick Haymes Society, Various Dates.

Downbeat Magazine. *Various Articles and/or Reviews*. New York, N.Y. 1950-1954

Ellington, Edward Kennedy. *Music is My Mistress*. New York: Doubleday & Co., 1973.

Erlewine, Michael, Editor. *All Music Guide to Jazz*. San Francisco, Cal.: 1996.

Feather, Leonard, and Ira Gitler. *The Encyclopedia of Jazz*. New York: Horizon Press, 1976.

Hall, Fred. *Diagogues In Swing*. Ventura, Ca.: Pathfinder Publishing, 1989.

Hall, Fred. *More Dialogues In Swing*. Ventura, Ca.: Pathfinder Publishing, 1991.

Harris, Jay S. *TV Guide: The First 25 Years*. New York: Simon and Schuster, 1978.

Haskins, Jim. *The Cotton Club*. New York: Hippocrene Books, 1977.

Hope, Bob, and Pete Martin. *The Last Christmas Show*. New York: Doubleday & Co., 1974.

Kennedy, Don, and Hagan Williams. *Big Band Jump Newsletter*. Atlanta, Ga: Various Dates.

Krivine, J., *Jukebox Saturday Night*. Secaucus, New Jersey: Chartwell Books Inc., Div. Book Sales Inc. 1977.

Laine, Frankie, and Joseph F. Laredo. *That Lucky Old Sun*. Ventura, Cal: Pathfinder Publishing, 1993.

Loescher, Greg, Editor. *Goldmine Magazine*. Iola, Wisconsin, January 29, 1999.

Palmer, Tony. *All You Need is Love: The Story of Popular Music*. New York: Grossman Publishers, 1976.

Pleasants, Henry. *The Great American Popular Singers*. New York: Simon and Schuster, 1974.

Rust, Brian. *The Complete Entertainment Discography*. New Rochelle, New York: Arlington House, 1973.

Settel, Irving. *A Pictorial History of Radio*. New Jersey, Castle Books, 1970.w

Shaw, Artie. *The Trouble With Cinderella*. New York, N.Y.: Da Capo Press, 1952.

Simon, George. *The Big Bands*, New York: Macmillan Publishing Co, 1967.

Simon, George. *Glenn Miller*, New York: Thomas Y. Crowell Co., 1974.

Sparke, Michael, with Peter Venudor. *Stan Kenton, The Studio Sessions*. Lake Geneva, Wisconsin: Balboa Books, 1998.

Walker, Leo. *Big Band Almanac*. Hollywood, Cal: Vinewood Enterprises, 1978.

WNEW. *Where the Melody Lingers On*. New York: Nightingale Gordon, 1984.

Index

226

De Betta, Robert, 138, 139, 203, 211
De Franco, Buddy, 107, 113, 166, 169
Delaney, Eric, 187
De Mars, Robert, 217
DeNaut, Jud, 30
Dennis, Matt, 191
De Niro, Angela, 209
De Nicola, Tony, 99, 100
De Vol, Frank, 153
De Pew, Art, 99
Desmond, Johnny, 161
Devlin, Johnny, 147
DeVito, Buddy, 99
Dickenson, Hal, 115
Diener, Christian, 196
DiFlorio, Anthony, III, 131
DiMaggio, Joe, 40
Disney, Walt, 204
Dodds, Baby, 215
Domino, Fats, 123
Donohue, Sam, 113, 117, 214
Doolittle, Jimmy, 160
Dorsey, Jimmy, 1, 2, 4, 7, 23, 101-111, 115, 120, 215
Dorsey, Tommy, 1, 2, 4, 13, 14, 17, 22, 23, 30, 38, 49, 70, 71, 94, 95, 98, 99, 101-111, 117, 119, 120, 140, 160, 165, 167, 175, 178, 179, 186, 187, 190, 201
Douglas, Mike, 135, 169
Drake, Ervin, 121, 122, 126, 131-137, 144
Drake, George, 203, 206, 208
Dressler, Marie, 141
Dubin, Al, 130
Dunphy, Don, 169
Dweck, Dave, 122
Dylan, Bob, 212

Eastman, Lee, 142
Eastman, Linda(McCartney), 142
Eberly, Bob, 101-104, 109
Eberle, Ray, 115
Eckstine, Billy, 113, 213
Edelhagen, Kurt, 193
Eldridge, Roy, 9, 30, 216
Elgart, Larry, 120, 121, 128, 204
Elgart, Les, 117, 120
Ellington, Duke, 1, 18, 19, 63, 64, 68-81,
128, 134, 137, 179, 190, 193
Ellington, Maria (Cole), 80
Ellington, Mercer, 74
Ellington, Ruth, 68, 72, 76-78
Elliot, Bill, 218
Elman, Ziggy, 94, 106, 108
Elmer, Ziggy, 99
Ellis, Gil, 208-210
Ellsworth, Dot, 203, 206, 207
Ellsworth, Jack, 124, 203-211
Empire Room, 4
Ennis, Skinnay, 54
Eppinger, Stephan, 196
Erikson, Rolf, 193
Erwin, Pee Wee, 114

Fagerquist, Don, 47
Faith, Percy, 219
Farlow, Tal, 30, 89
Farrell, Charles, 9
Farrelly, Dick, 151
Fazola, Irving, 93
Fatool, Nick, 30
Feather, Leonard, 81, 85
Ferguson, Maynard, 56, 66
Fields, Dorothy, 130
Feinstein, Michael, 218
Filaferro, Carlo, 176
Fields, Shep, 213
Finegan, Bill, 115, 118, 214
Fischer, Carl, 220
Fisher, Dan, 134
Fisher, Tony, 172, 181, 185-189
Fitzgerald, Ella, 15, 442, 128, 134, 135, 161, 187, 191
Flanagan, Ralph, 120
Fleming, Rhonda, 160, 163, 164
Ford, Art, 205
Ford, Mary, 152-155, 158, 206
Forgie, Barry, 188
Forrest, Helen, 26, 27, 95, 96, 99, 161, 162
Franchi, Sergio, 124
Franklin, Joe, 169, 210, 211
Frazer, Peter, 184
Freeman, Bud, 105
Froman, Jane, 131
Fromm, Lou, 30

227

228

Quinn, Freddie, 189

Raybin, Oscar, 160
Raeburn, Boyd, 120
Rael, Jack, 144, 154
Raisig, Al, 98
Raney, Jimmy, 86
Ray, Johnny, 220
Rayman, Morris, 30
Redman, Don, 9, 18
Rehbein, Herbert, 187
Reinhardt, Django, 161
Reisman, Leo, 1, 4, 5
Repole, Dan, 119
Rich, Buddy, 3, 27, 52, 99, 106, 108, 120, 174, 213
Richards, Ann, 58
Richards, Denise, 119, 120, 124
Riddle, Nelson,107, 169,182, 201
Riggs, Joe, 99
Rimes, LeAnn, 132
Rinker, Al, 85
Rizzi, Tony, 47
Roberts, Lynn, 92, 98-99, 110
Robin, Leo, 130
Robinson, Les, 27
Roche, Betty, 80
Rock, George, 213
Rockefeller, Nelson, 166
Rockwell, Tommy, 24
Rodgers, Richard, 130
Rogers, Buddy, 169
Rogers, Shorty, 56, 66, 88
Rolling Stones, 180, 197, 217
Rooney, Mickey, 44
Rose, David, 163
Rose, Billy, 130
Roseland, 4, 8, 9, 19, 42
Rosen, Bob, 123, 124
Rosolino, Frank, 56
Ross, Diana, 138, 175
Rowe, Vince, 15, 16
Rugolo, Pete, 44, 53, 58-60-64, 67, 74
Russell, Andy, 9
Russell, Della, 164
Russell, Jane, 160, 163, 164
Russell, Peewee, 23

Rydell, Bobby, 123
Ryan, Rodger, 213

Safranski, Eddie, 52, 128
Salden, Wil, 176, 177-179
Sampson, Edgar, 9, 42
Sanders, Joe, 6, 7
Sauter, Eddie, 87
Savoy Ballroom, 18
Schmid, Edgar, 176
Schonberger, Heinz, 193
Schudmans, Wiebe, 179
Schwartz, Jonathan, 207, 210
Schwartz, Wilbur, 114
Scott, Ronnie, 35, 51, 172
Scott, Raymond, 213
Seeger, Pete, 212
Severinsen, Doc, 98
Shavers, Charlie, 42
Shaw, Artie, 1, 20-33, 44, 46, 65, 66, 69-71, 102, 115, 118, 123, 153, 210
Shearing, George, 161, 191, 201
Sherill, Joya, 80
Sherock, Clarence "Shorty", 93
Shore, Dinah, 5, 140, 166, 168
Shulberg, Budd, 137
Simon, George, 39, 45
Sims, Ray, 47, 99
Simms, Ginny, 218
Sinatra, Frank, 13, 14, 38, 50, 89-91, 95, 99-101, 106-108, 122, 126, 135, 140, 141, 143, 144, 147, 162, 167, 168, 174, 175, 182, 188, 200, 204, 206, 207, 210, 216, 220
Sinatra, Frank,Jr., 117
Singer, Dan, 131
Singleton, Zutty, 215
Skelton,Red, 163, 164, 208
Slack, Freddie, 93
Smith, Bessie, 86, 87, 212, 215
Smith, Johnny, 56
Smith, Kate, 145, 155
Smith, Russell, 18
Smith, Willie "The Lion", 22, 99
Sousa, John Philip, 19, 35
Spanier, Mugsy, 7, 22
Sperling, Jack, 47

CELEBRITY PROFILES PUBLISHING

BOX 344 Main Street
STONY BROOK, NY 11790

(516) 862-8555 FAX 862-0139 RICWRITE 4 @ aol.com

THE BEST DAMN TRUMPET PLAYER   Copies _____
ISBN 1-57579-011-4   196 Pages   55 Photos
Price $ 15.95

****

THE SONG STARS   Copies _____
ISBN 1-57579-045-9   240 Pages   60 Photos
Price $ 17.95

****

THE MUSIC MEN   Copies _____
ISBN 1-57579-097-1   250 Pages   70 Photos
PRICE $ 17.95

****

JUKEBOX SATURDAY NIGHT   Copies_____
ISBN 1-57579-142-0   250 Pages   80 Photos
PRICE $ 17.95

****

NAME _____

ADDRESS_____

CITY, TOWN, STATE_____ ZIP CODE_____

Include $ 3.00 for Priority Mail (2 days arrival time) for up to 2 books.

Enclose check or money order. Order will be shipped immediately.

For CREDIT CARDS, please fill out as shown below:

Card #_____ Exp. Date_____

Signature_____

VISA ___AMEX ___ DISCOVER___MASTER CARD___(CHECK ONE)